May '68 and Film Culture

Sylvia Harvey

BFI Publishing
1980

Published by the
British Film Institute
127 Charing Cross Road, London WC2H 0EA

Typesetting by Dark Moon
Printed by Wise Printing Ltd., Hayes, Middx.
Cover by Julian Rothenstein

ISBN 0 85170 104 3

Copyright © British Film Institute 1978, 1980

First published 1978
Reprinted 1980

Contents

Introduction	1
1 The events of May and June '68	3
The Langlois Affair	14
The Estates General of the Cinema	16
The film groups	27
The film journals	33
2 Notions of cultural production	45
Post-revolutionary Russia: mass illiteracy and proletarian art	45
Post-revolutionary Russia: Formalists and Futurists	54
Modernist cinema and the 'materialist approach to form'	62
The critique of modernism	69
1. The means of representation	70
2. The question of form	72
3. The 'author as producer' and the apparatus	75
4. 'The realm of the merely enjoyable'	80
3 Ideology and the 'impression of reality'	87
The 'base and superstructure' debate	87
The 'impression of reality'	105
Film criticism and 'radical readings'	110
Appendices	121
The history (from *Cahiers du Cinéma*)	121
Film journals and politics (from *Le Monde*)	127
Polemic on *Coup pour coup* (from *Ecran '72*)	131
Interview with Paul Séban (*La CGT en mai '68*) (from *Cinéthique*)	139
Economic/Ideological/Formal (from *Cinéthique*)	149
Bibliography	165

Acknowledgements

Many people have contributed in different ways to the production of this booklet (though some of them would disagree strongly with its contents). I should like to thank staff and students at the Motion Pictures/Television Division of the University of California, Los Angeles, in particular the late Professor James Kerans; the members of the doctoral seminars in film, 1972-74; and the members of the Film Workshop, Spring 1974. I should also like to thank my parents, John and Greta Harvey, the members of the Women and Film Study Group, London, Sasha Brookes, Edward Buscombe, Denise Corner, Phillip Drummond, Richard Dyer, Christine Gledhill, Jeanne Hadfield, Jeremy Hawthorn, Angela Martin, Diana Matias, Elias Noujaim, Philip Simpson; and, finally, John Corner for generously giving up valuable writing time in order to read this manuscript.

Acknowledgement for permission to reprint 'Bad Times' by Bertolt Brecht, translated by Christopher Middleton, is hereby given to *Bertolt Brecht Poems* (1938-56), (eds.) John Willett and Ralph Manheim, Eyre Methuen, London 1976.

Vols. 5/6/7 of Gedichte Copyright © Suhrkamp Verlag, Frankfurt am Main 1964.

Dedication May 1980

To the members of the Independent Filmmakers Association, and in recognition of those real cultural needs to be served by the new cinema and the new television of the 1980s.

Bad Times

The tree tells why it bore no fruit.
The poet tells why his lines went wrong.
The general tells why the war was lost.

Pictures, painted on brittle canvas.
Records of exploration, handed down to the forgetful.
Great behaviour, observed by no one.

Should the cracked vase be used as a pisspot?
Should the ridiculous tragedy be turned into a farce?
Should the disfigured sweetheart be put in the kitchen?

All praise to those who leave crumbling houses.
All praise to those who bar their door against a demoralised friend.
All praise to those who forget about the unworkable plan.

The house is built of the stones that were available.
The rebellion was raised using the rebels that were available.
The picture was painted using the colours that were available.

Meals were made of whatever food could be had.
Gifts were given to the needy.
Words were spoken to those who were present.
Work was done with the existing resources, wisdom and courage.

Carelessness should not be forgiven.
More would have been possible.
Regret is expressed.
(What good could it do?)

Bertolt Brecht

Introduction

There are many ways of remembering, many rituals of remembrance; with a moment of silence we commemorate the dead. But this silence conceals two distinct positions. From the first we enter the past to remain caught within it, in flight from the present, enfolded in nostalgic fantasies. From the second we approach the past with an analytical purpose, moved by the need to view it and review it in the hopes of constructing a future as well as a past. This booklet cannot search out all of the secret places of the memory of May '68, but it can, in an introductory and tentative fashion, provide a review of some of the information that will allow us to begin an active and productive reading of that past, not raiding it for self-referential sectarian purposes, but reading, unravelling its complex fabric.

The purpose of this monograph is threefold. Firstly, it aims to give a brief account of the impact of the events of May '68 on the development of Marxist film criticism in France, particularly as manifested in the journals *Cahiers du Cinéma* and *Cinéthique*. Secondly, it considers this development in relation to earlier attempts at arriving at a materialist understanding of culture and of cultural production. Thirdly, it indicates the contribution made by the discussion of theories of ideology in France and elsewhere to the progress of a more general debate about materialist theories of culture. What is omitted here, not because these areas are regarded as unimportant but rather for reasons of space and time, and because they have been dealt with extensively elsewhere, are the post-'68 developments in cinema semiotics (the study of the cinema as a system of signs, often associated with the name of Christian Metz) and those re-developments of psychoanalysis (associated with the name of Jacques Lacan) which, based upon the insights of structural linguistics, have resulted in the radical re-thinking of the 'place' of the individual human subject in language; the implications of this for the systematic study of the 'language' of film have been considerable.

Slowly, and in many different ways, the landscape of film studies in Britain and in the United States has been transformed by post-'68 developments in French film theory. Many of these transformations would have been brought about without the particular impetus of the political crisis of the May events. Among them may be listed the interest in structuralism and semiotics, in theories of narrativity, and in notions of filmic specificity and of the textual operations that derive from that specificity. Sooner or later the crisis of impressionistic criticism, and a certain stagnation in the circulating currency of ideas out of which academic careers are made, would have required the injection of that theoretical rigour and complexity, that self-avowed 'scientificity' which the new French schools seemed to promise. But what is interesting about the way in which some of these ideas have been appropriated for English and American criticism is the precision of the operation through which they have been neatly cut free from that theory of the complex unity of the social formation and that mood of political militancy which engendered them in France. Those ideas which, in France, were the product of a momentary but radical displacement, a critical calling into question of all the levels of the social formation, have become in Britain and the United States little more than a hiccup in the superstructures, a slight grinding of gears in that social machine whose fundamental mode of operating has not changed.

It is here that the concept of ideology — in so far as it allows us to think through the relationships between the different levels or instances of the whole social formation — is crucial. The world of film studies, whether of the old-fashioned practical criticism variety, or of the newly-fashioned formalist semiotic variety (though not all semiotics are formalist in the sense of refusing that whole network of relations within which their object is placed) requires a very much more vigorous sense of the necessary difficulties engendered by the study of the cultural object or process in the context of a particular historical moment (something which was understood by the Marxist Formalists in Russia in the twenties), and a sense of the way in which both itself and its object of study are in a delicate, complex, but ultimately determined relationship with a particular mode of material production. The world of film studies, like the wonderful world of Oz, crammed with such colourful theoretical riches, threatens to obliterate the memory of that drab and repressive dustbowl from which it was generated. And what we are witnessing now, in certain quarters of the field of film studies, are the strenuous efforts of the exponents of traditional aesthetics to admit the word 'ideology' while excluding that whole system of materialist analysis to which — for some — the word properly belongs.

1 The events of May and June '68

In *The Civil War in France* Marx wrote of the Paris Commune of 1871: 'What is the Commune, that sphinx so tantalising to the bourgeois mind?' For the Left, as well as for the Right, the events of May '68 in France have something of the same fearful quality, that same sphinx-like silence. In many ways the events of '68 are as inscrutable, as full of riddles, as difficult to read as those of 1871. A record of 'what happened', checked off according to place and date, actor and edict, does not begin to give us an historical understanding of this period. We can recite the litany of events, but how we are to interpret them, how they are to become meaningful for us almost ten years later, is a much more difficult question. In every important sense the events of May '68 are in dispute. And while, within these disputes, the same factors are referred to again and again, their positioning within a multiplicity of scenarios changes with the position of each interpreter. To list these factors is only a beginning: the French Communist Party (PCF); the Government; the largest grouping of French Trade Unions, the *Confédération Générale du Travail* (CGT); the other, smaller, union groupings; the left-wing organisations; shop floor militancy and the notion of trade union bureaucracy; the mass media; the army; the students; as well as, more generally, the questions of alienation and spontaneism, of organisation and leadership, of the relationship between cultural production and the general mode of production: the re-emergence of the old question about the relationship of 'superstructure' to 'base', and a calling into question of the value of this model. Here, we can only be concerned with that delimited area, marked off from the larger political questions and yet insisting upon its relationship to them, the area that concerns itself with the analysis of culture, of cultural theory, cultural struggle, cultural production.

The Events of May and June 1968
'The movement of May is irreversible', wrote Jacques Doniol-Valcroze in the August 1968 issue of *Cahiers du Cinéma*. So many of the attempts which were subsequently made in France at theorising the place of the cinema within contemporary capitalism were premised upon a passionate acquaintance with the events of May, that it may be useful to attempt a brief account of these events here. What is most striking about the political upheavals which began with student unrest and culminated in a wave of massive strikes in the latter half of May is both the unexpected way in which they burst upon the scene, and the extreme rapidity with which they developed, and then apparently dissipated.

The 'Movement of March 22' founded at the University of Nanterre in '68 typifies many of the concerns of the student movement: opposition to the war in Vietnam; dissatisfaction with the bureaucratic and authoritarian structures of the university; a critique of the alienated and isolated character of student life; a suspicion of all organisation, all hierarchy, and of the traditional Left (in particular the PCF); and an at once powerful and confused equation of social and of sexual repression. This critique of the university which led to the critique of a whole mode of social organisation tended towards the affirmation of spontaneous action and self-expression, the validating of direct democracy in place of the mechanisms of representation and delegation, an emphasis on sexual liberation, notions of creativity and the work of the imagination and of desire.* The March 22 Movement organised a series of occupations of university buildings after the arrest of a number of student members of the National Vietnam Committee, and when the university was closed against them, students met to continue their discussions outside the buildings, developing the notion of an 'anti-university' and preparing to boycott examinations. This assault on the regulations of the university and on its methods of defining and transmitting appropriate knowledge was met with the threat of disciplinary action, and eight of the Nanterre students were ordered to appear before a disciplinary board at the Sorbonne on Monday May 6. However, the sudden acceleration of events in Paris subsumed this incident within a much larger framework of student unrest and 'contestation'.

On Friday May 3, the Rector of the University of Paris, Jean Roche, called the police into the university to disperse the students who were meeting inside the Sorbonne. Large numbers of these students were duly arrested, but the university authorities seem to have seriously miscalculated in assuming that they could take stern action against a few isolated troublemakers and thus ensure the smooth running of the institution, and in particular of the forthcoming examinations. In response to this police intrusion, large numbers of students gathered quickly throughout the Latin Quarter (the area around the Sorbonne) and numerous and violent clashes with the police followed with the students demanding the release of their comrades. Opposition from the students brought increased violence from the police using truncheons and tear gas, and fighting continued until the evening. The response of the students' union (UNEF) to this escalation of repression was to call for a nationwide strike, and the lecturers' union (SNESup), similarly concerned at the repressive intervention of the state in the affairs of the university, also called for a strike by its members. In addition the students called upon the labour unions for support, although it was clear that at this stage the PCF, which through its effective leadership of the CGT exercised considerable influence within the union movement, was more inclined to criticise what it called the adventurism of some of the students than to try to build support for them. The Communist Party paper, *L'Humanité* spoke, on May 4, of 'the

---

* The concern with the stultifying effects of what was regarded as a fundamentally repressive culture owed much to the influence of the surrealist-inspired *situationists* and to the latters' attack on the mechanisms of alienated consumption and the negative values of the 'society of the spectacle'. (See Guy de Bord, *The Society of the Spectacle*, Practical Paradise Publications, London 1977.)

serious consequences to which political adventurism inevitably leads, even if it is concealed behind pseudo-revolutionary phrases'.[1]

In the week of escalating violence which followed a series of large student demonstrations and marches was organised, and reports of police brutality seem to have resulted in considerable public sympathy for the students and for their aim of re-possessing the university, which had been closed against them by ministerial directive. The increasing solidarity and strength of the student movement, and the continued refusal of the government and university authorities to enter into any meaningful negotiations with them resulted in the 'Night of the Barricades' (May 10). Unable to march through the Latin Quarter because of the massive concentration of police forces, including now the riot police (CRS), the student demonstrators dispersed into smaller groups and raised a large number of barricades beginning in the Rue Gay Lussac, with the intention of holding key positions within the area against the assaults of the police. Several hours of tension and stalemate, with students confronting police and a series of last minute attempts at negotiation, were followed in the early hours of the morning by a long drawn-out and violent conflict when the police were given orders to clear the area and the students resisted, attempting to hold the positions which they had taken up behind the barricades.

Throughout the crisis the government-controlled radio and television network, the ORTF, had offered very little or very biased coverage of the student demands, and the night of May 10 is sometimes remembered for the role played by the two 'independent' radio stations, Europe One and Radio Luxembourg, which throughout the night broadcast detailed reports of the fighting around the barricades,[2] and in some cases assisted the students by giving information about the location and movement of the police.

The extensive and extremely violent rout of the students on the night of the barricades in fact secured for the students both a moral victory and a tactical advantage. It established beyond doubt the seriousness of their opposition to de Gaulle's government, and the horror of liberal public opinion at the clubbings by riot police of the sons and daughters of respectable professionals was accompanied by what was, politically, the far more weighty support of the CGT, which could no longer ignore the extent and severity of Gaullist repression, and, moreover, saw a way of linking the student demands to those of the organised working-class. The turning point in May was the demonstration which was organised for Monday May 13 and supported by an impressive alignment of forces, the students' union, the teaching unions and the labour unions, including the CGT and the CFDT. The banner at the head of the demonstration read: STUDENTS, TEACHERS AND WORKERS TOGETHER, and in the front ranks marched together student and labour leaders —among the former, Daniel Cohn-Bendit, Jacques Sauvageot, Alain Geismar (lecturers' union), and among the latter, Georges Séguy of the CGT and Eugène Descamps of the CFDT. Estimates of numbers for this Paris demonstration ranged from what contemporary news sources regarded as the conservative police estimate of 171,000 up to half a million or more. More-

over, this demonstration of solidarity and of radical dissatisfaction with
de Gaulle's government was not confined to Paris; the CGT had called for a
one-day strike, and there were reports of large demonstrations from all over
France.

However this great show of strength concealed some important differences
of analysis and of emphasis: there were those who felt that the current crisis
was only the beginning of a revolutionary transformation of French society,
and there were others who saw it as strictly a bargaining counter for obtaining
better wages and working conditions within the existing social system, and
without challenging the existing relations of production and existing class
relations; there were those who shouted the slogan: *'Ce n'est qu'un début,
continuons le combat'* ('This is only a beginning, continue the struggle'), and
there were the CGT stewards on the demonstration who quickly and efficient-
ly dispersed the demonstrators at the end of the day. The students went back
to the just re-opened Sorbonne.

The character of the opposition to the Gaullist regime changed after May
13. A series of strikes and factory occupations, numerous declarations of
'unlimited strike', developed throughout France, and workers came out without centralised directives from their union organisations. First, on May 14, was
the Sud-Aviation aircraft factory near Nantes, followed by the Renault plant
near Rouen and then by all the major Renault factories, including those at
Flins and Le Mans. By May 17 sit-ins and strikes had spread throughout the
engineering and chemical industries, and it was on this day that the film technicians' union, together with a large number of film directors, producers and
students established the Estates General of the Cinema, which will be discussed later in this chapter. By May 18 public transport was at a standstill,
trains were no longer running, post offices were closed, the mines were empty,
and the gas and electricity industries were disrupted, though supply to
domestic users was continued. The Cannes Film Festival was closed down,
after some angry arguments by the producers and distributors attending.

In the week of May 20 the textile industry was affected by the strikes and
the Paris shops, including Galeries Lafayette, closed their doors; the teachers
came out on strike. Nor were other professions, of middle management or the
arts, left untouched, and, as with the case of the Estates General of the
Cinema, there were some strange crossings over of the normal barriers of class
and cultural grouping. A group of young executives, calling themselves 'C4' –
from the initials of the organisation C*entre de* C*oordination des* C*adres* C*on-
testaires* – took part in a token occupation of the offices of the National
Council of French Employers (CNPF); a group of doctors occupied the
building of the Medical Order; and a number of architects, following the
occupation of the School of Fine Arts by the architecture students, declared
their own professional organisation to be dissolved; researchers at the Atomic
Energy Commissariat (CEA), were called out on strike, and a number of
government departments, including the Ministries of Finance and Social
Affairs, were affected.

All areas of the arts were touched by the crisis. The directors of provincial theatres and community arts centres (the *Maisons de la Culture*) met to discuss cultural policy, and issued a statement extremely critical of the government's existing cultural policy. They set up a permanent committee, and continued to meet after the May crisis, adopting the notion of 'politicisation' as the goal of all cultural activity — though it must be noted that such a theory of 'making political' was inflected in many different directions in accordance with a wide variety of political purposes.

In May also, those active in the field of the plastic arts set up an action committee which organised a march on the Museum of Modern Art in Paris, with the express intention of closing it down. Attack on the institutionalisation of art had, of course, for a long time been characteristic of the romantic tradition in the visual arts stretching from Delacroix's attack on the academicians, down to the anti-establishment fury of the Fauves, and Vlaminck's vituperative outbursts against the art of the museums. The writings of the Italian Futurists offer a summary of this tradition:

> We want to get rid of the innumerable museums that cover it [Italy] with innumerable cemeteries ... To admire an old picture is to pour out sensibility into a funeral urn instead of casting it forward with great spurts of creation and action ... museums, libraries and academies ... calvaries of crucified dreams ...[3]

This same language of provocation, of assault on the past in the name of the liberties of 'creation and action', deployed in the case of the Italian Futurists in the service of a fascist ideology, was also characteristic of the surrealist-inspired slogans of May which advocated, under many different guises, the notion of the work of the free imagination against the dead hand of an oppressive past and an authoritarian society. The ideas of May constituted a departure from this romantic tradition only to the extent to which they argued for the introduction of class struggle into the previously sacrosanct — the previously separate — sphere of culture. Pierre Gaudibert, the curator of the city of Paris Museum of Modern Art, has outlined this other argument, introducing the notion of the struggle within culture and of the potential, gradual, penetration of this sphere by class struggle:

> The predominant function of the cultural apparatus and of culture, that of integration into the ruling ideology and into the system, is not the only possibility, there also exist dominated, protesting ideologies and struggles within the cultural apparatus. Class struggle, class violence, little by little penetrates the field of culture, despite all the attempts to make this an area of free choice and common consensus.[4]

Not only in the visual arts, but in music and in literature, the May crisis resulted in frequently violent confrontation with the existing state of things: those musicians who were employed were able to withdraw their labour, after the manner of workers everywhere. The French classical music radio station was closed down because of a strike by the orchestras, and the Society of Men of Letters building was invaded and occupied by a group of dissident writers who set up a new Union of Writers open to all those who 'believed that the practice of literature is indissolubly linked with the present revolutionary process'.[5] The model of this occupation was obviously drawn from the many contemporary occupations of factories by workers; the problem with the application of the model in the case of the writers was that it brought them, of necessity, no closer to an analysis of the existing relations of production and exchange of cultural commodities.

By May 24, barely two weeks after the great demonstration of May 13, approximately ten million workers were on strike in France. In extent, in militancy and in inventiveness these strikes went far beyond that other great wave of strikes and of working-class militancy of the Popular Front period in France in 1936.[6] From the actions of a few discontented and apparently 'marginal' students, the escalation and organisation of discontent and opposition, firmly linked within that two-week period to the expression of the grievances of French workers against the government of de Gaulle, had resulted in a situation in which one of the most powerful and stable governments of Europe was on the verge of collapse.

On May 24 the government was finally forced to the point of calling together a conference (the Grenelle conference) of all the unions together with the employers' federation in order to search for a way out of the present crisis; thus falling back upon the mechanisms of wage-bargaining with the hope of preserving intact the fabric of the state and of the mode and relations of production which that state fostered and preserved. This day was also marked by a number of large demonstrations, one organised by the students, and separate ones organised by the CGT (a sign of the growing rift between the two 'wings' of the May movement, between the policies of the radical students on the one hand, and those of the traditional organisations of the labour movement and in particular of the French Communist Party, which is to be seen as the main force behind the policies adopted by the CGT). De Gaulle proposed a referendum, and later that night, the 'Night of the Bourse', fires were started by demonstrators who broke into the main building of the Stock Exchange. Once again there were battles all night with the police in the Latin Quarter.

On Saturday May 25, the day after the beginning of the Grenelle conference, the ORTF journalists came out on strike. Rather later than many of the other sections of organised workers, but in terms of the orchestration of public opinion they were among the most important. The pro-government bias of the television and radio networks during the first few weeks of May was, in a sense, too obvious to be of very much use to the government. The huge discrepancy between what was actually going on in the streets and factories and workplaces and what was allowed to appear on television, was too apparent. The lesson of May, from the point of view of the government, must therefore be that in a relatively 'advanced' society, based on the principles of mass education and mass literacy, what is almost more important than the control of the mass media is the creation of public confidence in those media,[7] and the skilful negotiating of the susceptibilities — and the code of ethics – of the professional journalists. Something which the British government understood very well during the General Strike of 1926.[8]

In France the censorship of information on the ORTF in May led, as has already been indicated, to the sudden and considerable increase in importance of the independent/commercial radio stations as alternative sources of news and information. The inflexible system of control within the ORTF made any struggle within the institution, around the point of production (that is, transmission) of news, for example, impossible, and meant that journalists could only conduct their debate about the principles of uncensored information from outside. And it must be said that despite the uneven nature of the combat, with the striking journalists (in conjunction with students of the *Atelier Populaire* (Popular Workshop of the School of Fine Arts) using wall posters, and the government using the airwaves, this debate was fairly successfully conducted. The posters of barbed wire drawn across a television screen, of helmeted riot police speaking into the ORTF microphone with the caption *'La police vous parle'* ('The police speaking'), taken in conjunction with the presence of alternative news sources, and the general experience of a massive social upheaval, did the government cause immense damage.

It must be noted, however, that the striking journalists' demands were not radical or revolutionary ones: the struggle which they conducted around the question of public information was based on notions of objectivity and impartiality; they were certainly not arguing that the mass media should serve the cause of the revolution (or, if some were, they were not speaking on behalf of their whole profession). But there can be no question that there was considerable public support for the ORTF journalists and technicians (some 13,000 of whom were out on strike by early June). Evidence of this wide support is indicated by 'Operation Jericho', launched on June 6 and which planned a series of large demonstrations, which for seven days on end were to wind their way, provocatively, around Broadcasting House. The demonstrations in fact went on for six days; on the seventh the police were out in force around the building and the march was called off.

It is important, now, to return to a consideration of the results of the Grenelle Conference in order to get an overall sense of the shape of the May events. On Monday May 27 the results of the urgent negotiations were made public. At this point the CGT seems to have miscalculated the likelihood of French workers accepting the deals that were offered, and Georges Séguy, CGT General Secretary, reporting on the negotiations to the Renault plant workers at Boulogne-Billancourt, was constantly heckled and interrupted. A clear veto against acceptance of the negotiations was expressed not only at Billancourt, but, in the next few days, repeated by striking workers throughout France. So the crisis lurched forward another step, but was offered neither impetus nor direction since the Communist Party was unwilling to go beyond wage demands, and the students, lacking political experience, organisational strength and any consistent history of involvement in working class struggles, were clearly incapable of playing any leadership role.

In this extremely unstable situation, with the question of state power in the balance, de Gaulle finally took decisive action, and after visiting French military leaders to assess the degree of support for the government from the army, returned to Paris and on May 30 announced the dissolution of the Assembly and a general election, adding in his broadcast speech dark references to the dangers of totalitarian Communism facing France. Séguy responded with the announcement that 'the CGT declares that it has no intention of impeding in any way the conduct of the election'.[9] It was this which the *'gauchistes'* ('leftists') branded as the *'élections-trahison'* (betrayal of the elections), with a greater bitterness against the CGT and the Communist Party than against the government, which was expected to act in this way.

The crucial problem, or difficulty, of May was that those who regarded the elections — and hence the 'parliamentary road' to social change — as a betrayal of revolutionary goals had been unable to propose a concrete political alternative. The French sociologist Alain Touraine, professor at Nanterre during the May events, summarises the situation as 'the encounter between a revolutonary movement and a non-revolutionary situation',[10] and suggests that by the last week of May, certain sectors of the radical student movement, together with left-wing trade unionists, regarded a change of government as the first priority and the possibility of a revolutionary transformation as no longer on the agenda:

> For all or almost all on the left, the overthrow of Gaullism was the most immediate objective. Cohn-Bendit proclaimed it several times. Barjonet made a careful distinction between the overthrow of Gaullism, which seemed to him possible, and the establishment of socialism, which seemed to him impossible . . .[11]

André Barjonet, Secretary of the CGT's Centre for Economic Studies for many years, had resigned from the CGT on May 23 and later from the French Communist Party, profoundly disturbed by the slow and inadequate response of both the CGT and the Party to the events of May. The problem was the lack of alternatives, and the student movement had nothing to compare with the organisational strength and the numbers of working-class militants of the CGT. Or, as Touraine puts it, the May movement 'had been too spontaneous and too hostile to political organisation to transform itself into an instrument for the seizure of power'.[12]

The gradual return to work in the first half of June was marked by various incidents which increased the bitterness between the *'gauchistes'* and the Communist Party. The Federal Committee of the CGT issued this declaration on June 5:

> Wherever the essential claims have been satisfied it is in the workers' interest to pronounce themselves overwhelmingly in favour of a return to work.[13]

It was, of course, the feeling of some on the left that the return to work was being orchestrated with indecent haste, and that the question of just precisely what constituted 'essential claims' was a matter of controversy. In addition, the wording of some of the CGT statements in early June seemed to suggest that the sudden eruption of the most extensive wave of strikes in French history was nothing more than a momentary diversion from the grand plan of action through parliamentary activity by the forces of the 'union of the left'. Perhaps what was in dispute, in particular, was the CGT's conception of 'victory':

> Since the elections open up concrete perspectives in our perennial struggle for democracy it is in the workers' own interests that we lead them to victory by first settling their claims so that the elections can take place normally.[14]

The return to work itself was marked by violent incidents, in particular at those rather more isolated factories where the government felt it might be in a better position to force its hand than in any of the militant Paris plants. On June 6 police forces were sent to take over the Renault factory at Flins. The car workers who organised resistance to the police in and around the plant were joined by students who came out from Paris to assist them, and for a couple of days there was open fighting in and around Flins. On June 10, in the course of one of these battles a young *lycée* (secondary school) student, Gilles Tautin, was drowned in circumstances which remained unclear. Large numbers of workers and students were arrested. At this time too *gendarmes* and the CRS moved into the Peugeot works at Sochaux, and as the workers there fought to retain control of their plant the police used their guns and two people were killed. The CGT organised a token, one-hour strike in protest at the killings, but seemed to reserve its most bitter criticisms not for the violence of the police, but for the actions of the radical students who by involving themselves in the battles at Flins were regarded as trespassing on the territory of the trade union organisation. The CGT published this statement:

> When the government had ordered the CRS into the (Flins) factory and while the workers were peacefully assembled, strangers to the working-class, led by Geismar, who is increasingly proving himself an expert on provocation, insinuated themselves into the meeting and incited the workers to re-occupy the factory. These groups . . . were quite blatantly acting in the service of the worst enemies of the working-class.[15]

On June 18 the Renault workers at Boulogne-Billancourt, the plant which had been the first to turn down the Grenelle agreements, returned to work; on the 20th workers at Citröen, Peugeot and Berliet returned; on the 26th journalists of the ORTF radio station, France-Inter, decided to go back, though the television journalists stayed out until July 12, and then many of them were fired; on June 30, one month after de Gaulle had announced the elections, the Gaullists were returned to power with a large majority.

Despite the defeat, despite the failures of policy and analysis, despite the hostility often expressed towards them by the Communist Party (quite apart from the hostility of the Gaullists), certain positive aspects of the student May movement — their memorable inventiveness — must be noted. Calling

everything into question, the students were able to generate an enormous
enthusiasm for the re-examination and criticism of all aspects of public and
private life. Two British journalists, Patrick Seale and Maureen McConville,
who were present in Paris during the events, described the feeling that was
generated thus:

> This very widespread revolt against the old forms of established
> authority was accompanied by an acute and profoundly enjoyable
> sense of liberation. All sorts of people felt it in all walks of life. A great
> gust of fresh air blew through dusty minds and offices and bureaucratic
> structures.[16]

Slogans, graffiti, wall newspapers and posters proliferated everywhere, and
the posters produced by the *Atelier Populaire* presented some of the clearest
and most powerful expressions of the goals of the May movement. The
slogans often owed less to that tradition of political slogans which aimed to
summarise the objectives of a political programme, and more to the deliberate
provocativeness, the deliberate 'unreality' of Surrealism. Hence the following
often quoted statements:

> It is forbidden to forbid.
> The Imagination Rules.
> Take my desires for reality, for I believe in the reality of my desires.
> Forget all you have learnt. Begin dreaming.
> As long as we have not destroyed everything, there will remain ruins.
> Art is dead. Let us create our daily lives.

These aggressive but non-programmatic slogans reflect both the strengths and
weaknesses of the May movement: both its searching for a more adequate and
more radical analysis of the reality of daily life under technocratic capitalism,
and its idealistic, often anarchistic, utopianism. From the perspective which
sought to contest, to oppose, all existing forms of authority, power and
organisation, what the radical students found particularly impossible to
accept were the policies of the CGT and the PCF, which it seemed to them
sought to bring about certain changes within the existing social, political and
economic system, not to overthrow that system. The CGT's attitude of
co-operation, of working from within the existing system, of adopting
electoral policies within the structures created and controlled by the capitalist
state, was regarded as unacceptable by the *'gauchistes'*.

There is, however, a sense in which the policies of the PCF must properly
be distinguished from those of the CGT, despite the inter-changeability of
personnel between the two institutions. The French CP would, in theory,
distinguish between its long-term revolutionary goals and its short-term participation in the often primarily economistic struggles (a larger slice of the
cake, not the question of ownership) of the trade union movement. The real
argument then is around the balance which it maintains, or fails to maintain,
between long-term perspectives, and immediate responses to the contemporary situation. It could be argued that in relationship to its response to the

May events the traces of its long-term goals were so faint as to be unrecognisable. The explanations for this must include the real fear of a right-wing militarist coup in France (particularly in view of de Gaulle's special relationship with the army), and the fear of engaging in adventurist politics in the face of what was judged to be a reluctance on the part of the mass of French workers to move from economic to (revolutionary) political demands.

Thus, throughout May, a bitter debate was conducted around the questions of reform or revolution, co-operation or confrontation, factory occupation or official trade union negotiation, direct action or the acceptance of the procedures of parliamentary representation. These arguments, conducted at the level of political theory, had important implications for the development of film theory and of a theory of cultural production in France, and the political debates were often the motive force behind the emergence of different conceptions of film-making and different conceptions of film criticism.

With respect to the larger issues raised by the May events, any evaluation of them must take into account both the extraordinary diversity of positions on the left (from Stalinist to anarchist across the middle ground of popular front socialism), and the central importance of the French Communist Party. For, despite the bitter hostility expressed by some sections of the French left towards the PCF, it remained a kind of touchstone *in relationship to which* other analyses, other positions, were expressed and defined. And if the criticisms of the part played by the PCF have been hard, sometimes savage, they have not always been made from outside the Party. Some of the most incisive criticisms have been made by those most sympathetic to its history and traditions. The British Marxist historian, E. J. Hobsbawm, while arguing, in his essay on May 1968, that the French Party was right in its general strategy, that it correctly assessed the May events as a 'basically non-revolutionary situation', nevertheless wrote in criticism:

> The test of a revolutionary movement is not its willingness to raise barricades at every opportunity, but its readiness to recognise when the normal conditions of routine politics cease to operate, and to adopt its behaviour accordingly. The French CP failed both these tests . . . It consistently trailed behind the masses, failing to recognise the seriousness of the students until the barricades were up, the readiness of the workers for an unlimited general strike until the spontaneous sit-ins forced the hands of its union leaders . . .[17]

Another criticism, made later but by someone very much more intimately involved with the assessment of the French situation, tends in the same direction. Thus the Marxist philosopher Louis Althusser, a member of the PCF since 1948, wrote some six years after the events:

> In these last years some Party militants have had to jump into a moving train, or have even got left on the platform. Why? Because they did not understand in time what was happening among the masses . . .[18]

With the failures of both the students and the communists laid out in the balance, Alain Touraine offers what is perhaps the best summary of the tensions, contradictions and achievements of the May movement:

> The May movement did not win a victory by defeating its adversary. It did not carry out the revolution. It did not even try to take power. It did destroy the illusion of a society united through growth and prosperity; it replaced the mirage of social rationality and the common good with a picture of society's struggles and contradictions. In the midst of a crisis of social change, it reinvented the class struggle.[19]

The Langlois Affair

The 'Langlois Affair' constitutes an interesting prelude to the May events, and helps to explain the extraordinary speed with which the film world in Paris organised itself during that month. Early in February 1968 the government intervened in the affairs of the Paris Cinémathèque, an internationally famous archive and film theatre, and removed Henri Langlois from his position at the head of the institution. Whatever criticisms might have been made of Langlois' methods as a curator and archivist, the government's interference in the internal administration of an independent cultural institution, and its attack upon Langlois in particular, one of the most venerable figures on the French film scene, was regarded as quite unacceptable by the vast majority of French *cinéastes*.

The Cinémathèque, although in receipt of government funds for its programme of film preservation and restoration, was nevertheless an independent organisation controlled by its own committee of members. In addition, it was an institution which had the support of most French film-makers, and many of the critics who had written for *Cahiers du Cinéma* in the late fifties — people like Truffaut and Godard who had subsequently embarked on careers as film directors — had praised the imaginative quality of the film screening programmes at the Cinémathèque, and were happy to attribute to it their knowledge of cinema history.

Within a matter of days public demonstrations were organised against Langlois' dismissal, outside the film theatre in the rue d'Ulm, and there were violent incidents when a group of some 1,500 people gathered to protest outside the theatre at the Palais de Chaillot. A systematic boycott of the two theatres was organised, and on February 16 the Committee for the Defence of the Cinémathèque was set up. The Honorary President was Jean Renoir, and members of the committee included the film-makers Resnais, Godard, Truffaut, Bresson, Carné, Chabrol, Lelouch, Rivette, Malle and Vadim, and the writer, professor and critic, Roland Barthes. With such well-established names in the film world involved, the affair quickly achieved an international fame, with telegrams and letters of support coming in from both Europe and America, and the list of French signatories to the petition for Langlois' reinstatement reading like a who's who of the world of arts and letters. What is interesting about the campaign is the extraordinary diversity of support which it elicited, with a range of people that included Picasso, Chaplin and Simone de Beauvoir.

By February 24 the whole matter had become sufficiently embarrassing to the government for the Minister of Cultural Affairs, André Malraux, to issue a public statement explaining the government's case. The statement which appeared in both *Le Monde* and the *Journal Officiel* cited administrative inefficiency, the problem of decaying film prints in storage, the failure to catalogue and locate prints, the charge that Langlois had refused to co-operate with a group of officials who had been appointed to investigate the current state of the prints, and the comment that Langlois had refused the compromise offer of collaborating with an official who would be appointed by the government to oversee the administrative and financial aspects of the Cinémathèque, and who would leave the artistic direction of the institution to Langlois. So, Malraux concluded, the state had been forced to use its powers under the law to appoint a new and 'responsible' director.

The campaign grew in strength and in volubility, uniting people as much around the principle of opposition to state interference as in defence of Langlois as an individual. Demonstrations continued throughout March, and the March issue of *Cahiers du Cinéma* carried an inset, central section with full details of 'L'affaire Langlois' which included publication of the vast lists of names of supporters. Moreover, with growing dissatisfaction with the government funded and controlled *Centre National de la Cinématographie* (CNC), the editorial of this same issue of *Cahiers* declared that 'Today the French Cinema aspires to take over the burden and the responsibility of managing itself', which was fair warning of the desire for self-management which erupted with such force – throughout France and far beyond the confines of cinematic production – in the month of May.

Early in April, when the Federation of French Cine-Clubs voted by an overwhelming majority to support the Defence Committee, the campaign had arrived at the peak of its success. The government, looking for a way out of the situation, began to investigate the possibility of separating out the work of film conservation from the organisation of screenings, and on April 21 the Minister announced the creation of a separate film conservation office, which meant that the Cinémathèque was henceforth free to pursue its own policies, but was also 'free' of government funding for the purpose of conservation. The next day Langlois was re-elected Secretary General of the Cinémathèque, and the April-May issue of *Cahiers* celebrated his re-instatement with a cover picture after the style of Magritte which showed a smiling Henri Langlois cradling in his arms a submachine gun fed not by bullets, but by frames of film. It was a slightly hollow victory which had won the re-instatement of the man, and a mobilisation of the French film world, but a loss to the Cinémathèque of the state subsidy of over 1 million francs.

The defence of Langlois was a liberal cause, not a radical one, but it provided a certain organisational infrastructure, a network of communication within French film culture which was to prove useful to those who, in the month of May, and through the Estates General of the Cinema, were seeking not to defend individual freedom but to place the cinema apparatus in the service of the French working-class.

The Estates General of the Cinema

The Estates General of the Cinema (EGC) should not be thought of as a single, homogeneous body, developing a unified position and a coherent policy. Rather, it was the site of those same tensions, conflicts and contradictions which characterised the rest of French society in the months of May and June.

The implications of the title of the organisation (which refer to a whole series of developments in the political and social history of France) are perhaps worth spelling out, since they are not self-evident in a British context. The illustrious ancestor, to which the EGC refers in its own title, was the States General of 1789, and what this deliberate reference back to the period of the French Revolution does is both to make apparent the enduring importance of the enormous political upheavals of 1789 for the France of 1968 and, at the same time, for anyone with an eye for the ironies of historical repetition and the tendency of the present to parody the past in reproducing it, to call into question the value of the comparison between 1789 and 1968. Any attempt at an evaluation of the EGC, ten years after the event, must take into account those tantalising remarks made by Marx on the relationship between past and present:

> The tradition of all the dead generations weighs like a nightmare on the brain of the living. And just when they seem engaged in revolutionising themselves and things, in creating something that has never yet existed, precisely in such periods of revolutionary crisis they anxiously conjure up the spirits of the past to their service and borrow from them names, battle cries and costumes in order to present the new scene of world history in this time-honoured disguise and this borrowed language.[20]

In borrowing this name from the past, the French film world of 1968 sought to express itself as a united and historically progressive force, but what the name itself tended to repress was both the bourgeois nature of the revolution of 1789, and the new class divisions, and some serious differences of political analysis which characterised the May movement, and the EGC itself.

The States General, that great three-tiered assembly of nobles, clergy and commons, met at Versailles in May 1789. Previously these three orders had received equal representation, but the already considerable power of the rising bourgeoisie had forced the monarchy to concede double representation to the commons (the 'Third Estate'). And, as George Rudé, one of the historians of the French Revolution, has pointed out: 'the urban bourgeoisie captured the great bulk of the seats among the deputies of the Third Estate'.[21] What the Third Estate then did, encouraged by popular support, was to declare its independence from the other orders and to claim for itself the title of

National Assembly, thus proposing itself as the sole legitimate representative of the French people and arrogating to itself the task of preparing and safeguarding a new constitution for the state. It was this Assembly which faced with the arrogance of the other orders, and locked out of its meeting place, had adjourned to a nearby tennis court where the massed deputies of the Third Estate 'took a solemn oath that the National Assembly should not disperse until the Constitution had been firmly established'.[22] It was this Third Estate of the States General which in 1789 both expressed and organised the massive transformation of class relations within French society, replacing the old order by the new, the clergy and nobility by the commons, but a commons firmly led and directed by the bourgeoisie.

The Estates General of the Cinema of 1968 was an infinitely more fragile affair, and yet one which reflected, perhaps, the new importance within an advanced capitalist society of the work of ideological opposition to existing social, political and economic relations. The EGC orchestrated this work of opposition at the level of the cultural apparatuses or institutions of the capitalist-technocratic state.

A couple of days after the great united student-worker demonstration of May 13 a special Cinema Commission was set up among the Action Committees at the Sorbonne, and a number of film screenings were organised in *lycées* (secondary schools) within and outside Paris, in various university buildings and in a number of factories. These screenings included both film classics and, more importantly, films (primarily agitprop documentaries) which had not been submitted to the censor and which therefore had no censor's certificate. The projection of these uncertificated films before the public was illegal. On Friday May 17 the Union of Film Production Technicians of the CGT (*Syndicat des Technicians de la Production Cinématographique*) called together a number of technicians, directors, and members of the French actors' union as well as students from the two main film and photography schools: the *Institut des Hautes Etudes Cinématographique* (IDHEC) and the *Ecole Nationale de Photographie et de Cinématographie* (ENPC). Out of this meeting and a subsequent meeting between members of the film technicians' union and the editors of *Cahiers du Cinéma* came the suggestion for a new institution to be called the Estates General of the French Cinema (*Etats Généraux du Cinéma Français*). An action committee and the film technicians' union itself issued invitations to all those active in or interested in French film culture to attend the first meeting of the EGC that evening (May 17), at the ENPC building in the rue de Vaugirard, which had been occupied by the film and photography students for a couple of days. More than a thousand people met together for the inaugural session. In the week that followed the EGC continued to meet in the premises of the occupied Film and Photography School, and then moved out to the Cultural Centre at Suresnes on the outskirts of Paris where three General Assemblies were held on May 26 and 28 and on June 5.

Although considerable efforts were made after June 5 to keep the EGC in existence and active, its major importance as a force expressing the needs and tensions of the French film world derives from the work which it accomplished between May 17 and June 5 — a period of just under three weeks. These were the three weeks which saw the spread of strikes and factory occupations throughout France, the strike by journalists and technicians at the ORTF, the constant repetition of massive demonstrations and, on occasions, of street fighting between demonstrators and riot police, the building of barricades and the attempted destruction of the Stock Exchange (the night of May 24), the rejection by the majority of French workers of the Grenelle agreements, de Gaulle's dissolution of the Assembly and the calling of a general election, and, finally, the gradual return to work beginning in the week of June 3. The major contradictions, the often confused debates and demands of the EGC, only begin to make sense in the light of the larger political questions of those three weeks; and first among these was the question: 'reform or revolution?' — was France witnessing the beginning of a major social transformation — the dissolution of the bourgeois state and its replacement by organisations representing the power of the workers, the organised power of the French working-class, or was it simply a crisis in the government to be resolved through the electoral process?

That the question of state power was thought to be in the balance by some during those weeks now seems the only explanation for the hopes expressed by them as to the 'revolutionary' potential of the EGC, the idea expressed, for example, in a *Cahiers du Cinéma* editorial (August 1968) that there was to be a 'Revolution in/through the cinema', and that 'making the revolution in the cinema' implied also 'making it before or at the same time everywhere else'.

Certainly the notion of 'direct action', of 'people's power', had penetrated to the sphere of culture, though its premise, that France was in a situation of dual power (that is, that there was a possibility of one sector of French society taking over power from another sector, of one class replacing another in the direction and organisation of the state) was not perhaps as closely scrutinised as it might have been. Given the political context, it was to be expected that certain groups within the cultural sphere should be arguing for the importance of 'direct action', and organising street demonstrations rather than trusting to the reforming zeal of an existing bureaucracy. *Cahiers*, for example, argued that the Langlois affair was to be seen as a prologue to the May events and that the lesson of the campaign around the Cinémathèque was that 'there must be no hesitation about demanding in the street what cannot be obtained in the offices'.[23]

One of the radical slogans of the great May 13 demonstration was 'Power is in the Streets'; such a statement, of course, cannot always be true, it must be based upon a careful estimation of the balance of class forces at a particular historical moment. In this respect, the tendency to 'take one's desires for reality' was in some quarters unproductively prevalent. It must be said immediately, however, that the fact that de Gaulle's government was returned to power with a large majority on June 30 does not detract from the long-term importance of the critical and creative energies unleashed in the course of the debates at the EGC.

It has already been suggested that the EGC was in certain respects a fragile organisation. This sense of fragility, of weakness, was echoed by the students in May (that is, by those students who were interested in seeing a revolutionary transformation of French society), and is summed up by the slogan which appeared on the banners of a student group which on May 16 had marched right across Paris with the intention of fraternising with the workers of the huge Renault plant at Boulogne-Billancourt:

> The workers will take from the fragile hands of the students the flag of the struggle against the anti-popular regime.

If the students, who had engaged large numbers of heavily-armed riot police in street fighting for several nights, regarded themselves as 'fragile' in terms of the larger scheme of things, how much more 'fragile' were the cultural workers: the film-makers, the film teachers, the film technicians, the journalists of the ORTF. And yet, there was a sense in which the weakness of those who worked in what has been called the 'consciousness industry'[24] was also their strength since they were in a position to analyse the production, and influence the dissemination, of the ideas, news, information, fictions of their respective industries; in other words they were in a position to engage in analysis and struggle at the level of ideology, and around the question of *hegemony* (that is, through the analysis of the variety of methods by which a ruling group organises the consent, rather than the compulsion of the majority to compliance with its own rule, its own dominance).

The difficult and contradictory nature of cultural production was apparent from the beginning of the EGC's work. For, on the one hand, on May 19 the Film Technicians' Union declared an unlimited strike, and on the other, a day later, the EGC made arrangements for filming to carry on, despite the strike (though not in opposition to it), so that films could be made about the workers' and students' movement. So that what was being attacked on the one hand as a commercial product, a 'mere commodity' whose owners moreover were to be bereft of their needed profit through the withdrawal of labour on the part of the workers, was at the same time being recognised as a valuable cultural product, if only it could be inserted into a different system of production and consumption. Thus the *Cahiers* editors argue for the value of those films which were being produced on the subject of the workers on strike and the radical students by film crews working 'outside of all existing structures';[25] and their attitude to mainstream cinema reveals the high hopes which were being expressed at that time for the development of an alternative cinema, what was rather loosely called the 'cinema of today':

> It is no longer a question of defending a 'parallel cinema' which will remain always the poor relative of the 'official' cinema: it is the whole or part of this latter cinema which has become for us marginal . . .

The *Cahiers* editors' purpose is rather to further the 'knowledge and dissemination of that which is truly the cinema of today.'[26]

The desired 'cinema of today' was to be defined largely in relationship to and in reaction against what were seen to be the negative aspects of existing structures. First among these was the *Centre National de la Cinématographie* (CNC), and one of the earliest motions discussed, voted on and passed by the EGC declared:

> The Estates General of the French Cinema deems the reactionary structures of the CNC to be abolished.[27]

The CNC had been founded in 1946 and was subject to two government ministries: the Ministry of Information and the Ministry of Cultural Affairs. It had various commissions which dealt with the employment of projectionists, the issuing of professional identity cards, the authorisation of feature films and shorts and the collection of statistics. The Centre also drafted legislation to cover most aspects of film production, distribution and exhibition and, most importantly from the film-makers' point of view, it administered the financing system known as 'advance on receipts' which gave film-makers block sums of money as a loan in anticipation of monies to be received from the box office upon completion of the film. It also financed a body known as Unifrance Films (which had the responsibility of promoting French films abroad), funded the IDHEC film school, and put money into the Cannes International Film Festival. Basically the Centre acted as the arm of the government, carrying out the policies of the government in so far as it wished to intervene in the organisation of the French film industry.

In May most areas of the Centre's work came under fire, but perhaps the most bitter criticism was reserved for the government, which could have used the CNC as a body that would genuinely be engaged in the protection and fostering of the French industry, but which rather chose to stand aside while the industry (if we include distribution as well as production) was massively infiltrated by foreign capital. This invasion of the film screens by foreign-financed and produced films was severely criticised and was seen to be responsible for, among other things, the chronic unemployment of the French film industry. A member of the Film Technicians' Union, interviewed by *Cinéthique* in 1969, gave the following break-down of distributors' receipts. Out of a total of 249 million francs:

> 108m went to 8 American or British companies (7 American, 1 British)
> 103m went to 9 French companies
> 6m went to the *Art et Essai* (Art house) circuit
> 32m went to 69 independent distributors.[28]

Most of the films sponsored by the EGC and made as a record of the May events were produced quite outside the kind of distribution and exhibition circuits referred to by the figures quoted in *Cinéthique*. It was agreed that these usually short documentary film projects were to be regarded as the result of collective efforts, and that they would not therefore bear the name of any one film-maker; a brief listing of the titles of some of them here will give an indication of the kinds of subjects to be covered in this way:

Université critique, Che Guevara, Paris—manifestation 13 mai, Sorbonne, Répression, Besançon-Rhodiaceta, Le pouvoir est dans la rue (Power is in the Street), Comités d'action (Action Committees), Ce n'est qu'un début (Only a Beginning).

Like the Committee for the Defence of the Cinémathèque the EGC was a broad front organisation, encompassing a fairly wide variety of political positions, and, in the absence of a revolutionary transformation of French society, it is difficult to see how this extraordinarily diverse collection of directors and producers, technicians and students, could have developed a working unity over a long period of time. In other words, without a revolution in society it is difficult to see how the EGC could have expected a working future for itself, given that the differences of interest between the members of the organisation could only be exacerbated within a capitalist mode of production. In a situation of scarce resources, with intense competition for jobs, and financing available for relatively few projects, the differences of interest between producers and directors, directors and technicians, and technicians and students, or (even more intensely) between technicians and amateurs, were bound, sooner or later, to break apart the precarious unity of the organisation. It is all the more extraordinary, therefore, that for those three weeks in May the EGC operated as a viable and efficient forum for the expression of the needs and aspirations of the French film world.

Among its most important achievements, apart from the sponsoring of a series of films, was the production of a number of plans for the transformation and re-structuring of the whole of the French film industry. These plans, drawn up by a variety of different groups, were finally submitted in the form of nineteen different projects, and were discussed and evaluated by the EGC general assembly early in June. The three projects which received the most votes at the assembly were numbers 16, 13 and 19, while number 4 was regarded as one of the most controversial, or one of the most utopian.

Before attempting a consideration of the major recommendations of each of these projects, it would be useful to summarise the more general questions or issues around which each of the projects revolves. As has already been indicated the larger political question which lay behind all of these deliberations was the question of 'reform or revolution?' From this larger question there stemmed other issues which may be listed thus: (i) the division of labour in the film industry and the organisation of production, and the notion of class relations around the point of production; (ii) self-management and the notion of workers' control; (iii) censorship; (iv) the relationship with the state, and the notion of a 'parallel' cinema; (v) finance and distribution; (vi) education or training; (vii) the relationship between film and television.

Project 16 (prepared by a group consisting of René Allio, Jean-Louis Comolli, Paula Delsol, R. Dembo, Jacques Doniol-Valcroze, Jean-Paul Le Chanois, Louis Malle, Jean-Pierre Mocky, Jean-Daniel Pollet, Alain Resnais, Jacques Rivette, Jacques Wagner) declared its intention to make a 'radical break' with the existing system, and spoke of the need to bring about the 'destruction of the old structures' of the French cinema.[29] It proposed the setting up of a public sector which would be in competition with the private sector of the industry, the abolition of all censorship bodies, the establishment of a central office which would organise the direct collection of all box office monies and their subsequent re-distribution, and the abolition of the existing division between the cinema and television industries. It was envisaged that the public sector would:

> ... operate on principles of autonomy and self-management and will be based on the total absence of profit-making as a goal.[30]

Project 16 argued that within the existing system ('slavery conditions engendered by the capitalist system') the search for profits reduced films to a 'mere commodity', and it set against this reductive process the need to consider films in terms of their 'more profound value'. Thus a notion of 'art' was being proposed, as against a notion of 'commodity'. The solution to the problem was seen to be the removal of artistic or cultural production into the sphere of state finance, not controlled by the profit motive. However, while the progressive nature of this proposal must be acknowledged, there may have been an underestimation of the extent to which the co-existence of public and private sectors might result in the same kind of restrictive determinations (including the dominant concept of 'entertainment') which characterised the private sector being placed upon, and holding back the development of, the public sector. To put the case in a more general way: the setting up of a sphere of cultural production not dominated by the profit motive, in a society which is dominated by the profit motive, would leave a number of unresolved problems.

The basis of the public sector system as outlined by Project 16 would be the formation of Production Units which would operate on the principles of autonomy and self-management. The officers with responsibility for managing one of these units would be drawn 'from all branches of film work', and would be elected every two years by the Permanent Council of the Estates General, and in terms of the detailed organisation of production would be free to choose a system of collective responsibility or one of individual responsibilities (that is, a system of collective decisions or of individual authority —normally that of the director). The concepts of individual authorship and of a production process controlled by a single person were not therefore abandoned, but the proposed appointment of unit officers from the different branches of film production, including technicians as well as directors, meant that the way was open for a gradual breaking down of the distinction between mental and manual labour and for a rejection of the assumption that decision-making should naturally be the job of the 'intellectual' workers.

A Finance and Re-Distribution Service (controlled by representatives of the Permanent Council of the EGC) would be responsible for collecting money direct from the box offices, and for channelling this money back into the financing of the Production Units. This national, public Finance Service, together with a public Promotion and Distribution Body, which would organise film distribution, would help to rationalise the industry by cutting out a whole range of 'middlemen' who not only controlled audience access to the product through their programming policy, but also, in raking out their own profits, reduced the global sum available to be ploughed back into film production. As well as setting up a nationalised and centralised distribution service it was envisaged that there would be a policy of progressive nationalisation of the cinemas also, so that while the private sector at all levels (production, distribution and exhibition) would continue to exist, all aspects of the industry, including that of film screening or exhibition, would gradually be brought under public control. The problem of reaching particular audiences was also acknowledged, and an account given of the inadequacies (even by the standards of an efficient capitalism) of the present system in this respect:

> ... the spectators' access to films is organised in an arbitrary manner by a small number of all-powerful programmers ... the operations of the exhibitors are equally marked by a commitment to routine. No account is taken of changes in the public and its artistic and cultural needs, nor of the profound transformation of methods of selling on the level of capitalism itself. In all spheres of modern commerce, the seller goes out in search of the buyer—the exhibitors sit back and wait for him.[31]

Project 16 therefore insisted on the full participation of representatives of Production Units in the work of distribution, so that the makers of the film might have a say in the manner of its distribution, and argued for 'a new commitment to audience research' on the part of the central Promotion and Distribution Body. In addition, a proportion of all box office monies should be allocated to 'theoretical research, education and the donation of copies of the works produced to the Cinémathèque Française'. The work of young or new film-makers would be encouraged through the allocation of a certain percentage of the annual budget of each Production Unit to the production of first films.

Projects 13 and 19 made proposals along the same general lines. Project 13 is of particular interest because it was put together by officers and members of the CGT Film Technicians' Union. It was proposed by Pierre L'homme and the working party included Henri Faviani, Philippe Arthuys, Jean Michaud-Maillan; moreover, it was approved by the majority of the members of the union. This project, like Project 16, emphasised the need to set up a public sector for film production, distribution and exhibition under the principle of workers' control. In addition it underlined the particular importance of education in film for both producers and spectators. Arguing from the premise that 'The cinema is a universal mode of language and as such belongs to all', the proposers demanded:

> ... the means for a permanent and democratic training in its *écriture* ['writing' or 'production'] and interpretation: (a) at the level of the teaching of audio-visual techniques within a school which brings together the disciplines as a whole; (b) at the level of access to film

culture, from primary to secondary education, as well as in all spheres of social life.[32]

In emphasising the importance of interpretation as well as of production (to use a more literal translation, the importance of both 'reading' and 'writing'), the proposers of this project acknowledged that a concept of film culture which discussed only the production and dissemination of films would be inadequate. What was seen to be equally important was the creation of a context for the reception of the films produced; in this respect a new kind of film education needed to be developed and was to be defended on the grounds that knowledge of the cinema (and the ability to 'read' films critically, which would derive from that knowledge) could not be gained from watching films alone. A living film culture could not grow simply out of the watching of movies, rather it would grow out of the *relationship* between the act of watching and a critical awareness of the techniques of the cinema. Film education would change the context within which the films were viewed, and make possible a more active role for the spectator: the role of challenging, analysing and criticising the spectacle, not simply consuming it. This desire to think about film culture in a broader sense, to consider not just the transmission and reception of films, not just production, distribution and exhibition as discrete entities, but to think also about the context of reception, the context of film exhibition – to think, in other words, about the level of knowledge of the film's spectators – was characteristic also of the concerns of Project 16. The proposers of Project 16 had noted, as a criticism of the existing system, that:

... the spectator, who must also be formed by a knowledge of the art of film, is given no access to the study of its techniques.[33]

They criticised the existing educational system on the grounds that it was 'aimed at an élite' and 'trains technicians to serve the system as it exists'. Precisely because this sytem of education in film production was *not* 'founded on any desire to spread a training for the cinema into traditional education' it therefore tended, so Project 16 argued, to support the existing system of film production and its financing by monopoly capital:

... to protect the monopolies by keeping back cinematic training from the majority.[34]

The educational system, in training technicians and not spectators, could only therefore reinforce the existing relations of production and consumption in the cinema. Only through the extension of film education to the majority of the spectators could a new kind of film culture be developed. This desire to change the context within which films are received led the proposers of Project 13 to consider not only the development of a new kind of film education, but also to take more seriously, and to regard as more problematic, the questions of distribution and of the promotion of individual films. Because the process of promoting a film is part of the preparation of a context of reception for that film, Project 13 recommended that:

A committee of experts specialised in promotion will be created to launch and support the career of *each* film.[35]

Project 19, drawn up by a group which included Michel Cournot, Marcel Carné, Claude Lelouch, Robert Enrico, Jean-Gabriel Albiocco, Serge Roulet, made proposals similar to those of Projects 16 and 13 for setting up a public sector for film production, distribution and exhibition. In addition, in relation to the work of distribution they emphasised the need to search out new projection sites, so that apart from traditional screenings in cinemas and film societies, films would also be projected in:

> factories and firms, schools and universities, youth clubs and cultural centres, ships, trains, aeroplanes and other means of transport, and mobile projection units created in suburban and country areas.[36]

The searching out of such non-traditional projection sites, apart from being a way of extending the market for the circulation of films, could also be seen as an aspect of the desire to produce a new kind of context for the reception of a particular film, and thereby also a new sort of relationship between audience and spectacle.

Projects 16, 19 and 13 were all characterised by both the search for new practices, and adherence to older formulae. This tension between the old and the new manifested itself clearly in the descriptions of the organisation of production: Project 19, for example, retained the traditional division of labour at the point of production by listing the categories of producer, director, technician, administrative personnel etc., characteristic of the existing system of production, yet at the same time it suggested an attack on the existing system through its support for the notion of workers' control and self-management and through a concept of profit-sharing which was, however, limited by acceptance of the principle of salary differential:

> Over and above a certain ceiling, what might be termed the excess amount in the highest salaries should be shared among the members of the group.

The same kind of tension between old and new is apparent in the advocacy of co-productions between the (proposed) public and the existing private sector. Moreover this policy on co-productions seemed to resolve the question 'reform or revolution?' in favour of reform of the existing system of film production, not its revolutionary transformation. Similarly the notion of profit-sharing could be seen at most as a transitional demand, certainly not, in itself, as a demand for the abolition of wage labour and of an economic system motivated by the need to produce profit on capital invested. The system is still to be motivated by the search for profit, but these profits are to be shared out a little more equitably. In terms of the relationship between film production and the state, these proposals assumed no revolutionary transformation of that state.

Project 4, supported by Thierry Derocles, Michel Demoule, Claude Chabrol and Marin Karmitz, was regarded by many at the EGC as the most revolutionary or the most utopian of the projects. It caused considerable controversy within the EGC, and was partly instrumental in the EGC's failure to agree upon a final platform or position statement. The Project 4 proposers refused to accept the 'synthesis project' which was put forward to the General Assembly of the EGC on June 5. This 'synthesis project' was put together by the proposers of Projects 16, 13 and 19, and represented an attempt by these proposers to produce a minimal programme around which the EGC might unite. Such unity proved impossible to achieve, and the final statement issued by the Estates General was very much shorter, vaguer and more general than even the compromise position outlined in the synthesis project. Project 4, by contrast, had all of the elegant aggressiveness of a no-compromise position. Emphasising the need for a thoroughly democratic mass medium the proposers of this project made this demand:

> As a participant in the cultural development of all, the audio-visual area must revolutionise its way of existing.[37]

To this end they outlined the development of a public service sector for both film and television, which was to be independent of the government, and financed by a national fee or levy (not unlike the system of the BBC licence fee in Britain). The money thus raised would be used to finance the whole of the national film industry; in this way, the proposers argued, 'the spectators become producers', and admission to all films would be free. This method of finance would allow for more films to be produced, and would reduce unemployment in the industry. In addition, the public service sector would operate according to the principles of workers' control, so that the makers of any film would take charge of that film throughout all the stages of production and distribution, and film workers would be paid a 'uniform monthly salary' which would end the casualisation of labour in the industry. In addition to this basic salary, each worker would also receive 'a second salary calculated on the basis of qualifications for every film he works on'. Thus a system of wage differentials is still envisaged, although it is proposed that any monies raised from the sale of a film abroad would be divided equally among the members of the production team, thus introducing, to some extent, the notion of equality between workers at the point of production.

Along with its provisions for the organisation and financing of production, Project 4 spoke of the need for a 'genuine decentralisation of culture'. This was to be achieved through the setting up of regional offices which would:

> ... not only provide for film exhibition, but also for film production and professional training in all regions of the country.[38]

The stranglehold of a metropolitan culture was also to be loosened through the proposal for an aggressive and innovative system for distribution and exhibition:

> New cinemas must be established, but mobile projection units must also be set up so that films may reach factories and rural communities where a cinema would not be appropriate.[39]

Neither Project 4, nor the less controversial Synthesis Project, were accepted at the final meeting of the general assembly of the Estates General on June 5. Instead, the EGC passed a rather brief and general final motion which, while making quite explicit the political nature of the EGC's opposition to the existing system, failed to produce a programme of concrete proposals to be agreed and acted upon by all. The motion began with the declaration:

> The Estates General of the Cinema were born of a popular movement of opposition and struggle against the economic, social and ideological order—that of capital protected by the state apparatus.[40]

Its main points can be summarised thus: the destruction of the monopolies and the creation of a nationalised industry; workers' control and a method of production not governed by the law of profit; the abolition of censorship; access for all social classes to practical or theoretical knowledge of the techniques of the cinema, and the linking of cinema and television 'independent of the political and financial powers'.

It could be argued that the return to work and the re-stabilisation of de Gaulle's government in early June rendered impossible the development of any revolutionary policies within the cultural sphere. But what marks the final statement of the EGC is not so much the absence of a revolutionary programme as the absence of even a reformist programme of action. It is as though this potentially powerful organisation, caught up within the political contradictions of May, was unable to clear for itself a space for action and for the collective implementation of policy. While summarising a range of radical objections to the existing system, it was unable to propose the means for the transformation of that system. Its legacy to the future is to be found in the comprehensive nature of its critique of existing practices. Those who inherit the legacy are left with the problem of making this critique politically effective.

The film groups

The *Cahiers du Cinéma* editorial of August 1968 ('Revolution in/through the Cinema') spoke of the work of certain film-making groups working outside of all existing structures, and emphasised the need to develop new film distribution circuits to disseminate their work. This oppositional practice at the level of both production and distribution gave rise to the notion of a parallel, marginal or alternative cinema, and many film-makers defended this parallel cinema as the only possible locus for a militant practice. The existing system of film production and distribution was criticised on the grounds that it operated only to market film-commodities to alienated spectators and that, further, the consumption of these spectacles contributed to the maintenance of that alienation. The parallel cinema was to contribute to the destruction of that endless circuit which began with alienated production and ended with alienated consumption.

It is important to realise in this respect that one of the effects of May was to open up the sphere of cultural production to a class analysis and to encourage the asking of the question: which classes were served by which forms of cultural production? The first issue of the new film journal *Cinéthique*, which appeared in January 1969, bore on its cover a photograph of a wall covered with posters which asked one of those insistent questions of May: 'Who Creates? For Whom?' This slogan then implied a further question 'who profits?', or more exactly, 'which class profits from the production of cultural objects?' Many highly reductionist answers were offered to this question, but what needs to be noted here is a certain significant ambiguity about the use of the word 'profit'.

The use of the verb 'profit' in this context fuses, and to some extent obscures, two specific, distinct but related operations: *firstly* the extraction of surplus value or 'profit' from the process of film production, and *secondly* the production of systems of ideas about the world which are helpful to and supportive of existing social relations, those relations which ensure the right of the profiteers to profit. The first of these operations is related to the economic, and the second to the ideological spheres of activity. Both these spheres of activity were regarded as important by the parallel cinema, and its adherents worked both to counteract the profit-motive of the existing industry and to counteract the production of ideas supportive of the *status quo*.

The radical film groups which came into existence in response to the May events attempted to mount an attack, from outside, on the existing structures of the film industry. Their mode of operating was in direct opposition to that which characterised the mainstream of the industry, and their means of distribution had therefore to be outside the existing distribution circuits. A statement issued by one of the student action committees made it clear that the radically committed film-makers were searching for a new political content, a new audience, and a new relationship between the two. Film was seen (in perhaps too unproblematic a way) as a weapon in the service of class struggle:

> It is urgent that we become aware of the absolute need to place in the service of the revolution all the means at our disposal. We must support the strikers. Films must be projected in the factories.[41]

A film projected in a factory is a rather different phenomenon from a film projected in a cinema, and the former was seen as part of an attempt at breaking down the 'normal' relationship that exists in capitalist society between the audience-consumer and the spectacle-product. The emphasis on new locations for screenings indicated the beginning of a realisation that it was not enough simply to change the *content* of films, but that the whole socio-economic structure in which they operated had also to be changed. Film as a consumer product was seen as an intrinsicially non-revolutionary phenomenon, and to simply use the film content to show a condition of misery, of contestation or of struggle was regarded as an inadequate, an incomplete solution.

It is interesting in this respect to contrast the remarks made by Paul Séban, maker of the film *La CGT en mai*, with a point made some three decades earlier by the critic Walter Benjamin. Benjamin, in his essay 'The Author as Producer', pointed out the dangers of:

> ... a certain type of fashionable photography, which makes misery into a consumer good ... I must go a step further and say that it has made the *struggle against misery* into a consumer good.[42]

Séban, in an interview with *Cinéthique*, discusses the way in which television has developed a method for showing reality without ever explaining or analysing that which is depicted, without ever indicating certain causal connections between the elements depicted, presenting these elements rather as a spectacle to be consumed:

> Television always stops at the moment when things are becoming interesting ... it is terrible to think that, finally, on television misery and struggle are presented as a spectacle. They show the rats, and the children who are going to eat them, the sordid picturesque, but they never say anything about imperialism which is the cause of it.[43]

The argument of both Séban and Benjamin is that the media (film, photography and, for Séban, television) present spectacles — e.g., given instances of suffering as 'the way things are' — for consumption, rather than offering the kind of exploration of social inequality which would give the audience the conceptual framework necessary for, firstly, the recognition, and then the analysis, of this inequality. What Séban and other radical film-makers propose, therefore, is a method of film production and exchange based on a new kind of relationship between the film-maker and his/her subject (e.g., engagement with a particular social struggle, not its observation from a distance), *and* a new kind of relationship between film and audience. Changing that latter relationship was seen to entail the development of new film screening circuits in order to serve those audiences for whom the cinema could become a means for the exploration of social reality and whose interest was ultimately in the transformation of that reality.

In addition to the attempt at developing new methods of distribution and exhibition, the radical film groups attempted a re-organisation of the practices of production: in particular the development of a collective mode of working which refused the hierarchisation of tasks typical of the mainstream of the industry. Thus decisions about script and treatment were taken collectively and the clear distinction between those filmed and those doing the filming (and taking the decisions about the organisation of meaning in the finished film) began to be broken down as the film-makers entered into extensive consultation with those about whom they were making the film. In this way the method of organising around the point of production developed as a genuinely co-operative endeavour, and the mental-manual distinction characteristic of the division of labour within the existing industry began to

be replaced by a less alienated and less alienating mode of production.
With the emergence of a collective mode of working the concept of individual authorship was gradually discarded, or at least called into question. It is interesting in this respect to note one of the more radical attacks on the notion and the value of individual authorship in the cinema mounted in a leaflet that was distributed at the 1969 film festival at Hyères. The leaflet attacked the notion of individual authorship and the way in which the festival itself worked to enshrine the value and importance of the director as the sole producer of meaning. It spoke of the cinema of directors as a cinema defending the interests of private property (the concept of authorship being linked with the concept of ownership in a way which was perhaps more problematic than the writers of this document were willing to allow), and summarised the role of the author as that of *'patron du sens'* (the 'boss of meaning').[44] The notion that a film director was to be found lined up on the side of the owners, rather than on the side of the workers, in the production of any film was an idea that was also developed by the militants of the film technicians' union. The film groups tried to develop a practice which would lead them out of what were seen as the twin traps of individual authorship and, beyond that, of private ownership.

The most well-known of these film collectives is probably the *Dziga Vertov* group which was set up, in the words of Jean-Luc Godard, one of its members, 'to make politically a political cinema':

> . . . to make concrete analysis of a concrete situation . . . to understand the laws of the objective world in order to actively transform that world . . . to know one's place in the process of production in order then to change it.[45]

Interviewed on the question of how the group came into existence, Godard noted that it was a union between himself, wanting to leave the cinema, and Jean-Pierre Gorin, a political militant, wanting to come into the cinema. The work of Godard and of the *Dziga Vertov* group in attempting a revolutionising of the language of the cinema has been well documented elsewhere and will not be discussed here. In terms of the larger political configurations of May it should be noted, however, that the *Dziga Vertov* group was committed to a leftist position extremely critical of the French Communist Party. Indeed, despite all of the arguments which have been made about the 'open' structure of a film like *Tout va bien* (produced by the group in 1972), this film operates as a sustained defence of the leftist position, offering finally an unproblematic endorsement of the politics of spontaneity, and thus reproducing an ideology which, it might be argued, constituted one of the chief weaknesses of the May movement. The radical rejection of the policies of the PCF left the group in the uncomfortable position of arguing that film is one of the weapons in the class struggle, that film production should be subject to, and accept, the leadership of the vanguard organisation directing that class struggle but, crucially, that no such organisation existed in France. Godard expressed the problem in this way:

> The cinema is a party instrument and we find ourselves in countries
> where the revolutionary party is far from existing.[46]

The films of the group include: *British Sounds, Pravda, Vent d'est, Struggle in Italy, Vladimir and Rosa, Tout va bien* and *Letter to Jane.*

A second film group whose existence in fact preceded the May events but whose work was stimulated by them was SLON (*Société pour le lancement des oeuvres nouvelles* — Society for the promotion of new works). The group arose out of a contribution made to the film *Loin du Vietnam (Far from Vietnam)* and its first project as a group developed out of co-operation between film-makers and militant workers at Besançon in December 1967. Two members of the group, Chris Marker and Mario Marret, made *A bientôt j'espère* (1967/8). This film was criticised by the workers for being too sad, too romantic, an outsider's view of industrial struggle, and *Critique/autocritique* was made from the video recording of that discussion.

SLON criticised the smooth, technical perfection of mainstream cinema, and opposed this technical perfection in their practice; this criticism, however, did not lead them in the direction of the formal avant-gardism of the *Dziga Vertov* group. And while they praised Godard as 'the purest, the most courageous, the most universal film-maker for a long time', yet they had reservations about his experimentation with new forms, and drew a parallel with the attempts of the nineteenth century romantics to smash the accepted conventions of communication:

> Godard strives to break down the old forms. But perhaps he will end
> up in the silence of Rimbaud.[47]

Subsequently the group, now under the name *Groupe Medvedkine*, changed its composition and internal modes of organisation in order to represent more adequately the workers' own views and priorities, and the decision-making role of the film-makers themselves was reduced or disappeared entirely. The group took its title from the name of a Soviet film-maker who had worked extensively in the countryside in the 1930s with propaganda units which were organised around the famous agit-prop cinema trains, characteristic of the work of Soviet education after the revolution. The films of *Medvedkine*, under the workers' own direction, included: *Rhodia 4/8, Nouvelle société, Classe de lutte (Class Struggle)* and *On vous parle,* which consisted of a whole series of newsreel-type films on a variety of subjects including Latin America, Greece and Brazil.

SLON and *Medvedkine* were non-sectarian groups, but a fourth organisation, *Dynadia*, was linked with the French Communist Party. *Dynadia*, while sympathetic to the notion of a militant cinema operating as part of the overall propaganda work of a national political organisation, seems to have been somewhat hostile to the notion of a parallel or marginal cinema. This hostility derives from, or can be explained in terms of, two positions. Firstly there was the notion that a marginal cinema could only be the work of a minority speaking to a minority, and, moreover, that both of these minorities tended to be more interested in the freedom of self-expression and in notions of individual creativity than in taking an active and progressive part in contemporary class struggle. Secondly there was the idea (regarded as mistaken or dangerous by other groups on the left) that art was to be regarded as a neutral province or a universal language, that it could not be directly related to class struggle or to the development of a particular political programme. It is interesting to recollect in this context that the project for the re-organisation of the French film industry submitted to the Estates General of the Cinema by the CGT Film Technicians' Union (Project 13), spoke of the cinema as a 'universal mode of language', and two members of this union, in an interview with *Cinéthique*, while acknowledging the importance of a militant cinema practice referred to this practice as a 'work of struggle' not a 'work of art';[48] the world of art is more-or-less marked off from the world in which political struggles take place: 'The entity called ART is universal. No need to apply to it the notion of class'.[49] *Dynadia* in an interview in 1970 expressed the position in this way:

> We do not wish to replace art with politics, neither mechanically to confuse the two.[50]

While there might have been considerable agreement, on the left, on the need not to confuse 'art' and 'politics', a number of left-wing groups would have wished to insist that the domain of art, or of cultural production, was itself one of the domains (or, perhaps more properly, one of the dimensions) of class struggle; that it was not a question of saving up some existing entity called 'art' to be handed over to the working-class, but rather that the domain of cultural production was already an area of struggle between competing ideas, and often mutually contradictory systems of values and beliefs, and that it was the task of those on the left engaged in cultural production to enter into and to intensify these struggles. The members of *Dynadia* were committed to the development of a militant and propagandist cinema practice, but for them this did not entail the development of a parallel cinema or of an alternative or oppositional culture; their films were seen as a contribution to the propaganda work of the Communist Party, not as a contribution to the development of art or to the history of the cinema. The questions of the specific nature and problems of struggle at the level of cultural production were not therefore raised, and there was a tendency to instrumentalise film-making, that is, to see film as one of the instruments of propaganda, as one of many possible vehicles for the dissemination of ideas, without taking into account the ways in which the nature of the 'instrument' might affect the dissemination of the ideas. The films made by *Dynadia* include *Dix ans de Gaullisme* (1968); *Les communistes dans la lutte* (1969); *Le témoignage de Pham Thi Lien; Les immigrés en France: le logement* (1969); *Laos images sauvées* (1970); *Le choix* (1970).[51]

One final group should be mentioned briefly, the *Cinéastes révolutionnaires prolétariens* (Revolutionary Proletarian Film-Makers). This group put forward the positions and analyses of the Maoist left in France, and filmed the strikes and confrontations between workers and police at the Renault works at Flins; they also covered the trial of Alain Geismar. They speak of making films 'under the direction of the workers' and were often forced to explore unusual venues for their screenings (in one case out in the street) because their films, often without visas from the censor and highly controversial because of their strong criticism of official trade unionism, could not be shown easily in public. They seem to have depended in many instances on the protection of the working-class community for whom the films were being screened. Supporting the Maoist paper *La cause du peuple*, they put forward constant criticisms of what they saw as the reformist, not revolutionary, policies of the French Communist Party. Despite this difference of political position, the *Cinéastes révolutionnaires* seem to have subscribed to an instrumentalist notion of the cinema, similar to the views adopted by *Dynadia*; the question, therefore of the particular ways in which the cinema mediates social reality was not explored, and the major problem was seen to be one of content. The question of the particular means of representation to be selected for the investigation of an aspect of social reality was left to one side.

The film journals

The impact of the May events can be traced through the pages of a number of French film journals, though the two which most explicitly and consistently referred themselves back to the events were *Cahiers du Cinéma* and *Cinéthique* (the latter founded in January 1969). It is arguable that the journal *Positif* should be linked with *Cahiers* and *Cinéthique* in this respect. However, despite *Positif*'s long-established (pre-May) tradition of left-oriented criticism, its subsequent frequent references to the May events and to the work of *Cahiers* and *Cinéthique*, and its explorations of the arena of political cinema, it would be fair to say that the May events had less radical, traumatic and far-reaching consequences for the development of its critical work.

Already, before May, *Cahiers* had involved itself in extensive and polemical coverage of the Langlois affair; its June-July issue (1968) referred to his victorious re-instatement, made brief reference to the political events of May and to the founding of the Estates General of the Cinema, but was mostly given over to an examination of the history of the French avant-garde film. It was not until the August issue that the detailed coverage of May began with the publication of the deliberations of the EGC and a full account of the more important proposals for the radical reorganisation of the French cinema put forward by that body. Moreover a number of the *Cahiers* writers had themselves been involved in the founding of the EGC. The September issue, indicating a desire to maintain the momentum of the spring, placed at the head of its table of contents this quotation from Roland Barthes:

> Since Marx, Nietzsche, Freud, *criticism*, the tearing away of the ideological wrappings with which our society surrounds knowledge, feeling, behaviour, value, is the great work of this century. We must not each time begin again from zero.[52]

But this hopeful assertion of a programme of theoretical and critical work was not immediately followed up, and the magazine reverted to the production of more traditional work on the American cinema, including the films of Warhol, to an examination of the work of Rivette, Buñuel, Jacques Demy, an account of the Venice film festival, and ended the year with a special issue on the films of Carl Dreyer. The August editorial of *Cahiers* had indicated that it would no longer be the policy of the magazine to concern itself with the products of the major distribution circuits or with the first-run films released in Paris, rather the locus of attention was to be shifted to films only shown in the Cinémathèques and cine-clubs and to those films threatened increasingly by political as well as commercial censorship.

The implications of this shift for the theoretical work of the magazine only began to be apparent early in 1969 with the initiation of a series of translations from the writings of Eisenstein (beginning in February 1969), and with the appearance of a number of articles addressing the theoretical problems raised by the concepts of *cinéma-vérité* (or *cinéma direct*) and film montage.

The spring of 1969 also saw the publication of a two-part article, '*La Suture*' by Jean-Pierre Oudart,[53] which marked the introduction into film studies of psychoanalytic theories of the formation or 'constitution' of the individual human subject, derived from the work of the psychoanalyst Jacques Lacan. '*La Suture*' attempted a reconsideration of the relationship between 'film' and 'spectator' in terms of a theory of reading based on the accounts offered by Lacanian psychoanalysis of the processes involved in the formation of the reading subject (the film reader or spectator). This work has had considerable repercussions for the development of film theory both in France and in Britain.[54]

Cahiers' most explicit statement of its post-'68 position, its clearest presentation of a programme of work, and one which precipitated a crisis in the ownership of the magazine, was made in the autumn of 1969 in a two-part article, 'Cinema/Ideology/Criticism' by Jean-Louis Comolli and Paul Narboni.[55] This article spoke of the need to develop a 'critical theory of the cinema . . . in direct reference to the method of dialectical materialism'.[56] Their approach, as outlined here, was based upon the assumption that film could and should be considered as an aspect of ideology, as a vehicle for the expression of dominant social systems of values and beliefs:

> Cinema is one of the languages through which the world communicates itself to itself. They constitute its ideology for they reproduce the world as it is experienced when filtered through the ideology . . . The film is ideology presenting itself to itself, talking to itself, learning about itself . . . it is the nature of the system to turn the cinema into an instrument of ideology . . .[57]

Later the notion of ideology as some kind of distorting filter (with the implication that, in cinema, it might some day be removed to reveal 'reality as it really is'), as well as the idea that an art form (the cinema) could be totally and simply subsumed within the category of 'ideology', could be entirely explained in terms of 'ideology', was called into question.

The main achievement of this article, however, was to propose a number of categories of films with the aim of assisting the film critic in differentiating between types of films, and allowing the following questions to be answered:

> ... which films ... allow the ideology a free, unhampered passage?
> ... And which attempt to make it turn back and reflect itself, intercept it and make it visible by revealing its mechanisms ...?[58]

Comolli and Narboni suggest that there are seven types or categories of films; it may be useful to list them briefly here:

(a) films which are 'imbued through and through with the dominant ideology in pure and unadulterated form';
(b) films which 'attack their ideological assimilation on two fronts'; these both 'deal with a directly political subject', and are involved in the process of 'breaking down the traditional way of depicting reality';
(c) films in which the content 'is not explicitly political, but in some way becomes so through the criticism practised on it through its form'; certain experimental films are cited here which operate the principle of self-reflexivity, of reflecting back on, and making explicit, their own devices for producing meaning;
(d) films which 'have an explicitly political content ... but which do not effectively criticise the ideological system in which they are embedded because they unquestioningly adopt its language and its imagery';
(e) films which seem at first to be caught within the dominant ideology, but which reveal on closer inspection that:

> An internal criticism is taking place which cracks the film apart at the seams. If one reads the film obliquely, looking for symptoms, if one looks beyond its apparent formal coherence, one can see that it is riddled with cracks: it is splitting under an internal tension which is simply not there in an ideologically innocuous film. The ideology thus becomes subordinate to the text. It no longer has an independent existence: it is *presented* by the film. This is the case in many Hollywood films, for example, which, while being completely integrated in the system and the ideology, end up by partially dismantling the system from within.[59]

It is this *Cahiers* category (e) which has subsequently provided the most food for thought for those critics who are primarily interested in the analysis of popular, mainstream, commercial cinema (*Cahiers* cite the films of Ford, Dreyer and Rossellini as examples of this category.)

(f) films which make use of *cinéma-vérité* techniques, and which are based on actual political events, but which, like category (d), 'do not challenge the cinema's traditional, ideologically-conditioned method of "depiction" ';
(g) films which make use of *cinéma-vérité* techniques and which are based on actual political events, but which also operate critically at the level of

their form, which call into question the conventions of documentary film.[60]

The crucial point which is introduced in relation to the seven categories is the notion that a film's capacity either to reproduce or to call into question dominant ideology is related to the formal devices adopted by that film. Certain formal devices, certain means of representation, facilitate a more thorough-going critique of dominant ideology than others.

The explicit advocacy of a Marxist approach, the emphasis on adopting the methods of dialectical materialism in order to develop a theory of the cinema, led to a crisis within the editorial board of *Cahiers* and to a change in the ownership of the magazine. This change ensured the continuance and development of the kind of critical programme outlined in 'Cinema/Ideology/Criticism'. Issue number 217 (November 1969) appeared with a note to the effect that a decision had been made to publish the articles contained within it despite the fact that fierce arguments over policy called into question the future of the magazine. Regular production was then interrupted for a period of about four months during the winter of 1969-70, and it was not until March 1970 that issue number 218 appeared with the news of the solution to the conflict. Ownership was transferred from Daniel Filipacchi to Francois Truffaut and Jacques Doniol-Valcroze, and Doniol-Valcroze took over the legal liability for *Cahiers* by accepting the position of director. An editorial reaffirmed *Cahiers*' interest in a theory of cinema: 'founded on the Marxist science of historical materialism, and the principles of dialectical materialism'.[61] The second part of 'Cinema/Ideology/Criticism' engaged in some fierce criticisms of aspects of the work of a new (also explicitly Marxist) film journal: *Cinéthique*. And it would be appropriate at this point briefly to review the history of the latter.

Cinéthique was established in January 1969. Its title indicated an intention to shift film analysis away from the plane of pure aesthetics, and towards the question of the relationship between aesthetics and ethics; an ethics, moreover, firmly linked to a left-wing political perspective. Unlike *Cahiers*' interest in exploring the contradictions characteristic of mainstream cinema, *Cinéthique*'s early position is based on a straightforward and complete denunciation of that mainstream, with an accompanying tendency to propose the rigorous difficulties of an experimental and avant-garde cinema (later to be defined by *Cinéthique* as the only truly 'materialist' cinema) as an alternative to that commercial mainstream.

The impulse behind the editorial comment of the first issue seems to be not so much to understand the popular cinema as to obliterate it (an operation that is as easy in theory as it is difficult in practice). Behind the denunciation lies a sense of horror at the crass vulgarities of the 'society of the spectacle', the horror of a consumer society with so many apparently contented consumers. The metaphor of 'enslavement' is used to describe the relationship between spectator and screen, and there seems to be little attempt at understanding what amounts to the voluntary complicity of the 'slaves' in the process of their enslavement — most spectators not only having chosen to be present but also *paying* to be present. There seems to be little desire to investigate those social processes which bring the spectators willingly into the cinema, and little interest in analysing the nature of the pleasures offered and consumed therein. An anathema is pronounced against the commercial cinema, but one is left wondering who are the faithful who will respect the force of the curse? The editorial states:

> We denounce the cinema as a luxury and consumer product or as a cultural gimmick for the enslavement of a public.[62]

It would be inappropriate to expect of a manifesto-like editorial the laying out of a programme of cultural action, but there is a disturbingly moralistic tone to the piece which seems to be, as it were, demanding temperance rather than asking why people get drunk. There is a tone of indignation at the moral impurity of the masses who succumb to, who allow themselves to be hoodwinked by, the grosser fantasies purveyed by the commercial cinema. This is not to suggest here that the commercial cinema offers, in general, ideologically wholesome fare, simply to argue that the pleasure-generating mechanisms of mainstream cinema (mechanisms which allow it to retain a mass audience) need to be carefully studied, not moralistically rejected, if a different sort of cinema is to be constructed. And while one must be in sympathy with a later statement in the editorial:

> We affirm that the cinema is an art of cutting-off, of the cutting-off of that necessary involvement of effort and intelligence on the part of the spectator-reader . . .[63]

the difficulty lies precisely in the production of a cinema which awakens the intelligence, the critical awareness of an audience, without falling back into a position which puritanically asserts the notion that the audience must enter the cinema in order to work (to 'think hard'), not in order to be entertained. There can be no doubt, however, that *Cinéthique*'s dedication to the production of cultural alternatives was a serious one, and among their considerable subsequent achievements was the fostering of alternative distribution and exhibition circuits.

The first issue indicates its commitment to such a task by inviting filmmakers to bring their films which have not found any commercial outlet to twice weekly screenings organised by *Cinéthique*, and promises also to devote critical attention to such films, ignored by mainstream film critics on the grounds that they have received no commercial distribution. The intention is thus to break the stranglehold of silence which the pressures of commercial (and sometimes more overtly political) censorship had operated upon the world of film criticism.[64] Despite this open invitation, the general commitment of the journal to the cinema of the avant-garde is apparent from the list of film-makers referred to in the first issue: Jacques Rivette, Jean-Marie Straub, Marcel Hanoun and Jean-Luc Godard.

In later issues, *Cinéthique* continued to explore what they saw as the progressive political implications of aesthetic modernism (the modernism of an experimental cinema which self-consciously sought to explore and to make apparent to its audience the devices of its own construction, attempting to call attention to the illusory nature of the film image and thus holding the audience back from an unproblematic identification with the events and characters portrayed on the screen).

But other aspects of the cinema were also considered; issue no. 3, for example, included interviews with the documentary film-maker Jean Rouch and with the Argentinian film-maker Fernando Solanas (one of the makers of *Hour of the Furnaces*), and issue no. 4 was devoted to 'Production', although, as *Cinéthique* themselves later acknowledged, this particular issue offered a highly reductionist, economistic account of the complexities of ideological production in the cinema.

Cinéthique no. 5 (September/October 1969) tried to offer an account of the indirect relationship between film and politics. In an article entitled 'Parenthesis or Indirect Route' the terminology of the Marxist philosopher Louis Althusser is adopted and it is proposed that the complex social formation consists of four practices: economic, political, ideological and theoretical. The cinema is then allocated to the arena of ideological practice rather than political practice, and it is argued that the cinema both reproduces existing ideologies and produces its own specific ideology: the 'impression of reality'- the illusion-generating power of the cinema, its 'impression of reality', is regarded as its central ideological function. The only possible 'escape', as it were, from the realms of ideology is via the production of a 'materialist' cinema which 'does not give illusory reflections of reality', and which is able to produce knowledge about the world only on condition that it first produces knowledge about the cinema, thus breaking the cinema's illusion-generating mechanisms.[65] This 'materialist' cinema is then promoted from the category of ideological practice to the category of theoretical practice.

And just as, for Althusser, theoretical practice produces scientific knowledge, so for *Cinéthique* theoretical cinema (and *Cahiers* were later to argue that such a thing could never exist) produces scientific knowledge; it escapes the limitations of a non-materialist cinema which is condemned to the endless reproduction of 'mere' ideology. The only way in which the cinema can circle back into an adequate, productive relationship with 'politics' is thus through the transformation of itself into a 'theoretical' practice.

This emphasis on a cinema which is able to produce knowledge about itself, and which can thus be promoted up the league table from 'ideological practice' to 'theoretical practice', is closely bound in with the political defence of modernist aesthetics. And *Cinéthique* shares in common with the literary journal *Tel Quel* (a journal with which they had many links)[66] an interest in what are regarded as the politically progressive aspects of the modernist 'text' — whether film, painting, poem or novel — the text which strives to make apparent its own textual devices, its own process of production, to reveal, not to hide, the work which has gone into its own making. While this defence of the modernist text has important implications for any attempt at rethinking and then restructuring the relationship between spectator and spectacle, reader and text, the general advocacy of the experimental, modernist tradition in twentieth century aesthetics tends to leave on one side the question and the problem of reaching a mass audience. In any case, by 1972, with a shift from its earlier position, *Cinéthique* had become critical of what it saw as the formalism implicit in *Tel Quel*'s defence of modernism.[67]

In its November 1969 issue (just prior to the change in ownership), *Cahiers du Cinéma* criticised *Cinéthique*'s notion of theory, in particular its notion of a theoretical cinema capable of producing scientific knowledge. *Cahiers* argue that according to Althusser's own definitions (the writer from whom *Cinéthique* claim to have derived their general approach):

> ... *the cinema is an ideological product*; its field of definition and exercise is ideology and not science. The basic problem is very simple; the cinema today is the instrument of the dominant ideology (bourgeois, capitalist); tomorrow we hope it will be the instrument of another kind of dominant ideology (socialist). But in between these two states of affairs, the nature of the cinema will not be transformed; it can never become a science, all that will be changed is the way it is used, and the purpose it is intended to serve.[68]

So, while indicating a general sympathy with *Cinéthique*'s aims the *Cahiers* writers argue that, in this respect at least, *Cinéthique* has done theoretical work a disservice through the importation of scientific-sounding concepts in order to dress out a not very rigorous argument; the cinema can never itself become scientific, it can only serve different ideologies. *Cinéthique* was later to concede the point, and within the year three journals: *Cinéthique, Cahiers* and *Tel Quel* had entered into an alliance against what they saw as the antitheoretical position being taken up by another film journal: *Positif.*

The immediate cause of the academic row was *Positif*'s publication of an article by Robert Benayoun '*Les enfants du paradigme*' ('The children of the paradigm') in its December 1970 issue.[69] This article, while relatively respectful of the work in cinema semiotics being conducted by Christian Metz, attacked the work of his disciples, which was presented as pretentious and obscurantist. *Cahiers, Cinéthique* and *Tel Quel*, in a joint letter written in December 1970, retaliated by accusing *Positif* of waging an 'obscurantist campaign' of its own against 'all revolutionary theoretical work', and argued that articles like Benayoun's could only stand in the way of, or hold back, the development of a Marxist-Leninist theory of 'signifying practice'[70] (that is, a theory of the processes for the production of meaning, characteristic of different sorts of cultural products, of different 'texts', films, poems, novels etc.). Metz responded by writing to *Positif* in defence of the 'children of the paradigm', expressing 'esteem, sympathy and a lively intellectual interest, in the work of the three journals criticised by Benayoun, and stating:

> As far as the cinema is concerned, in my opinion the most serious effort at theoretical reflection today is to be found on the side of those whom your revue attacks.[71]

Apart from the joint attack on *Positif*, one other issue which united the three journals was the question of China, in particular the Chinese Cultural Revolution, and the critical attitude of the French Communist Party towards this. It may be convenient to mark as the turning point here the criticisms made by the PCF of a book on China (*De la Chine*) written by a member of the Italian Communist Party, Maria-Antonietta Macciocchi. The book offered a positive evaluation of the achievements of the Chinese Cultural Revolution, and was taken up with enthusiasm by many of the *gauchiste* and pro-Maoist groups in France. What finally infuriated the non-communist left (the left which, not being aligned to a pro-Soviet position, had nothing to fear from public praise for China) was the refusal of the PCF to allow the distribution of the book at the *L'Humanité* fair (one of the most important annual cultural events of the PCF) in 1971.

Tel Quel referred to, and criticised, the attacks made by *L'Humanité* on *De la Chine* in its Autumn 1971 issue, and followed this up with two special issues on China in the spring and summer of 1972.[72] *Cinéthique*'s issue nos. 13-14 carried reviews of three Chinese films[73] and an attack on the Russian, French, Italian and Spanish Communist Parties.[74] *Cahiers* included in its Winter 1971/72 issue attacks on what it regarded as the revisionism of the PCF, and a defence of the Chinese Cultural Revolution,[75] and its subsequent issue contained letters from various readers criticising the stand taken by the PCF on the question of China.[76] *Cahiers*' defence of China merged into the period of its concern to develop a 'Revolutionary Cultural Front', from 1972-73. The building of such a front was seen to entail the development of a new revolutionary party in France, the forging of closer links with the French working class, a careful study of the forms of popular culture, and the gradual infiltration of cultural centres throughout the country (the *Maisons de la Culture*), by groups who were conscious of the productive contradictions within the cultural apparatuses of the French bourgeois state.[77]

If the theoretical trajectories of *Cahiers* and *Cinéthique* can be most clearly and consistently related back to the impact of the May events, there is also a sense in which the events changed the whole climate of French film culture. There were few journals which did not in some way or another acknowledge the importance of May, though for some this was frequently limited to the marking out of a new area of study to be called 'political cinema', and did not involve a radical transformation of the critical methods which they brought to bear upon their object of study — the cinema in general.[78]

NOTES

1. Quoted by Daniel Singer, *Prelude to Revolution: France in May 1968*, Hill and Wang, New York 1970, pp.122-3.
2. 'Le dialogue Geismar-Chalin' in Mark Kravetz (ed.), *L'insurrection étudiante*, Union Générale d'Editions, Paris 1968, pp.331-9, is a transcript of negotiations between the teachers' union leader, Geismar, in the streets, and assistant rector Chalin of the

university of Paris in his office, conducted on Radio-Télé-Luxembourg, on the 'night of the barricades'.
3. 'First Manifesto of Futurism', in *Le Figaro*, Paris 1909, translated in Joshua C. Taylor, *Futurism*, Museum of Modern Art, New York 1961.
4. Pierre Gaudibert, *Action culturelle: intégration et/ou subversion*, Casterman, Paris 1972, p.106.
5. Patrick Seale and Maureen McConville, *French Revolution 1968*, Heinemann and Penguin, London 1968, pp.136-7.
6. See Goffredo Fofi, 'The Cinema of the Popular Front in France (1934-38)' from *Giovane Critica* 10, Winter 1966, translated in *Screen*, v13 n4, Winter 1972-3, and *Screen Reader 1*, SEFT, London 1977.
7. Cf.,. Group Lu Hsun, 'On Equal Terms: analysis of a television programme', translated by Paul Willemen from *Cahiers du Cinéma*, nos. 236/7, 1972, in John Caughie, *Television: Ideology and Exchange*, BFI, London 1978, p.13. *A armes égales* is a current affairs debating programme which, claim the authors, emerged from the events of May '68,
8. See Richard Collins, *Television News*, BFI Television Monograph 5, London 1976.
9. Quoted by Singer, op. cit., p.205.
10. Alain Touraine, *The May Movement: Revolt and Reform*, translated by Leonard F. Mayhew, Random House, New York 1971, p.64.
11. Ibid., p.228.
12. Ibid., p.230.
13. Quoted by Gabriel and Daniel Cohn-Bendit, in *Obsolete Communism: The Left-wing Alternative*, Penguin, London 1969, p.159.
14. Ibid., p.159.
15. Ibid., p.161.
16. Seale and McConville, op. cit., pp.94-5.
17. Eric J. Hobsbawm, *Revolutionaries*, Pantheon, New York 1973, p.240.
18. Louis Althusser, *Essays in Self-Criticism*, Humanities Press, New Jersey 1976, p.215.
19. Touraine, op. cit., p.27.
20. Karl Marx, 'The Eighteenth Brumaire of Louis Bonaparte', in *Selected Works of Marx and Engels*, Lawrence and Wishart, London 1968, p.96.
21. George Rudé, *Revolutionary Europe 1783-1815*, Harper and Row, New York, 1966, and Fontana, London 1964, p.86.
22. Ibid., p.91.
23. 'Le retour de Langlois', *Cahiers du Cinéma*, no. 202, Jun-Jul 1968, p.68.
24. Hans Magnus Enzensberger, 'The Consciousness Industry', *New Left Review*, no. 64, Nov-Dec 1970.
25. *Cahiers du Cinéma*, no. 203, Aug 1968, p.24.
26. Ibid., editorial.
27. Ibid., p.26.
28. *Cinéthique*, no. 4.
29. *Cahiers du Cinéma*, no. 203, Aug 1968, pp.29-30, translated by Diana Matias in *Screen*, v13 n4, Winter 1972-3.
30. Ibid., p.66; all subsequent quotations from Projects 4, 13, 16 and 19 are from this source.
31. Ibid., p.62.
32. Ibid., p.70.
33. Ibid., pp.64-5.
34. Ibid., p.65.
35. Ibid., p.72.
36. Ibid., p.77.
37. Ibid., p.74.
38. Ibid., p.75.
39. Ibid.
40. Ibid., p.87.

41. *Cahiers du Cinéma*, no. 203, Aug 1968, p.26.
42. Walter Benjamin, 'The Author as Producer', translated in *New Left Review*, no. 62, Jul-Aug 1970, p.91.
43. 'Entretien avec Paul Séban', *Cinéthique*, no. 5, Sept-Oct 1969, p.10.
44. This leaflet is reprinted in an article on the 1969 Hyères Festival by Louis Séguin in *Positif*, no. 108, Sept 1969, p.36.
45. Jean-Luc Godard, 'What is to be done?', *Afterimage*, no. 1, April 1970.
46. *Cinéma 70*, p.83; the members of the *Dziga Vertov* Group are listed here as Jean-Luc Godard, Jean-Pierre Gorin, Gérard Martin, Nathalie Billard and Armand Mario.
47. Ibid., p.90.
48. 'Entretien avec J·M Lacor et J-P Lefèbvre du syndicat CGT des techniciens du film' *Cinéthique*, no. 4, p.30.
49. Ibid., p.28.
50. *Cinéma 70*, op. cit., p.99.
51. *Dynadia* later changed its name to *Unicité*; for further details on *SLON* and *Dynadia*, see 'Dynadia-SLON' by Bertrand Duffort and Michel van Zele, *Image et Son*, no. 249, April 1971, pp.36-54; for further details of the film groups discussed here see *Cinéma 70*, op. cit., pp.81-104, special issue on 'Politics and Cinema'.
52. *Cahiers du Cinéma*, no. 204, Sept 1968, p.3.
53. Jean-Pierre Oudart, 'La suture', *Cahiers du Cinéma*, no. 211, Apr 1969, and no. 212, May 1969, translated by Kari Hanet in *Screen*, v18 n4, Winter 1977-8, pp. 35-47.
54. *Screen*, v18n4, also includes a translation by Jacqueline Rose of 'Suture (elements of the logic of the signifier)' by Jacques-Alain Miller, pp.24-34, and an article by Stephen Heath, 'Notes on suture', pp.48-76. For an introductory bibliography on this general area see *Edinburgh '76 Magazine*, no. 1, 'Psychoanalysis/Cinema/Avant-garde', pp.87-90.
55. 'Cinéma/Idéologie/Critique', *Cahiers du Cinéma*, no. 216, Oct 1969, and no. 217, Nov 1969, translated by Susan Bennett in *Screen*, v12 n1, Summer 1971, pp.145-55; v13 n1, Spring 1972, pp.120-31; and reprinted in *Screen Reader 1*, op. cit.
56. *Screen*, v12 n1, Spring 1971, p.35.
57. Ibid., pp.30-1.
58. Ibid., p.29.
59. Ibid., p.33.
60. Ibid.; for *Cahiers'* account of categories (a)–(g), see pp.31-4.
61. Editorial, *Cahiers du Cinéma*, no. 218, March 1970.
62. 'Editorial-en-forme-de-manifeste', *Cinéthique*, no. 1, Jan 1969, p.3.
63. Ibid.
64. See 'Cinéma vivant', *Cinéthique*, no. 1, Jan 1969, p.19.
65. 'La parenthèse et le détour', *Cinéthique*, no. 5, Sept-Oct 1969, pp.5-21, translated by Susan Bennett in *Screen*, v12 n2, Summer 1971, pp.131-44, and reprinted in *Screen Reader 1*, op. cit.
66. *Cinéthique* had in common with *Tel Quel* an interest in the devices for the production of meaning (the 'specific signifying practices') characteristic of any art form, and both defended those modernist texts which sought to make apparent their own signifying practices. A number of *Tel Quel* writers also wrote for *Cinéthique*: see 'Economique, idéologique, formel', *Cinéthique*, no. 3, May-June 1969, pp.7-14, translated in this monograph by Elias Noujaim; Marcelin Pleynet, 'Le front "gauche" de l'art', pp.23-32, and Philippe Sollers, 'Cinéma/inconscient/sacré/histoire', pp.33-5, *Cinéthique*, no. 5, Sept-Oct 1969. *Cinéthique's* interest in the specific signifying practices of the cinema led it to investigate the work of Christian Metz: see 'Sémiologie/linguistique/cinéma–entretien avec Christian Metz', *Cinéthique*, no. 6, Jan-Feb 1970, pp.21-6; and Michel Cegarra, 'Cinéma et sémiologie', *Cinéthique*, nos. 7-8, 1970, pp.25-63, translated by Diana Matias and Paul Willemen in *Screen*, v14 ns 1-2, Spring-Summer 1973, pp.129-187.
67. See 'Programme pour une lecture publique de *Méditerranée*', *Cinéthique*, no. 13, pp.78-9; and *Tel Quel*'s attack on *Cinéthique* in 'Le dogmatisme à la rescousse du

révisionnisme', *Tel Quel*, nos. 48-9, Spring 1972, p.176.
68. 'Cinema/Ideology/Criticism', *Screen*, op. cit., p.148.
69. *Positif*, no. 122, Dec 1970, pp.7-26.
70. The letter from *Cahiers*, *Cinéthique* and *Tel Quel* is printed in *Cinéthique*, nos. 9-10, p.80.
71. *Cinéthique*, nos. 9-10, p.96.
72. See *Tel Quel*, nos. 48-9, Spring 1972, and no. 50, Summer 1972.
73. 'Trois films chinois', *Cinéthique*, nos. 13-14, 1972, pp.72-7.
74. 'Des conditions inter-révisionnistes', *Cinéthique*, nos. 13-14, 1972, p.80.
75. *Cahiers du Cinéma*, nos. 234-5, Dec-Jan-Feb 1971-2.
76. *Cahiers du Cinéma*, nos. 236-7, Mar-Apr 1972.
77. See 'Pour un front culturel révolutionnaire (Avignon '73)', *Cahiers du Cinéma*, no. 248, Sept 1973, pp.5-26.
78. A number of film journals ran special issues or articles on film and politics, for example: 'La politique', *Positif*, no.113, Feb 1970; 'Politique et cinéma', *Cinéma 70*, no. 151; information on the film groups SLON and *Dynadia* in *Image et Son*, no. 249, April 1971, pp.36-54; Albert Cervoni, 'Vers un cinéma politique', *Image et son*, Jan 1969; Philippe Esnault, 'Cinéma et politique', *L'Avant-Scène: cinéma*, Oct 1969; Jean-Marie Carzose, 'Propos sur le cinéma politique', *Cinémonde*, no. 1838, 2 June 1970; Guy Hennebelle, 'Brève rencontre' (interview with the film-makers of *La CGT en mai*), *Ecran 72*, no. 1, Jan 1972, pp.62-4; '*Coup pour coup*: polémique entre Gérard Leblanc (*Cinéthique*) et Guy Hennebelle (*Ecran 72*) 'à propos du film de Marin Karmitz', *Ecran 72*, no. 4, April 1972, pp.41-4; '*Tel Quel*, Mao et la révolution', *Ecran 72*, no. 5, May 1972, p.19.

Abbreviations

CEA	— Commissariat a l'Energie Atomique
CFDT	— Confédération Française Démocratique du Travail
CGT	— Confédération Générale du Travail
CNPF	— Conseil National du Patronat Français
CNC	— Centre National de la Cinématographie
CRS	— Compagnies Republicaines de Securité
EGC	— Etats Généraux du Cinéma
ENPC	— Ecole Nationale de Photographie et de Cinématographie
IDHEC	— Institut des Hautes Etudes Cinématographique
ORTF	— Office de Radio-diffusion et Télévision Française
PCF	— Parti Communiste Français
SLON	— Société pour le lancement des oeuvres nouvelles
SNESup	— Syndicat National de l'Enseignement Supérieur
UNEF	— Union Nationale des Etudiants de France

2 Notions of cultural production

The impetus which the May events offered to the development of a radical film practice and to the critical examination of all aspects of the existing system of film production had certain consequences, also, for the development of various theories of cultural production. The desire to make a radical intervention within the existing modes of cultural production led, necessarily, to a re-thinking of the various assumptions underlying that practice and led, in particular, to a re-examination of some of the debates around the questions of culture and class, attitudes to the art of the past and the development of new forms of art which had been conducted in Russia in the decade or so following the Revolution of 1917, and in Europe in the thirties by writers like Bertolt Brecht and Walter Benjamin.

This chapter will explore certain aspects of these debates as they were conducted in French journals like *Cahiers du Cinéma* and *Cinéthique*, but will not be limited to the ideas as developed in these journals. A broader overview of some of the issues at stake will be attempted here, for there is a sense in which both *Cahiers* and *Cinéthique* are not so much mapping out new territory, as making their own contribution to the development of certain long-standing debates within twentieth century Marxism about the possibilities of a radical aesthetic. A consideration of some of the earlier discussions offers the possibility of gaining some critical purchase on the ideas subsequently developed in France. The ferocious polemics conducted after May around, for example, the question of what constituted a 'materialist' cinema did not emerge from nothing. What the May events did was to stimulate a re-examination and a re-evaluation of some of the arguments about the revolutionising of cultural production which had been simmering within Western Marxism for sixty years.

Post-revolutionary Russia: mass illiteracy and proletarian art
Cahiers du Cinéma in their article 'Cinema/Ideology/Criticism', the first part of which appeared in October 1969, saw that in order to advance they had first to go back:

> To us the only possible line of advance seems to be to use the theoretical writings of the Russian film-makers of the twenties (Eisenstein above all) to elaborate and apply a critical theory of the cinema, a specific method of apprehending rigorously-defined objects, in direct reference to the method of dialectical materialism.[1]

Cahiers had in fact been publishing translations of texts by Eisenstein for nearly a year (beginning in February 1969), but with very little in the way of complementary material exploring the economic and political context of Eisenstein's work. Their special issue on Russia in the twenties, which did attempt such contextualising work, did not appear until May/June 1970 (nos. 220/1). Meanwhile, Marcelin Pleynet in an article published in *Cinéthique* no. 5 (October 1969), accused *Cahiers* (but perhaps more particularly the journal *Change*) of a hasty and ill-considered publication of texts drawn from these early debates, arguing that without adequate historical contextualisation such publication would, at worst, contribute to anti-communist notions about the suppression of debate in Russia and, at best, contribute to an idealist history of ideas which permits the consideration of ideas about art divorced from the economic and political context within which those ideas were first developed. Thus Pleynet writes:

> There is a conspiracy of silence about the general history of the articles, except for vague references to their 'revolutionary' origin. (By this is meant that they were produced at the same time as the October Revolution, and were later condemned by it.)
>
> In short we have a choice between camouflaged anti-communism and what may well be its natural concomitant, the Ivory Tower of Absolute Ideas.[2]

Pleynet goes on to consider the attitude of Lenin and Trotsky towards the work of the Formalists and Futurists in the early 1920s and regrets Trotsky's hasty condemnation and inadequate theorisation of the work of both schools. He argues that both Formalists and Futurists could have produced a very much more adequate account of cultural production if they had themselves, in the twenties, been subjected to a more rigorous Marxist critique. He suggests, moreover, that the reason for the absence of such a critique is to be found in the condition of Russia at this time, referring in particular to the massive social and political problems engendered by illiteracy: in 1914 76% of the Russian population could not read or write. As Pleynet indicates, debates in Russia about the art of the past, and about the abolition of bourgeois culture could only assume a strictly secondary importance for a society in which the vast majority had remained untouched by such art and culture. He quotes Lenin on the enormity of the problems to be faced:

> There is no country in Europe apart from Russia which is so uncivilised, where the masses are so without education, culture or general knowledge . . . a genuine bourgeois culture would have been quite enough for us to start with . . .[3]

Pleynet accompanies his critique of the under-development of the ideas advanced by the Russian Formalists and Futurists, and of the too-easy praise of such work evident in the moments of its re-publication in France, with a comparable critique of the translations of Eisenstein, referring to his work as 'theological', 'metaphysical', 'impressionistic', and dependent on 'Hegelian idealism'. He argues for the need to read Eisenstein critically, not simply to reproduce his ideas, precisely because:

> Eisenstein's huge, and extraordinarily rich body of writing is . . . historically determining for any possible scientific approach to that ideological monstrosity: the cinema.[4]

Pleynet's warning against the reproduction of texts and ideas in an uncritical manner, and divorced from any understanding of the particular historical conjuncture within which they appeared, may serve as a useful warning for those whose interest in cultural production in Britain leads them to a consideration of those debates on the subject generated in France in the wake of the May events. And whatever account may be offered here of the notions of cultural production developed either in Russia in the twenties or in France in the late sixties and early seventies, it must be emphasised that such notions need to be rethought in relationship to the specific history of a country (Britain) which, unlike France, has a labour movement that is moved, in general, by the principles of social democracy and by the rejection or avoidance of Marxist theory, in which the analysis of class struggle can only be undertaken in the light of the apparent success of the 'social contract' proposed by a Labour government, and in which there is no mass communist party and no recent experience of a general strike.

Moreover certain problems arise when impatience at what some see as the political backwardness of the British labour movement leads to an exclusive concentration on the small number of 'advanced elements' within or around it, and to a corresponding emphasis on political (the class conscious elements of the proletariat) and cultural (the counter cinema) cadre building. For this emphasis tends to draw attention away from analysis of the real strengths and the appalling weaknesses of the labour movement, and the real strengths and weaknesses of popular culture and the organs of mass communication.

Pleynet warns of the need to consider discussions about the development of new cultural forms in Russia in the twenties, in relationship to an awareness of the particular problems of mass illiteracy. We must go further and point out that in our reconsideration of the debates of the twenties, the central problem which confronts *us* is not that of mass illiteracy, and therefore of the relationship between mass illiteracy and the values generated within an élite, high culture. Rather it is the problem of mass literacy, 'mass culture', 'popular culture', and the pervasive influence of, and the cultural binding operations performed by, the mass media. The great disparity of cultural 'levels' characteristic of post-revolutionary Russia is thus to be contrasted with an advanced western industrial society whose members are constantly being, as it were, worked into cultural homogeneity through the operations of the mass media. If the problem for Russia in the twenties was that the nearest primary school was fifty miles away and the roads were bad, the problem for France or Britain in the seventies (apart from the question of who owns the means of production, a question that should not be too easily or quickly bracketed out of the discussion) may be that every child goes to school and that there is a television in each home.

In a society whose institutions of public instruction and communication — schools, press, television, radio — constantly affirm the principle of presenting all sides of the question and strive to 'reflect' the rich complexity of what is proposed as a basically stable mode of social organisation, any kind of understanding of social contradictions, of irreconcilable differences of interest, can only be arrived at in spite of — not because of — the marvellous facilities offered by these institutions. Or, to pull the argument back a little from the brink of such elegant pessimism — and such a totalising view of monolithic institutions — this understanding of social contradictions can only be arrived at and disseminated by those working to open up the contradictions within these institutions.

Just as it is important to understand the differences between Russia in the twenties and France or Britain in the seventies, so also it is important to understand the differences between France and Britain in the present period. Some of these have been very sketchily suggested, and a further one (particularly pertinent to discussions about the difficulties posed for any understanding of class conflict by those institutions which work to produce cultural homogeneity) can be indicated here: the difference between the BBC and the ORTF, and the extent to which the BBC has been more successful than its French counterpart in generating consensus and in creating a general public confidence in its work as neutral and objective. It may well be time for the discussion about the development of new cultural forms (often derived from the Soviet debates of the twenties) which has contributed so much to the theory and practice of a counter cinema in Britain to be rethought, re-applied in that area which concerns itself with the analysis of the mass media and the notion of 'mass culture' in Britain.

Returning to a consideration of the situation in Russia in the twenties, it is important not to underestimate the extent of the disagreements about cultural policy in the immediate post-revolutionary period. *Cahiers*, in their special issue on this period, pointed out, for example, Eisenstein's early interest in and later rejection of the policies of the *Proletkult* group, but did not explore the policies of the group as such (it is sufficient for *Cahiers* that they are rejected by Eisenstein) and did not examine the often critical attitudes of Lenin and of Lunacharsky — head of the Commissariat for Education and the Arts (NARKOMPROS) — towards *Proletkult*, nor the different positions from which Lenin, Lunacharsky and Eisenstein offer their criticisms of *Proletkult*. Although some of Lenin's key statements on culture are published, *Cahiers* introduce these statements in this way:

> ... the political position is made clear by Lenin's famous text on 'proletarian culture'.[5]

No account is offered of the debate to which these statements were a contribution, or of the positions which are implicitly attacked by Lenin. The reference to 'the' political position evacuates a polemic, and proposes in place of a struggle between positions, a single position which Lenin, simply, clarifies.

Proletkult, an amalgamation of various proletarian cultural organisations, was founded in the autumn of 1917 and held its first All-Russia Conference a year later. Members of *Proletkult* set up the All-Union Association of Proletarian Writers (VAPP) in 1920; this was later reorganised as RAPP (Russian Association of Proletarian Writers). RAPP was to be referred to later, by the Soviet film-maker Mikhail Romm, as 'an organisation very — today we would say "dogmatic"; then, we said "party-line" ideological'.[6] The 1918 Conference of *Proletkult* put forward a number of policies which were later to be opposed by Lenin: the two most controversial tendencies being *firstly* an insistence upon the independent nature of struggle within the sphere of culture, a struggle which was seen as independent of but developing in relationship to political and economic struggles; and *secondly*, an emphasis on the need for the Russian proletariat itself to develop a 'new culture', a 'proletarian culture' which would 'vanquish the bourgeoisie not only materially but also spiritually.' The first tendency is summarised by the Conference declaration thus:

> That the cultural movement among the proletariat should have an independent place alongside the political and economic movement.[7]

The Conference also argued for the need to defend *Proletkult*'s 'independence from the standpoint of organisation, so that proletarian creativity of a strictly class character may develop to the fullest extent.'[8] This notion of organisational independence designed to safeguard the class character of cultural production was to be opposed by Lenin who argued, successfully, in 1920 that *Proletkult* should operate:

> Not apart from the People's Commissariat for Education, but as part of it . . .

and insisted upon *'Proletkult*'s close link with and subordination to the Commissariat for Education'.[9] Lenin himself drafted these resolutions for the First National Congress of *Proletkult* in October of 1920; with the enormous weight of his authority behind them, the resolutions were adopted by the Congress and *Proletkult* merged with, and became organisationally subject to, the Commissariat of Education (NARKOMPROS), which, as one of the organs of the Soviet state, was itself subject in the last instance to the Communist Party. It should be noted at once, however, that subordination to the Commissariat of Education in this early period was no great hardship, and NARKOMPROS under the leadership of Lunacharsky (1917-1929) quickly established an extraordinary record of encouraging the widest and most fertile variety of tendencies within the arts, the widest variety of modes of production within the cultural sphere.

The tendency of *Proletkult* towards organisational independence remains an interesting one and has the merit of emphasising the specificity of struggle within the cultural sphere and the notion that the workers themselves must become involved in the struggle at the level of cultural production (most importantly, in the first instance, that they should become producers). But the tendency is also problematic in a number of ways.

Firstly, since in its early days *Proletkult* argued that it should exercise the same kind of authority in the cultural sphere that the Bolshevik Party exercised in the political sphere, and since it further argued that the task of cultural production was the task of the workers themselves (many of its workshops were only open to those of proletarian origin and closed to those of petit-bourgeois origin who were active in the arts before the Revolution), it tended towards a certain kind of dogmatism which, had it been given the authority it originally requested, would almost certainly have led to the abolition, to the driving out, of the tendencies which opposed it, namely those of Futurism and Formalism. Moreover, in proposing and pursuing a single line for artistic production it would have pre-empted any efforts at policy-making which might have been attempted by the Bolshevik Party.

The second problematic aspect of this tendency to organisational independence derives from the assumption that the taking over of artistic production by proletarians would necessarily mean the production of proletarian art. Thus, while the policies of *Proletkult* had the merit of emphasising the specificity of cultural struggle in relationship to political struggle (when Lenin's position seemed to be that the political victory of the proletariat would in itself solve the problems of cultural production, the workers simply having to understand the mode of production of bourgeois culture as they had to absorb and understand the skills of bourgeois scientists and specialists)[10] they perhaps underestimated the problems arising from the specificity of art itself. In proposing simply to change the producers of art (yesterday bourgeois producers, today proletarian producers) *Proletkult* underestimated the strength of that particular dead hand of the past grasping out to the present from the history of art itself. In France, the Cinéastes Revolutionnaires Prolétariens made perhaps the same mistake. The new producers might thus become the prisoners of the old ways of seeing and saying, and in adopting existing narrative structures, existing poetic forms, existing cinematic conventions, they might be negating the possibility of producing precisely that new class content which it was their aim to express.

This kind of criticism takes us close to the kind of objections to *Proletkult* which were made in Russia in the twenties by Eisenstein and by the Futurists and Formalists — the members of the Left Front of the Arts who published the journals *Lef* (1923-5) and *Novy Lef* (1927-8). Such criticisms will be examined in greater detail later in this chapter. But first the disagreements about the notion of 'proletarian culture' — which are evident from the different positions on this subject taken up by *Proletkult*, by Lenin, by Lunacharsky and by Trotsky — require further consideration.

Proletkult argued that it was for the workers themselves to develop a 'proletarian culture', and that while this new culture would absorb those elements in previously-existing culture which bore 'the imprint of common humanity', crucially there would be a *transformation* or 'recasting' of those elements. According to the 1918 declaration:

> The proletariat . . . must undertake this assimilation in a critical way, and recast the material in the crucible of its own class-consciousness.[11]

Lenin's formulation, which is certainly better known now than that of *Proletkult* — *Cahiers* reproduce it in their special Russian issue — was rather different in emphasis:

> Not the *invention* of a new proletarian culture, but the *development* of the best models, traditions and results of the *existing* culture, *from the point of view* of the Marxist world outlook and the conditions of life and struggle of the proletariat in the period of its dictatorship.[12]

What Lenin's formulation seems to suggest is that existing culture, the culture of pre-revolutionary Russia, is characterised by certain values which can be taken over, developed, by those engaged in building the new society; that existing 'models' and 'traditions' are there to be adopted in much the same way that factory machinery might be taken over. There may be an underestimation, in this position, of the extent to which a particular mode of communication, a particular form of art, a particular means of representation may have a determining effect on what can be said in that mode, with those means; certainly this was the kind of limitation that Eisenstein had in mind when he spoke of the need for 'a new form of cinema as a consequence of a new type of social demand';[13] but Lenin was not alone in emphasising the importance of the culture of the past, and the need to preserve a certain continuity with its valuable traditions. Lunacharsky also spoke of the need for the new art to be developed on the basis of a thorough understanding of the art of the past, not simply on a rejection of that art; and he warned against the notion of a spurious inventiveness, what he saw as an artificial striving for the new, for its own sake:

> ... the independence of proletarian art does not consist in artificial originality but pre-supposes an acquaintance with all the fruits of the preceding culture.[14]

Of course part of the work of NARKOMPROS consisted in preserving the art treasures of czarist Russia and in making them available and comprehensible to the masses of the people: in this sense it is not surprising that Lunacharsky speaks of the 'fruits of the preceding culture'. Moreover, despite certain problems with the notion of cultural continuity, with the assumption that there could and should be an orderly and regular digestion of the art of the past, Lunacharsky's attitude becomes more understandable if we view it in relationship to the appallingly low level of educational provision in pre-revolutionary Russia: Pleynet offers the information that in 1914 only 3% of all children received a secondary education.[15] Lunacharsky, as Commissar of Education with responsibility also for the arts, could not fail to be primarily concerned with the general level of education, and to be motivated by that feeling as to the general cultural and educational backwardness of the Soviet Union which is so evident in Lenin's remark (already cited): 'For a start we should be satisfied with real bourgeois culture'. Lunacharsky's desire to see the educational level of the Russian masses raised to the standard (at least) of their European counterparts is accompanied by a concern that new and experimental developments in the arts will be incomprehensible to them; despite his sympathy for such experiments and the tolerance which NARKOMPROS extended to the artistic avant-garde, he wrote in 1920:

> I have not only seen how bored the proletariat was at the production of a few 'revolutionary' plays, but have even read the statements of sailors and workers asking that these revolutionary spectacles be discontinued and replaced by performances by Gogol and Ostrovsky.[16]

The way forward, for the creation of new forms of art appropriate to the new form of society being constructed in Russia, for both producers ('artists') and readers or spectators, is thus seen to be via a thorough understanding and absorption of the art of the past; this process of understanding and absorption is moreover seen to be an integral part of the production of new cultural forms. It is only this notion of a process of understanding that contributes ultimately to the *transformation* of a culture that saves Lunacharsky's notion of cultural production from the accusation that it proposes a static model according to which the men and women of the new society swallow, unquestioningly, the pearls of wisdom from the past, as valuable today as they were yesterday. Rather, for Lunacharsky, it is precisely so that the new can be produced that the old must be understood:

> Before creating its own culture, or more correctly, as the first shoots of that culture begin to appear, the proletariat must do a tremendous job of studying, that is, of assimilating the old culture.[17]

The old danger here was of that empty antiquarianism which speaks of the good old days (a prescriptive speech characteristic of certain aspects of Soviet cultural policy in the 1930s) and which is born of a too close and loving acquaintance with the past and its forms of art. Such investigations of the cultural past must be treated with care, bearing in mind that maxim of Bertolt Brecht cited by Walter Benjamin in 1938:

> Don't start from the good old things, but the bad new ones.[18]

Like Lunacharsky, Trotsky also emphasised the need for a certain continuity with the art of the past, and the need for writers and artists to be aware of the actual level of education and knowledge of the workers and peasants. In the development of cultural forms he argues for a two-way interchange between cultural producers and the advanced sections of the workers, and in the context of a discussion of the Futurist avant-garde he writes:

> ... the new forms must find ... an access into the consciousness of the advanced elements of the working-class as the latter develop culturally ... The cultural growth of the working-class will help and influence those innovators ...[19]

Thus he insists that the working-class itself must be engaged actively in the process of transforming culture, in terms of influence at least, if not in terms of direct production, for 'it is impossible to create a class culture behind the backs of the class'.[20] This new class culture, which the Formalists and Futurists argued required entirely new means of expression in order to be adequately constructed, could, from Trotsky's point of view, only develop on the basis of a coming-to-terms with the culture of pre-revolutionary Russia. Thus he argues that what the workers must take from the writings of Shakespeare, Goethe, Pushkin or Dostoyevsky is 'a more complex idea of human personality, of its passions and feelings, a deeper and profounder understanding of its psychic forces and of the role of the subconscious etc.'[21] The trap which Trotsky seems to be falling into here is that of an essentialist and universalist notion of the 'human personality', the idea that there is a basic, trans-historical, unchanging phenomenon called personality which is illuminated from different directions, in different periods, by various writers. While it is relatively easy to mount a criticism of this apparently a-historical notion of 'human personality', it would be very much more difficult to argue that Trotsky's — or Lenin's, or Lunacharsky's — defence of the values of the art of the past is always a-historical in this way. What is at stake here is not so much the question of 'to read or not to read' the literature of the past, as the question of precisely what use is to be made of these readings in the development of new cultural forms appropriate to the new society (a question which, of necessity, also haunted radical film-makers of the post-'68 generation). This was not an issue which Trotsky or Lenin or Lunacharsky explored in any detail, believing perhaps that the problem could be more properly considered by the cultural producers themselves.

A sense of the value and importance of the literary and artistic classics is a recurrent and striking feature of the contribution to the debates of the early twenties which Trotsky makes in his book *Literature and Revolution*. The counterpart to his attack on the Futurists for what he calls the 'Bohemian nihilism' of their 'exaggerated' rejection of the past, is his statement that:

> A new class cannot move forward without regard to the most important landmarks of the past.[22]

The defence of the art of the past offered by Lenin, Lunacharsky and Trotsky can be contrasted with certain tendencies apparent (some forty years later) in the Chinese Cultural Revolution. In some respects the Cultural Revolution sought to do precisely what Trotsky warned against, namely to break with the 'landmarks of the past'. In the post-'68 period in France there were Maoist groups which took up the Chinese notion of rejecting the art of the past, and creating a new, proletarian culture — a culture, moreover, to be produced *by* the proletariat and not by artists of bourgeois or petit bourgeois origin (a policy clearly very close to that advocated in Soviet Russia by *Proletkult*). But those who in France defended the principles of the Chinese Cultural Revolution encountered certain problems stemming from the radically different economic, political and ideological organisation of French society. The most significant of these problems was perhaps the dominance of bourgeois forms of popular art, and the near impossibility of adapting these forms to serve the interests of the French working class. Certain elements within this pro-Maoist position would have defended the post-'68 slogan 'The Camera to the Workers', and tended to see the problems of the production of proletarian art in capitalist France only in terms of facilitating access to the means of artistic production, and not in terms of a struggle within artistic production, within ideology. The slogan 'The Camera to the Workers' in effect ignored the major difficulty caused by the dominance of systems of values and beliefs (including assumptions about the organisation of art and entertainment) in general supportive of bourgeois interests. Such a slogan makes very much more sense in a post-revolutionary situation. In a pre-revolutionary situation it runs the risk of ignoring one of the key factors which holds back the working-class from the political realisation of its interests, namely the predominance of ideologies supportive of bourgeois social relations.

The situation in Russia in the twenties, of course, was different. Trotsky suggests that the call to break with the past (in the sphere of culture) may be meaningful to the intelligentsia, but can have little meaning for the illiterate masses who know nothing of this past: without a knowledge of bourgeois culture (that is, of cultural production during the period of the political ascendancy of the bourgeoisie), the concept of a 'revolution' in art can have no meaning for them:

> The working-class does not have to, and cannot, break with literary tradition, because the working-class is not in the grip of such tradition. The working-class does not know the old literature, it still has to commune with it, it still has to master Pushkin, to absorb him, and so overcome him.[23]

It should be noted here that, as in the case of Lunacharsky, it is only the putting together of an argument about absorbing the culture of the past ('to master') *together with* an argument about going beyond that culture and creating a new one (to 'overcome'), which saves Trotsky from proposing a notion of the passive consumption of classical cultural objects, whose particular value remains unchanged by the social context within which they are consumed.

It is important to have some sense of the notions of cultural continuity proposed by Lenin, Lunacharsky and Trotsky in the early twenties before turning to an examination of the notions of cultural production proposed by the Formalists and Futurists during the same period. For although it is the ideas of the Formalists and Futurists (rather than those of Lenin, etc.) which have seemed very much more productive for the development of more recent theories of cultural production, these ideas have tended to be taken over with scant regard for the particular historical context within which they were generated, and with little regard for the extraordinary problems confronted by those engaged in the transformation of Russian society in the twenties.

Post-revolutionary Russia: Formalists and Futurists

That Lenin's ideas about cultural production were unfinished, did not go far enough, is beyond doubt, as is the fact that he had more pressing problems to solve. *Cinēthique* in their issue (nos. 9-10) devoted to a lengthy examination of the cultural policies of the Soviet Union in the twenties and thirties, pointed out one significant area in which his theorisation of cultural production simply stopped short. While, in his text 'Party Organisation and Party Literature', Lenin succeeded in outlining the new organisational basis for cultural production, premised upon the assumption that literature was henceforth to be deployed in the service of the proletarian revolution, what he was unable to do, *Cinéthique* suggest, was to:

> ... think the specific transformations implied by such a change of basis within literary and artistic production.[24]

To put the point more simply, it was clear that cultural production in the Soviet Union was henceforth to serve new masters: the workers and peasants; but the question which remained unanswered was *how* was it to perform this service, how was it to reorganise itself internally, how were the various modes of communication to be transformed so as to be able to fulfil their new function? It was these sorts of questions which the Formalists and Futurists, as well as film-makers like Eisenstein and Vertov — later to be accused of Formalist deviations — were theoretically better equipped to answer, and, indeed, were more interested in answering.

The term *formalist* was initially used to describe the work of close formal study of literary texts conducted by members of The Society for the Study of Poetic Language (OPOYAZ) founded in St. Petersburg in 1916 and the Moscow Linguistics Circle founded a year earlier. Texts by two members of OPOYAZ, Boris Eichenbaum and Yury Tynianov, are published in the Russian issue of *Cahiers*. The term *futurist* was used generally to designate the work of a range of avant-garde writers and artists working in Russia, though the movement was in fact a European phenomenon — the beginning of which is most conveniently marked by the appearance of the first *Futurist Manifesto*, written by the Italian painter F.T. Marinetti in 1909. Unlike the Italian Futurists, however, who were among the founders and supporters of Mussolini's fascist party, the Russian Futurists by and large declared themselves to be on the side of the Bolshevik Revolution. Pleynet in his article in *Cinéthique* on 'The "Left" Front of the Arts' quotes the Futurist poet Vladimir Mayakovsky as saying: 'To accept or not to accept? I never even asked myself. This revolution was my revolution'.[25] Nonetheless, as the writings of Trotsky and Lunacharsky attest, there was considerable contemporary controversy as to the value of Futurism, Trotsky claiming that:

> Futurism originated as an eddy of bourgeois art ... its violent oppositional character does not contradict this in the least ... Futurism carried the features of its social origin, bourgeois Bohemia, into the new stage of its development.[26]

And Lunacharsky indicated very clearly the contradictory nature of contemporary attitudes towards this movement, on the one hand welcoming, on the other hand critical:

> Every time an attack on futuristic or LEF art was mounted, even from high Party bodies, the Education Commissariat unfailingly defended its right to exist and develop. But the Commissariat never failed to warn the LEF group against certain of their tendencies, to disclose their roots which link them with the hangovers of bourgeois

culture, to remind them that bizarre trappings went with a lack of content ... .[27]

By the 1930s, with the development and official promulgation of the literary doctrine of Soviet socialist realism, both 'formalist' and 'futurist' became terms with highly pejorative connotations. Although various political criticisms were made of both groups (and often their membership merged) in the twenties, the attitude of official tolerance originally extended towards them by NARKOMPROS is made clear in Lunacharsky's statement:

> As People's Commissar I have imposed no bans on the futurists; I say there must be freedom in the cultural sphere.[28]

In fact the Futurists were extremely influential in the Fine Arts Section (IZO) of NARKOMPROS, and the official journal of this section, *Art of the Commune* (1918-19), functioned as their mouthpiece. A statement in that journal makes clear the kind of position which this group took up in relationship to the kind of line on cultural questions being proposed by *Proletkult*:

> If we, destroying old forms of human culture, created new forms appropriate to new content, we have the right to state that we are doing great revolutionary work. And you? You are pouring new wine into old wineskins.[29]

A similar debate was conducted in France after May '68 between those film groups who saw the primary concern as being the search for new formal structures, and those who saw it as being primarily a question of swift and effective communication in a language already understood by the mass of the people. In Russia in the twenties it was the Futurists who most vigorously proposed the arguments about the need for new forms of expression to be developed in order to express the new social realities of post-revolutionary Russia; it was they who were concerned to think through what *Cinéthique* called 'the specific transformations ... within literary and artistic production'.

But the argument was not only about producing new form for new content, it was also about changing the nature of the relationship between reader and literary text, between spectator and spectacle, and the changing of this relationship was itself premised upon new ways of thinking about the relationship between art (or more generally 'representation') and reality. In particular, the notion of art as reflection of reality, of art as a transparent window on the real world, faithfully showing or reflecting its substance, was discarded in favour of a notion of art as 'work', as 'practice', or as 'production', as a particular *transformation* of reality, a version of reality, an account of reality. As has been pointed out elsewhere, even Trotsky himself, often suspicious of what he regarded as the a-historical aestheticism of the Futurists. is in fact influenced by futurist- or formalist-inspired notions of art when he argues that artistic creation is:

> ... a deflection, a changing and a transformation of reality, in accordance with the peculiar laws of art.[30]

This notion of 'the peculiar laws of art' is crucial to an understanding of the ways in which Futurists and Formalists were attempting to rethink a notion of the specificity of cultural production, and the ways in which art had to be understood as much in terms of the specific history of artistic practices as in terms of contemporary social reality. This emphasis on the 'laws of art' and the importance of studying the history of art, considered as a process of production in its own right, the nature of which required close scrutiny if it was ever to be transformed, can be contrasted with the rather more pragmatic or instrumentalist approach to art evident in the writings of Lenin, and occasionally in the writings of the film-maker Dziga Vertov (a contemporary of Eisenstein's). Both Lenin and Vertov propose a partisan notion of art as an account of reality *from the point of view of* a particular world outlook (Marxism) deployed in the service of a particular social class (the proletariat). Thus Lenin speaks of:

> ... the *development* of the best models, traditions and results of the *existing* culture, *from the point of view* of the Marxist world outlook and the conditions of life and struggle of the proletariat . . .[31]

And Vertov, quoted in that issue of *Cinéthique* which examines the Soviet debates of the twenties, states:

> ... there is no cinema above classes, no cinema above class struggle: also we know that the cinema is a secondary task and our programme is very simple: to see and show the world in the name of the world proletarian revolution.[32]

What these ideas of 'from the point of view of', and of showing the world 'in the name of', seem to suggest is the notion that 'art' is a given entity, not unlike a machine, it simply has to be taken over and used by different people, deployed in the service of a different class. If yesterday the given entity 'art' showed the world from the point of view of the bourgeoisie, today it is to show the world from the point of view of the proletariat. The internal structures of art, its traditional modes of operating are not seen to be in themselves problematic, and, most importantly the notion of a single and coherent point of view is not problematised, art is simply an instrument like a gun or a steam engine, to be used to the best advantage of its new owners.[33]

What the Futurists and Formalists, by contrast, are interested in making problematic is the very notion of point of view itself, the idea that what the art object offers is a single position or point of view from which the world can be viewed by the reader or spectator. As has already been suggested, part of the argument about cultural production was about not just changing the forms of art but changing also the nature of the relationship between reader and literary text, or between spectator and spectacle. The notion of art work as offering a single point of view is therefore called into question. What is offered in place of this notion is the idea that the work of art might rather propose a number of points of view — perhaps conflicting with each other — and that the spectator will consequently be invited to engage in the work of producing the meaning of the art work; the spectator will be invited to work out, for him- or herself, the relationships between the various points of view. These ideas are first filtered into Russian aesthetics via the absorption of Cubist principles and techniques in painting, in the period just before and during the First World War; their first exemplification is to be found in the work of the Russian Cubo-Futurist painters.

According to these principles, what the work of art offers is not a resting point for the reader or spectator, the comfort of a single position from which to view the world, but something rather more like a crisis point, a troubling, a calling into question of the single point of view and, by extension, of given knowledge and existing values, and an invitation to the spectator to engage in this crisis of meanings, and to resolve them for him- or herself. Thus the art work does not set out to produce a single position, or 'line', which is then simply absorbed by the spectator. It does not set out to — as it were — cast a spell over the spectator so that there is a temporary forgetting of self and an acceptance of the view of the world proposed by the spectacle. Rather it intends to call into play the critical consciousness of the spectator, offering an invitation to actively 'read' the art work, and thus to produce its meanings, not to swallow or consume a meaning-as-given. Vertov, despite the apparently instrumental nature of his call to 'show the world in the name of the world proletarian revolution', was in fact himself well aware of the need to produce a new kind of art which would not perpetuate and reproduce the mystifying processes of the old kinds of art. He refers to the relationship between spectator and spectacle in the old forms of art as a relationship of 'enchantment'. and argues for the need to break this 'enchantment' by developing new methods of communication. In the new kind of cinema which he proposes the spectator will subject the image to a new kind of conscious criticism:

> We rise against the collusion between the 'director-enchanter' and the public which is submitted to the enchantment.
> The conscious alone can fight against magical suggestion of every kind . . .
> We need conscious people, not an unconscious mass ready to yield to every suggestion.[34]

This notion of the need to activate an audience, to encourage a critical consciousness of the account of reality proposed by the film spectacle, is developed by *Cinéthique* through the attack which they mount on what they refer to as films which permit the audience to 'live an imaginary life within a non-existent reality',[35] and through their advocacy of:

> . . . work on the part of the audience: they must decipher the film, read the signs produced by its inner working.[36]

The task of encouraging an audience to take part in the active and critical reading of a text (literary, painted or filmic) could only be undertaken if the producers of that text were able to develop new methods of communicating, new techniques. We can trace this kind of interest through the work of the

Cubist painters in the period before the First World War, to the writings of Eisenstein on montage, of Bertolt Brecht on the concept of the 'alienation device', and of Brecht's friend Walter Benjamin on the techniques of literary and dramatic production. This interest in developing new techniques is forcefully expressed by Sergei Tretyakov, Russian poet and dramatist, member of the Left Front of the Arts which brought together formalist and futurist artists and critics. Tretyakov's work was known and respected by Brecht, but like many experimental writers he did not survive the period of Soviet socialist realism and he was arrested and executed in the late thirties. He wrote:

> Every aesthetically constructed work of art must strive to smuggle in new techniques to remould language, new propaganda forms, new militant sympathies and sources of joy, hostile to outmoded tastes . . .[37]

The argument advanced by Tretyakov, and other members of the Left Front of the Arts, was not for the development of new techniques for their own sake, rather it was an argument that new forms of art were required if the radical changes in social life after the Revolution were to be adequately represented. Moreover these new forms or techniques would not develop inevitably, but had to be carefully and consciously worked out, *produced* by practitioners working in the various branches of cultural production. Simply because reality was changing it could not be assumed that therefore cultural production would change; these changes had to be brought about within artistic production by those who were conscious of the specific histories of the modes of artistic production within which they worked. Only those who were conscious of the historically accumulated devices or conventions of their respective 'crafts' would be in a position to bring about these transformations. A number of formalist critics felt that their own particular contribution to the cultural revolution consisted of the careful and systematic work which they were able to undertake in analysing what one writer called the 'devices of the poetic craft . . . the history of the development of the devices of linguistic fashioning'.[38] It was their:

> . . . knowledge of the laws of production instead of a 'mystical' penetration into the 'secrets' of creation[39]

which, these critics felt, made their work 'the best educator for the young proletarian writers' (O.M. Brik).

Brik was one of the key figures in that group of Formalists who, sympathetic to the aims of the Bolshevik revolution, sought to reconcile their methods of textual analysis with the principles of dialectical and historical materialism. The members of the group set out to study the artistic text both in terms of its internal formal organisation, and in terms of certain, 'external', historical and social determinants. Such attempts were of considerable interest to radical cultural theorists of the post-'68 generation in France, though academic interest in the Formalists preceded the May events, and can be traced back to the publication (sponsored by the journal *Tel Quel*) of a collection of formalist writings: *Théorie de la littérature*, in 1965. After '68, *Cinéthique* printed the Brik article from which the above quotations are taken, and *Cahiers* in their special Russian issue insisted on the importance of the Russian Formalist school of criticism. Publishing translations of articles on the cinema by Yuri Tynianov and Boris Eichenbaum, from a Russian collection entitled *Poetica Kino, Cahiers* argued that what the formalists achieved was:

> ... the evolution of a method of research for thinking about literary practices as articulated with other practices within the social totality and in a dynamic and multiple interaction with them.[40]

The writings of the Formalists were not to be seen as of mere antiquarian interest, but, *Cahiers* claimed, had a vital contribution to make to the development of contemporary cinema and cinema criticism. As examples of contemporary film-makers who were influenced by the same sorts of ideas as those which had preoccupied the Formalists, they cited the work of Godard, Jean-Marie Straub and Danièle Huillet, Robert Kramer and the Taviani brothers.

The Formalists' emphasis on the 'devices' of artistic representation, the practices by which art is able to give an account of, to re-work or to mediate reality, can be traced also in the work of the Cubist painters; although in their work this emphasis is developed in different ways and for different ends. What links the Cubists and the Formalists is both this emphasis on the artifices or devices with which art gives its account of reality, and an accompanying rejection of the notion of art as a transparent window through which we see reality. According to the new type of artistic production proposed by both Cubists and Formalists, the attention of the spectator begins to be drawn away from an examination of the content or subject matter of the work, and towards an examination of the *means* whereby the subject matter is represented. A productive tension is thus established between the means of representation and the subject matter, between the 'how' and the 'what', between the point of view and the object of attention.

The most important difference, however, between the Cubists and the pro-revolutionary avant-garde artists in Russia, is that while the former were more interested in an exploration of the problems of representation, the latter were more interested in the contribution which a revolutionising of the mode of cultural production (a revolutionising of the means of representation) would make to the transformation of Russian society. In comparing the two groups, therefore, it is important to note that while the Cubists were exploring the problems of the means of representation in relation to the representation or depiction of landscapes, or tables, or guitars, the Soviet avant-garde (whether in literature or painting or film) were exploring the problem of representation in relation to the depiction of industrialisation or collectivisation.

However, a comparison of the characteristic subject matter of the Cubists on the one hand, and of the Russian avant-garde on the other, must not be used to underestimate the significance of the Cubist revolution in the history of attempts at theorising the means of representation. A brief account of the particular break in methods of depiction which is constituted by the work of the Cubists may be useful here, not least because a similar kind of break can be discerned in the work of various film-makers, including Jean-Luc Godard in France and in the work of the Structuralist/Materialist film-makers in Britain. It is this same kind of break which *Cinéthique* propose when they speak of the need for a new kind of 'materialist' cinema in which:

> ... films are produced which say everything about themselves: their economy and their means of production.[41]

And *Cinéthique's* definition of a 'materialist' film owes a great deal to the emphasis on the fact of representation which is characteristic of the Cubist movement in painting. A materialist film, for *Cinéthique*, is one which:

> ... does not give illusory reflections of reality. In fact it reflects nothing. It starts from its own material nature.[42]

If the concerns of such 'materialist' film-makers must therefore be to call attention to the fact of the film, the fact of representation, to the presence and operation of those artistic/cinematic devices which allow the film as a construct to give an account of reality, but never a candid-camera glimpse, an unmediated looking at reality itself, a similar concern marks the work of the Cubists in painting. To return to the problematic metaphor of the 'window on the world', the attention of the spectator (for both Cubist painters and 'materialist' film-makers) is no longer concentrated solely on that which is seen beyond the 'pane of glass' (the content), but rather upon the particular distortion or mediation of that which lies beyond it, which constitutes the 'work' performed by the mode of production specific to art.

The aim of the Cubists was to make explicit the 'work' (the specific mode of operation) and the 'devices' of the art of painting. They were concerned to call into question the illusionism of western perspectival art, the aim of which since the time of the Renaissance had been the creation of spatial illusion, the illusion of looking at the world as though through a window — through the development of techniques for representing a three-dimensional world on a two-dimensional canvas. The work of Cubism was both to reduce the dimensions of the object depicted to a single plane, that of the canvas, *and* to go beyond the limitations of Renaissance single-point perspective by representing the object as seen from a multiplicity of viewpoints. Thus they rejected the traditional (western) mode of visual depiction from a single vantage point, the position of the controlling gaze of the static spectator. The elements of form, of the means of representation, are stressed, the illusions of a three-dimensional content discarded. So, Cubism both calls attention to the material fact of painting, the facts of colour, line and the surface of the canvas, and calls into question the hitherto unchallenged notion of representing or depicting the world from a single point of view.

Modernist cinema and the 'materialist approach to form'

There is a sense in which both the Structuralist/Materialist film-makers (associated with the London Film Makers Co-op) in Britain, and European film-makers like Godard, Straub and Huillet explore some of the same kinds of problem as those considered by the Cubist painters. Indeed we may generalise and see the work of all these individuals and groups as different aspects of the same modernist project in painting, literature and film. For both *Cahiers* and *Cinéthique*, Godard and Straub and a number of other experimental directors have made a considerable contribution to the development of a new kind of cinema because their work has indicated as much interest in the problems of the means of representation as in content or subject matter. Unlike certain other groups and individuals in France, during and after May '68, for whom the production of a militant cinema which would serve the interests of the workers and/or of a particular political party was a fairly straightforward process, for *Cahiers* and *Cinéthique* the production of a progressive, radical or 'materialist' cinema was not a simple matter. It certainly was not simply a matter of changing the content of a film: of showing the struggles of the workers instead of the pleasures and the intricate sorrows of the bourgeoisie.

What both journals speak of is the need to transform the mode of communication, the means of representation. Thus *Cahiers* write of the need for 'breaking down the traditional way of depicting reality', and applaud those films which, struggling at the level of form as well as at the level of content, seek to break down traditional ways of thinking about the world, of seeing the world and of representing the world. For *Cahiers*, these are films which 'challenge the concept of "depiction" and mark a break with the tradition embodying it'.[43] There is more at stake here than the notion of developing new means of representation, new forms of expression for their own sake. Like the Russian Futurists and Formalists before them who were interested not only in formal innovation but also in *changing the relationship* between the cultural object produced and its reader or spectator, *Cahiers* and *Cinéthique* also are interested in the new sorts of critical relationship which can be established between spectator and spectacle. The writers of *Cinéthique*, like the film-maker Vertov long before them, thus speak of the need to produce films which, in making apparent the processes of their own construction, do not 'enchant' the viewer into an acceptance of the reality of the spectacle, but rather, in calling attention to their own devices, invite the viewer to a critical consideration of the *account* of reality offered by the spectacle:

> These films do not offer the audience any pseudo-satisfactions; instead they take the entirely new step of inviting them to stand on the same footing as the makers of the film and take a conscious part in the work that produced (and through them continues to produce) the images and sounds. In these films, images and sounds at last no longer deny the process by which they came to be imprinted on the film stock . . . This break is materialism.[44]

In the emphasis which they placed on the importance of the means of representation, on the 'making apparent' of the process or devices which enable the production of meanings, *Cahiers* and *Cinéthique* were thus engaged in a battle against certain of their contemporaries, and against what they would have regarded as an unproductively instrumentalist view of art, that is, the view of art which sees it as simply an instrument which can serve whoever 'uses' it or produces it. In place of this instrumentalist view that the same forms of art, the same structural devices, could be used by different people to say different things, they proposed the need for struggle and change at the level of form itself. It is not therefore surprising to find *Cahiers*, in their special Russian issue, resurrecting the debate between Eisenstein and *Proletkult*, to the advantage of the former, and publishing a translation of Eisenstein's essay 'On the Question of a Materialist Approach to Form', in order to underline Eisenstein's interest in questions of form.

The going back to the debates of the twenties is a way of gathering ammunition in defence of certain positions on film theory and film practice in 1970. Christian Zimmer, a frequent contributor to the journal *Temps Modernes*, summarises the central difference of position nicely in the title of one of the chapters of his book on cinema and politics: 'To film something different or to film differently'.[45] Both *Cahiers* and *Cinéthique* were as interested in finding different ways of constructing films (and therefore in different ways of placing the audience in relationship to the spectacle) as in filming different 'subject matter'.

Eisenstein is presented by *Cahiers* as one of the great masters of the modernist tradition, and the importance of his theoretical contribution to an understanding of the cinema is emphasised and contrasted with what are seen as the much vaguer formulations of an organisation like *Proletkult*. The logic of his trajectory through and then beyond *Proletkult* is outlined in an article by Bernard Eisenschitz who contrasts Eisenstein's early interest in *Proletkult*:

> The Proletkult theatre busily sought new art forms that would correspond to the ideology of the new Russian state structure . . . at that time their artistic ideas and demands fully concurred with mine . . .[46]

with his later rejection of them and of their policies:

> In 1922 I became director of the First Moscow Workers' Theatre and completely broke with the views of the Proletkult administration. The Proletkult staff adhered to Lunacharsky's position: to maintain old traditions and to compromise on the question of revolutionary artistic efficiency.[47]

Eisenschitz goes on to discuss Eisenstein's adherence to the position developed by the Left Front of the Arts and his formulation of the demand for a new form of cinema 'appropriate to a new type of social demand'.[48] He also refers readers to Eisenstein's article 'Perspectives' (1929, translated in *Cahiers du Cinéma*, no. 209) in which the problem of the relationship between the need to create new forms in order adequately to express social reality and the actual educational and cultural level of the masses of the Russian people is touched upon. Thus Eisenstein writes in 'Perspectives':

> In the jostlings and contradictions between the urgency to find forms equal in height with the post-capitalist forms of our social construction and the cultural capacity of the class that is creating this construction ... we have no right to establish limits or theoretical solutions to this problem.[49]

What was finally at stake in the twenties and in the late sixties was just precisely what constituted 'revolutionary artistic efficiency' and, indeed, the adequate expression of social reality, in relation to 'the cultural capacity of the class'. The problem for those engaged in cultural production was just how to develop certain progressive or radical artistic practices which would not, in reality, cut themselves (and, more importantly, the questions which they were trying to raise) off from the masses of the people whom they were trying to reach. Godard's solution (and that of a number of people working in the area of 'counter cinema') to the problem of a radical aesthetic colliding with an aesthetically conservative mass audience was to speak of producing films for an advanced, 'cadre' audience. How this problem might have been solved in Russia, but for the advent of the policies of Soviet socialist realism in the thirties, we can never know.

Eisenschitz, in his article on Eisenstein, also underlines the latter's interest in the question of the 'formation' of the spectator, quoting Eisenstein on the 'tasks of the theatre', as of all spectacle in general, as being 'the "elaboration" of the spectator' ... 'the old representative-narrative theatre is worn out. To replace it there arrives the theatre of "agit-attractions", dynamic and eccentric'.[50] The theatre of 'agit-attractions', heavily dependent on the experimental work of the theatre director Vsevolod Meyerhold, was designed to introduce a variety of extraneous elements, often drawn from the circus, music hall and other forms of popular entertainment, into the conventional space of the theatre, disrupting the hitherto dominant conventions of a naturalist theatre. In place of a unified narrative, the presence of psychologically realistic characters, and the logical unfolding of conventional plot structures, the theatre of 'agit-attractions' offered the spectator an interplay of discordant elements, and very little in the way of a single viewpoint, a unified position from which to see and judge the world as represented in the theatre. The spectator is thus not 'formed' in an unproblematic way, invited to take up and accept a given position, but rather invited to take part in the construction of the play's meaning by working upon the various discordant elements offered within the spectacle. It was clear, also, to Eisenstein's contemporaries that this idea of a collage of discordant elements in theatre owed a certain amount to the Cubists' introduction of collage into painting in the period before the First World War. Thus we find Sergei Yutkevitch, a student of Meyerhold, writing of Eisenstein's work in the theatre in this way:

> He built a proper ring in the proscenium, taught the actors to box

properly ... and he appeared extremely proud of having been the first to introduce an authentic sports exhibition in a legitimate theatrical presentation. It was the same kind of daring as when Picasso or Braque introduced bits of coloured paper or fragments of newspaper into their pictures, when 'collage' made its appearance and people dared to introduce new elements, never hitherto utilised, into painting.[51]

It is the theatre of 'agit-attractions' (with all that this in turn owes to the work of the Cubists in terms of problematising the notion of point-of-view and of the 'organic' composition of the representation) that lies behind Eisenstein's concept of montage in the cinema. For Eisenstein, montage is a matter of juxtaposing shots not on the basis of a principle of *'linkage'*, of simple addition, one element added to another, but rather on the basis of the principle of *'collision'*. He explains this idea in terms of the operation of Chinese ideograms: when the character that signifies 'water' is juxtaposed with the character that signifies 'eye', a third term is generated — the verb 'weep':

... the combination of two hieroglyphs of the simplest series is to be regarded not as their sum, but as their product, i.e., as a value of another dimension, another degree; each, separately, corresponds to an *object*, to a fact, but their combination corresponds to a *concept*.[52]

Thus, just as the traditional unity of narrative is broken down in the theatre of 'agit-attractions' and the way opened up for productive work on the construction of meaning by the spectator, so with the concept of montage-as-collision the way is opened up for the spectator in the cinema to produce meaning out of the juxtaposition of disparate shots. It is the orchestration of conflict both within and between shots that provides the overall dynamic of the film, and while this orchestration is developed in such a way as to maximise the part that must be played by the spectator in producing the final meaning of the film, the interaction of the elements of the film is not completely anarchic, since the purpose, at the end of the day, is what Eisenstein calls the forging of 'accurate intellectual concepts'. Montage-as-conflict is therefore designed to:

... form equitable views by stirring up contradictions within the spectator's mind, and to forge accurate intellectual concepts from the dynamic clash of opposing passions.[53]

It is important not to underestimate the extent to which Eisenstein is interested in opening up certain questions and problems, rather than in closing them down and resolving them after the fashion of more traditional narratives (whether of the novel or of the theatre, or of the cinema of Hollywood). His concern is to open them up in such a way as to encourage the conscious participation of the spectator in the work of producing the meaning of the film. However, it must also be said (particularly in view of some of the notions of the 'open text' proposed by certain experimental film-makers and

by theorists of modernist cultural production) that Eisenstein is not interested
in a complete 'openness' or anarchy of meaning, but in 'accurate concepts'
(presumably defined as those deriving from the principles of dialectical
materialism). Moreover, the 'work' which he offers to the spectator is motivated by the desire to understand and to change the world and not by some
kind of puritanical belief in the value of work as such. It is interesting in this
respect to compare Eisenstein's concept, and employment, of montage in
relationship to *Cahiers*' discussion of the employment of montage within
French modernist cinema. Jean Narboni, for example, in discussing Pollet's
film *Méditerranée*, speaks of this film as 'an interrogation of montage' . . . 'a
question unendingly asked and asked again of montage: when, how and why
to pass from one thing to another?'[54]

It is this kind of interest in montage as formal operation that is characteristic of some of the concerns of the Structuralist/Materialist film-makers in
Britain, and of others like Godard and Straub-Huillet, operating within the
modernist experimental tradition. Like the Cubist painters who called attention to the facts of painting, the Structuralist/Materialist film-makers call
attention to the material facts of film: the presence of sprocket holes, the
grain and texture of the film; the movement of film through the gate of the
projector; the factor of light in the registration of any image on film; and, at
a more complex level of signification, investigate the devices of film narrative,
the techniques of story-telling in the cinema. There is a paring down to
essentials in order to examine and to make explicit the conventions of film
'language'. The codes and conventions of depiction specific to the cinema are
systematically taken apart, so that the spectator may learn something about
the tricks and devices of the cinematic mode of communication. For Pollet, in
Méditerranée, it is the conventions of montage that are the subject of
scrutiny: in a series of self-reflexive movements the film sets out to uncover,
or to make explicit, the means of representation which it itself employs.

A similarly self-reflexive interest in its own formal operations is characteristic of certain aspects of Godard and Gorin's film *Tout va bien* (1972)
(though this film makes many more concessions to the transparent style of
mainstream Hollywood narrative film than any of Godard's other films made
between 1968 and 1972). Godard's interest in the means of representation, in
that particular reality of the devices which the cinema adopts in order to offer
its account of that social reality that lies beyond itself, is apparent in an interview which he gave in 1970:

> A movie is not reality, it is only a reflection. Bourgeois film-makers
> focus on the reflections of reality. We are concerned with the reality
> of that reflection.[55]

The danger of this position is that in concentrating on the 'reality of the
reflection', on the means of representation alone, the sense of a productive
tension between means of representation and that social reality which the
means of representation strive to analyse and account for is lost. Although, to
expand on the point made earlier, it could be argued that *Tout va bien* avoids

this particular danger and, further, that the film-makers work hard to maintain another tension, between familiar and unfamilar means of representation, holding in balance on the one hand the pleasures of the star system in the cinema, the operation of psychological realism (identifiable characters), recognisable locations and an almost coherent plot and on the other hand certain devices calculated to throw into relief the operations of dominant narrative cinema.

To cite examples of this self-reflexivity, a calling into question of the 'normal' operations of narrative in *Tout va bien*, we might list: the cheque-signing sequence at the beginning, listing payments to the various people involved in making the film; the discussion on the soundtrack of what elements are needed to make this a popular film, a love story; an undercutting of the romantic mode in the ironic shots of the lovers by the side of the river; the parallel tracking shot over a cross-section of the occupied factory, in which all the rooms are open at one side to the viewer/camera, as in an architect's model — showing the 'factory' to be clearly a stage set, built in a studio; the non-naturalistic use of sound-over — the presence of voices without naturalistic spatial or temporal contexts; the rigidly formalised parallel tracking shots in the supermarket sequence and the obvious choreographing of action in relationship to the position of the camera; the long tracking shot along the surface of a brick wall at the end of the film which seems to suggest the two-dimensionality of the cinema screen and to hint at the illusory nature of the screen's representation of three-dimensional space. All these elements work to call the spectator's attention to the means of representation which the film itself employs, and allow *Tout va bien* to be included in that rare category of films which, as *Cinéthique* (in a moment of somewhat unhelpful exaggeration) puts it: 'say everything about themselves: their economy and their means of production'.

For both *Cahiers* and *Cinéthique* this modernist project is seen to be an important one, and crucial for the development of any radical and 'materialist' cinema. A self-conscious reflection upon the *material* of any artistic expression, upon the means of representation employed, is presented as a kind of cornerstone without which the edifice of a genuinely progressive cinema cannot be constructed. The force of their polemic emerges more clearly if we contrast those films which they applaud with others which, although they may engage with certain progressive political positions at the level of their content, are found to be lacking in terms of the way in which they organise that content, or, in terms of the means of representation which they employ.

In pursuit of their argument about the need for change at the level of form as well as at the level of content, we find *Cahiers* stating:

> We would stress that only action on both fronts, 'signified' and 'signifier', has any hope of operating against the prevailing ideology. Economic/political and formal action have to be indissolubly wedded.[56]

The terminology is drawn from a definition of the *sign* (that is, a minimal unit of meaning in verbal language or in any other communication system) offered by the linguist Ferdinand de Saussure as the union or conjunction of a signifier (a vehicle of meaning, a word, a series of sounds, an image) with a signified (a concept or meaning). The equation of the signifier/signified distinction with the form/content distinction is a problematic one, but will have to stand here.[57] An example which *Cahiers* give of the operation which attacks what is called 'ideological assimilation' at the level of the signified is of a film which deals 'with a directly political subject'; operations at the level of the signifier, by contrast, are involved with a 'breaking down of the traditional way of depicting reality'. *Cahiers* then go on from this to criticise those films within the *cinéma verité*, or 'direct cinema' traditions, which arise out of political events, but which:

> ... make no clear differentiation between themselves and the nonpolitical cinema because they do not challenge the cinema's traditional, ideologically-conditioned method of 'depiction'. For instance a miner's strike will be filmed in the same style as *Les grandes familles*.[57]

What *Cahiers* seems to be proposing here is some kind of notion of contamination by the characteristic forms and methods of dominant narrative film. In an article in *Cahiers* a year later (October 1970), we find Straub-Huillet's *Othon*, the Taviani brothers' *Sotto il segno dello scorpione* and Kramer's *Ice* being cited as examples of a progressive, genuinely 'political' cinema, as against a film like *L'aveu*, which has an ostensibly or 'obviously' political content. The article argues that it is not enough for a film to deliver a 'political message', rather, like any political discourse, the film must examine its own 'means and conditions of existence'. It must call into question an unproblematic 'practice of cinema as the representation of the lived', the 'self-satisfaction of the shown'. In place of this unproblematic 'showing' of a highly problematic social reality, the film must rather strive to make apparent its own devices, its own mode of production of meaning. It must also call into question its relationship with the 'economic and cultural norms of the dominant social system' within which it is inserted. Thus, it must say something about its own mode of production (the techniques which it adopts in order to produce certain meanings), about what might also be called its own *specific signifying practice* as these are inserted within those dominant systems of production and exchange.[59]

Similar kinds of criticism of those films which fail to reflect upon their own signifying practice are to be found in *Cinéthique*. And we find one of the *Cinéthique* writers criticising Marin Karmitz' film *Coup pour coup* (a film which, revolving around the subject of a spontaneous occupation of a factory by the rank and file workers, is often compared with the similar subject matter but radically different treatment of *Tout va bien*).[60] The criticism is made on the grounds that Karmitz has fallen into the trap of 'taking up without criticism bourgeois filmic practice',[61] and that the film reproduces the 'ideology of the lived, of the "well expressed", of the authenticated, exact detail: the ideology of the mirror'.[62] Leblanc argues that in reproducing faithfully the details of surface appearance, after the manner of the naturalist theatre or novel, Karmitz is unable to develop a method for penetrating below or beyond surface appearance in order to give some account of the 'internal mechanisms' of society. In failing to give any account of society's mechanisms, of how a particular social formation works, Karmitz maroons himself in a position within which he is unable to propose any possible means for the transformation of that society.

In the world of left-wing film theory in France the method of naturalism, the 'ideology of the mirror', has had an extremely bad press, and we might, briefly, at this point compare this position with the much more sympathetic attitude which Trotsky expressed in the twenties in a statement which perhaps constitutes one of the earliest defences of progressive realism:

> To reject art as a means of picturing and imaging knowledge because of one's opposition to the contemplative and impressionistic bourgeois art of the last few decades, is to strike from the hands of the class which is building a new society its most important weapon. Art, it is said, is not a mirror but a hammer: it does not reflect, it shapes. But at present even the handling of a hammer is taught with the help of a mirror, a sensitive film which records all the movements.[63]

Cinéthique specifically reject the notion of art as reflection or 'mirror' of reality,[64] and propose instead the notion of *transformations* (something much closer to the model proposed by the Russian Formalists). Thus the article on *Coup pour coup* notes two chief problems: firstly, the need to establish a political line (in relation to that particular aspect of social reality which is to be 'transformed' through artistic/filmic practices); and secondly, the need to determine 'the specific transformations implied by putting this line into operation within filmic practice'.

The critique of modernism

Both *Cahiers* and *Cinéthique* emphasise the transformative work of art, the specificity of artistic or filmic practices, and the need for any 'materialist' film to make apparent the devices of its own specific signifying practice. However, having rehearsed the arguments about the importance of this self-reflexive activity, certain reservations must now be expressed about the modernist project. These reservations can best be detailed through a consideration of some of the ideas developed by the German dramatist Bertolt Brecht and by his friend and critic Walter Benjamin. Both Brecht and Benjamin are acknowledged by *Cahiers* and *Cinéthique* as seminal figures in the history of attempts at theorising a revolutionary artistic practice. Criticisms will be proposed here of four tendencies within the modernist tradition.

1. The tendency to replace an interest in the *relationship* between specific means of aesthetic representation and a social reality conceived of as distinct from those means, with an exclusive concern with the means of

representation (quite often an exclusive concern with the means of representation which make up the range of artistic practices).
2. The tendency towards an essentialist position on the question of form, for example the argument that a particular style is essentially progressive or essentially reactionary.
3. The tendency to think through the question of formal innovation only in terms of the internal organisation of the literary, dramatic or filmic 'text', and not in terms of the insertion of that text within a particular apparatus, within a system of consumption, distribution or exchange specific to a particular society and a particular historical moment.
4. The tendency to offer a puritanical defence of the 'work' (of reading, of meaning production) which the modernist text invites the reader to perform, and an accompanying underestimation of the importance of pleasure and of entertainment.

1. *The means of representation*
In relation to the first tendency it is important to distinguish between the critique of illusionist art as developed by Brecht and the anti-illusionism of the Structuralist/Materialists and other modernist film-makers, and of the consequent differences of emphasis which are placed upon the foregrounding of the means of representation. Brecht's starting point is the desire 'to apply to the theatre the saying that one should not only interpret but change the world'. His concern with the 'illusion of reality' in the theatre, therefore, is a concern with the way in which that illusion tends to present reality as static, unproblematic, given. It is a concern with the problems of a naturalist art which says: 'things simply are like that'. What Brecht therefore sets out to develop is a criticism, or at least an account, of the limitations of a naturalist art which is capable of presenting all the details of the surface appearance of phenomena, but incapable of penetrating below the surface to reveal those processes or laws according to which these phenomena change and develop.

The kind of artistic production which Brecht advocated, therefore, was one which went beyond the mere recording of surface appearance and that sought to penetrate to some understanding of the material and historical processes which 'produced' the phenomenon. The purpose is to present reality not as a given, unchanging and eternal, but as a process subject to change and able to be changed. Thus Brecht's anti-illusionism seeks not to call the attention of the audience to the 'lies' of art, but rather to call the attention of the audience to the ways in which the forms of art strive to give an account of a social reality which lies beyond them, and *at the same time* to invite the audience to take part in the work of transforming that social reality. Like the modernist film-makers, Brecht certainly places an emphasis on the fact of representation, and on the problems entailed in the selection of certain means of representation. *But* this emphasis is made only in terms of a tension which exists between the fact of representation and a 'that which is represented'. What is preserved is a sense that there is something *outside of* and beyond the fact of representation, that there is a 'something else', a social reality to which the representation refers.

If we compare this approach with the position of even an overtly 'political' modernist film-maker like Godard, we can distinguish an important difference of tendency. Godard has remarked, in a comment similar to the one quoted earlier, that 'A photograph is not the reflection of reality, but the reality of that reflection'; what a remark like this does is to place emphasis solely on the fact of representation. Brecht by contrast remarked 'A photograph of the Krupp factories doesn't tell you very much about those factories'. What emerges from the latter statement is the notion that there is a whole complex social and political reality beyond the fact of representation of this particular photograph, and the implication that it is the task of the progressive photographer or film-maker to analyse this reality and to find a means of representation (photomontage?) adequate to the task.

To summarise the point, for Brecht the desire to go beyond illusionism, to go beyond the mirroring of an apparently unproblematic reality, is intimately connected with the desire to explore the operations of social reality, and to invite the audience to take part in the work of transforming that reality. For many of the modernist film-makers, on the other hand (and it would not be fair to think of the work of Godard as being simply subsumed within this latter category), the desire seems not so much to go *beyond* illusionism in order to engage in an analysis and transformation of the real, as to engage in a constant critique of illusionism, to remain caught up in a permanent meditation upon the nature of illusion, which is much the same thing as a permanent meditation on the nature of art. The point has been put succinctly elsewhere that the anti-illusionist method developed by Brecht in the theatre:

> ... was not simply to break the spectator's involvement and empathy in order to draw attention to the artifice of art, i.e., an art-centred model, but in order to demonstrate the workings of society...[65]

However, this criticism of the limitations of the tendency within modernism which shackles itself to an 'art-centred model', should not be taken as an endorsement of the position which regards the question of the means of representation as an irrelevancy. The Russian Formalist and Marxist Osip Brik spoke of the importance of a knowledge of the 'laws of production' of art, the need for a systematic study of what he called the 'devices' and what we may call the means of representation employed by any art form. Moreover this was not proposed as simply some kind of addition to general knowledge, but rather as a kind of knowledge that was particularly important for those who wished to intervene within cultural production. Trotsky referred disparagingly to the work of the Formalists as 'sterile syllable counting', and similar kinds of criticisms have been made of writers like Christian Metz who, in the course of the sixties and early seventies, have undertaken the slow and arduous task of 'counting', of enumerating the specific devices, conventions or codes of the cinema.

If the categories of 'production' and of 'work' can begin to be accepted as ways of reconceptualising those theories of art which are dependent upon notions of 'individual creativity' and 'genius', then it becomes apparent that an understanding of the laws of artistic production, of the mode of production of meaning specific to art, is a prerequisite for any writer, painter, photographer or film-maker who is interested in changing the direction of, in transforming, cultural production. The argument that anyone who is interested in transforming a society must first understand how that society works, is thus applicable also in the field of cultural production.

Thus we may argue that any film-maker (for example) who intends to conduct a political struggle within the terrain of cultural production, must know about the specificity of that terrain. The attempt to inject a bit of radical political content into the ancient terrain of narrative structures will fail without some understanding of how these narrative structures have worked and therefore how they can be reworked. What is still frequently underestimated is the resistance of old structures to the expression of new ideas, and the need for what Gérard Leblanc of *Cinèthique* called 'the formal filmic transformations made necessary by our concrete situation'.[66] Form is something more than the random, casually selected clothing draped across the body of a political 'content'. To advocate the development of new formal structures in order to express new ideas is not to defend those avant-garde forms which express no ideas at all, but to emphasise the resistance of existing forms to the representation of new struggles, new aspects of an always changing social reality.

It is here that the work of analysing the existing devices, conventions or codes of mainstream narrative cinema is indispensable, for without an understanding of the specific mode of operation of an object or process, we can never hope to change it. If we want cultural production to operate in a different way and to a different sort of purpose, it is not enough simply to place it beneath the control of new masters, we need to understand it in its own way of working in order to change it. What is being proposed here is not the sudden creation of radically new communicative structures, but the breaking down of existing popular forms which is made possible through an understanding of the weak points of those forms, an understanding of the points of internal contradiction and tension. When we begin to understand, for example, what a soap opera television serial, or a disaster movie, or a soft-porn sex film, seem to promise but never deliver[67] — the values respectively of community, intense experience and pleasure — then we have discovered the point of entry into the form, the point of ideological tension, which will enable us to take it apart, to destroy it from within, and on this basis to construct new forms.

2. *The question of form*

In many respects Brecht's arguments about the need to develop new forms of art rest upon the same premises which support the writings of the Russian Futurists. The central point is made in a *Novy Lef* editorial:

> Old art deforms fact — to grasp fact use new methods.[68]

It is because social reality ('fact') is changing, Brecht argues, that new forms of art must be developed; and the substance of his criticism of Georg Lukacs' defence of the style and structure of the nineteenth century realist novel is that Lukacs is proposing to force the writers of the present into the straitjacket of the artistic forms of the past. He calls Lukacs' theory of realism 'formalistic' because Lukacs proposes a particular style from a particular period ('a few bourgeois novels of the previous century') as being essentially adequate to the task of representing social reality. He distinguishes a certain utopianism in Lukacs' desire to go back to the art of the past and to propose it as a model for the writers of the present, and insists that the way forward for writers 'does not involve undoing techniques but developing them'.[69]

Just as Brecht distinguishes a certain a-historical essentialism in Lukacs' arguments in defence of nineteenth century realism, so we should now be equally ready to distinguish essentialist arguments at work in the defence of certain modernist methods of textual/filmic construction; to believe that, for example, some of the anti-illusionist devices of a modernist 'counter' cinema are *essentially* more adequate to the representation of social reality than the devices drawn from those styles labelled 'realist' or 'naturalist' would be to make the same mistake that Brecht criticises in the writings of Lukacs. Because the kind of 'realism' which Brecht has in mind does most importantly have to do with a notion of adequacy to the representation of reality, he is not willing to pin this 'realism' down to a particular style or set of devices. Rather the adequacy or effectivity of the devices employed depends entirely upon the historical moment or 'conjuncture' within which they are manifest.

Terry Eagleton puts the point well in discussing the crucial difference which Brecht's contribution has made to the terms of the debate about realism:

> You thus cannot determine the realism of a text merely by inspecting its intrinsic properties. On the contrary, you can never know whether a text is realist or not until you have established its effects — and since those effects belong to a particular conjuncture, a text may be realist in June and anti-realist in December.[70]

Brecht's notion of realism develops from the demand that the writer take up a position within contemporary class struggle, and that he/she works to uncover the hidden mechanisms of a society's mode of operation, presenting these mechanisms not as fixed entities, but as subject to process and change:

> Realist means: laying bare society's causal network/showing up the dominant viewpoint as the viewpoint of the dominators/ writing from the standpoint of the class which has prepared the broadest solutions for the most pressing problems afflicting human society/emphasising the dynamics of development...[71]

And since social reality is always changing, the methods for representing it must change; new forms are never to be introduced for their own sake but only in order to serve better the aims of this freshly defined realism:

> Time flows on ... methods wear out, stimuli fail. New problems loom up and demand new techniques. Reality alters; to represent it the means of representation must alter too. Nothing arises from nothing; the new springs from the old, but that is just what makes it new.
>
> The oppressors do not always appear in the same mask. The masks cannot always be stripped off in the same way.[72]

One of the most important devices which Brecht develops in the service of this new realism is the 'alienation' effect, a method of distancing the audience from the spectacle, of breaking down the mechanisms of identification. That which is familiar is presented in an unfamiliar way, so that the audience is invited to 'see differently' the normal. For Brecht the alienation device:

> ... consists in turning the object of which one is to be made aware, to which one's attention is to be drawn, from something ordinary, familiar, immediately accessible, into something peculiar, striking and unexpected.[73]

The idea can in certain respects be traced back to the notion of the work that literature performs in 'making strange', developed by the Russian Formalist Viktor Shklovsky, and to the notion of 'eccentrism' which Eisenstein and many others developed as the theatre of 'agit-attractions'. An interesting sidelight is thrown on the relationship between the notion of 'eccentrism' and Brecht's notion of 'alienation' in a remark reportedly made by Lenin on the subject of 'eccentrism', which is quoted by Shklovsky. The remark is all the more interesting in view of Lenin's usual impatience with the formal experiments of the avant-garde:

> There is a certain satirical and sceptical attitude to the conventional, an urge to turn it inside out, to distort it slightly in order to show the illogic of the usual. Intricate but interesting.[74]

The same point is put rather differently by Walter Benjamin in his discussion of Brecht's 'Epic Theatre':

> ... the conditions of our life ... are not brought close to the spectator, they are distanced from him. He recognises them as real — not, as in the theatre of naturalism, with complacency, but with astonishment. Epic theatre does not reproduce conditions; rather, it discloses, it uncovers them. This uncovering of the conditions is affected by interrupting the dramatic processes; but such interruption does not act as a stimulant; it has an organising function. It brings the action to a standstill in mid-course and thereby compels the spectator to take up a position towards the action ...[75]

The last point made here by Benjamin is the crucial one in that it makes clear the purpose of the alienation device which is to change the relationship between spectator and spectacle. The attempt to put such notions into practice can be traced in certain post-'68 French films, and one obvious example would be the tracking shot (mentioned previously) in Godard and Gorin's *Tout va bien* which shows all the rooms of the 'factory' like a cross-section through a doll's house. As the dramatic action is suspended and the camera pulls back the audience is given the opportunity of rethinking, as it were 'with astonishment', the action represented. This device of pulling back in order to reveal the artifice of the studio set cannot, of course, be regarded as essentially or necessarily a radical or progressive device. This will rather depend on the relationship of this device to other devices in the film, and beyond that on who is watching the film and under what circumstances.

3. *The 'author as producer' and the apparatus*
Within the modernist tradition the question of revolutionising the means of representation has too often been considered apart from the question of the 'apparatus', that is, the mode of production and distribution of artistic texts (literary, filmic etc.) within a given society. As Benjamin points out, in his essay 'The Author as Producer', it is not sufficient to consider:

> ... the rigid, isolated object (work, novel, book) ... it must be inserted into the context of living social relations.[76]

In order to do this, the work has to be considered, to use *Cahiers'* paraphrase of Benjamin, 'not as a reflection of the relations of production, but as having a place within these relations'.[77] The author is himself/herself a *producer* and must therefore think of his/her work as not simply reflecting social relations but as inserted within a system of production, and as manifesting certain techniques which can either perpetuate or call into question what Benjamin calls the 'literary production relations' of the time. There is, in other words, a struggle specific to artistic production, the struggle of one technique against another technique; art does not simply reflect struggles which take place elsewhere.

This does not mean that the work of cultural production can be thought of as taking place without reference to aspects of contemporary social reality. Rather, it must be thought of as transforming these aspects in terms of its own specific signifying practices. Thus the textual productivity of the art work has to be understood in its own specificity, in terms of its own formal operations, as it were 'before' it can be understood in its relationship to contemporary economic, social and political reality. What characterises cultural production, therefore, is not a complete autonomy within history or within the social formation; we may rather speak of what has been called the relative autonomy, or the semi-autonomous nature of that production.[78]

Of course Benjamin's emphasis on literary or artistic work as production, as construction, is a familiar one from the earlier polemics of the Russian Futurists. The *Proletkultists* had argued that art should reflect the life of the workers; the Futurists came along and insisted that art was itself a kind of work with its own mode of production. The point has been summarised very well by Masha Enzensberger in the context of a discussion of the work of the Marxist Formalist Osip Brik:

... the Futurists turned the tables on *Proletkult* (which expected workers to become artists) by urging artists to become workers.[79]

Returning to Benjamin's analysis, each of these artist-workers, who understands the importance of technique, then has the task of transforming himself/herself:

... from a supplier of the production apparatus, into an engineer who sees his task in adapting that apparatus to the ends of the proletarian revolution.[80]

The work of adapting the apparatus of cultural production and consumption depends upon how its function is conceived, and which class it is to serve. (To digress momentarily on the controversial question of the 'service role' or the 'instrumental nature' of art, it is not the idea that art should be an instrument for, or should serve the interests of, a particular class that is incorrect; rather, what is to be rejected is the notion that the instrument can be taken over unchanged.) As Benjamin points out, the key role is to be performed here by those who are able to make suggestions 'for changing the function of the novel, of drama, of poetry'.

To raise this question of function or purpose is to avoid the formalist trap which proposes formal innovations as in and of themselves radical. What the struggle of one technique against another technique should lead to, in the opinion of both Benjamin and Brecht, is a calling into question of the social relations of artistic production and consumption, that is, a calling into question of – and an attack upon – the apparatus. Moreover, Brecht makes a distinction between those kinds of innovation in artistic production which can be absorbed by the existing apparatus, and those kinds of innovation which threaten its very existence, and criticises those who do not see the necessity for making this distinction:

The *avant-garde* don't think of changing the apparatus, because they fancy that they have at their disposal an apparatus which will serve up whatever they freely invent ... But they are not in fact free inventors; the apparatus goes on fulfilling its function with or without them...[81]

The notion of the apparatus as that which organises consumption as well as production is extremely important, and it could be argued that in its early days *Cinéthique* (and it was certainly not alone in this) tended to emphasise the latter at the expense of the former. Thus great stress was laid upon the need to revolutionise the mode of production/the means of representation, to produce a self-reflexive and hence 'materialist' cinema, the work of the *Dziga Vertov* Group being proposed as exemplary in this respect, but there tended to be an underestimation of the problems of consumption, of who was watching, when, how and where.

Thus, in an article entitled 'Which Avant-garde?', in *Cinéthique* nos. 7-8, which operates as it were under the banner of a quotation from Benjamin, we find a lengthy examination of the cinematic practice of the *Dziga Vertov*

Group, presented as a 'struggle against the bourgeois concept of representation',[82] and only at the end of the article is the question of distribution and therefore of consumption raised. It is also only at the end of the article that the question is raised as to how a cinema which will serve the 'avant-garde of the proletariat' is to be developed. The article ends with the hopeful and correct proposition that (speaking of a militant cinema):

> ... the problem of its insertion within existing struggles can only be resolved through the encounter in front of the screen of the film-makers/film enthusiasts whose researches develop the real work done by the *Dziga Vertov* Group on the material of film *together with* militants from the avant-garde of the proletariat.[83]

But no indication is given as to how these encounters might be facilitated, nor is there any exploration of the problems which are likely to arise when the most advanced cinematic techniques are encountered by spectators who are better acquainted with the self-effacing ('transparent') techniques of 'popular' (that is, dominant) narrative cinema than with the principles of self-reflexivity. So, *Cinéthique* propose a questioning of the apparatus at the level of the 'how' of production, but they do not carry this question through to the 'for whom' of consumption. While considerable attention is devoted to revolutionising the means for the production of meaning within the text, the question of social function, the social siting of the text is left to one side.

This failure to think through the problems of cultural production in relation to the exigencies of contemporary class struggle is in a sense acknowledged in a later *Cinéthique* article:

> ... we were sure then of having traced the line of demarcation between two class cinemas when in fact we had done nothing more than to decide between two classes of films.[84]

In the same article they speak of their earlier defence of the self-reflexive cinema of 'deconstruction' (that cinema which sets out to analyse, to break down and to make apparent the conventions or devices of dominant narrative cinema) as having suffered from a failure to 'put politics in command'. And though they are still clearly interested in developing that 'materialist' cinema which is premised upon a revolutionising of the means of representation, they speak of the limitations of their own earlier 'reductionist conception of signifying practices (deconstruction)'.[85]

What *Cinéthique*'s self-criticism involves is a return to the questions of purpose and function; as Brecht put it: 'The means must be asked what the end is'.[86] What needs to be proposed in place of a single type of radical signifying practice is the possibility of a multiplicity of methods, of which 'deconstruction' is one. We find Brecht speaking of the attitude of the workers to the theatre in this way:

> 'The universally-applicable creative method': they didn't believe in that sort of thing. They knew that they needed many different methods in order to reach their objective. If you want an aesthetic, there you are.[87]

The tendency in the earlier work of *Cinéthique* referred to to discuss the apparatus in terms of the problems of production, rather than in terms of the problems of distribution and consumption ('which audiences are watching, when, how and where?'), finds its counterpart in certain aspects of the development of film theory in Britain. For there has been a tendency in Britain for the single-minded and extremely important investigation of concepts like 'film language' – and the question of the mode of production of meaning specific to the system of the cinema (together with suggestions as to the possibilities for revolutionising that mode of production) – to be accompanied by an ill-considered and unhelpful assumption that all attempts at sociological research into the conditions of reception or consumption of filmic texts can only be manifestations of the rashest empiricism. The baby (the study of the conditions of consumption) has too often been thrown out with the bathwater (the inadequacy of many of the methods employed).

In Britain there has also been a tendency to rethink the problems of 'adapting the apparatus' in terms of the setting up of an alternative apparatus (the clearest example of this would be the setting up of the Independent Film-makers Association). The question then becomes, what is the relationship between the dominant apparatus (mainstream film production, television, radio etc.) and the alternative one? While the alternative apparatus has often provided the conditions for a revolutionising of the means of representation (the mode of production of meaning), it has often evaded the question of consumption, it has often failed to ask whether it can do more than reproduce the 'normal' conditions of consumption (art centre location, petit-bourgeois intellectual audience) of avant-garde art. The question that must be posed of such an alternative apparatus is whether it offers a non-hostile alternative or a hostile opposition to the dominant apparatus.

To constitute itself as a hostile opposition, this other apparatus must fulfil two conditions: firstly it must engage in a struggle at the level of consumption as well as at the level of production. That is, it must engage with the question of audiences; it must be able to draw certain audiences away from the dominant apparatus. And secondly it must search out contradictions and possible allies within the dominant apparatus. Too often the advocacy of the 'oppositional space' of alternative film and video production and distribution practices has allocated to progressive elements within the dominant institutions (most obviously within television) little more than the performance of routine trade union activities in defence of pay levels and working conditions. It is not surprising, therefore, that such a theory of 'oppositional space' has been found largely irrelevant by those working within the mass media. Little has been done (and the cultural theorists are culpable in this respect) to develop, in conjunction with those working within the apparatuses of the mass media, a theoretical understanding of the parameters of a struggle specific to work within those institutions. Consideration must increasingly be given (and is already being given in some quarters) to the development of a policy of intervention with respect to the *nature* of the media product, a policy which goes beyond the more 'normal' trade union intervention with respect to the working conditions within which the product is produced. There has been a tendency for a theory of oppositional practice 'free' from the ideological contaminations of dominant institutions to stand in for, or to block out, an analysis of the contradictions and therefore of the possible areas of struggle within these dominant institutions. Such an analysis must now be developed.

One final notion, that of the 'popular', needs to be considered in relation to the problems of 'adapting the apparatus'. Clearly the notion is often employed to displace the question of class and class interest as did the notion of 'the people' deployed within American populist ideology in the thirties. And once a distinction has been made between that which is 'popular' (that which is enjoyed by the working-class) and that which objectively serves the interests of those who enjoy it, it is no longer possible for those who have an interest in the socially progressive uses of popular art to equate the popular with the unproblematically good. For something can be popular but not serve the interests of those who enjoy it. Brecht negotiates a way out of this problem by explicitly defining popular art as:

> ... art for the broad masses of the people, for the many oppressed by the few, 'the people proper', the mass of producers that has so long been the object of politics and now has to become its subject.[88]

What he has in mind, therefore, as he goes on to explain, is 'a fighting people and also a fighting conception of "popularity" '. It is with such definitions in mind that we might turn to a consideration of the discussions conducted by *Cahiers* and others in the summer of 1973 around the question of the need for research into popular forms. With a sense of some of the difficulties generated by avant-gardist practice — at least in terms of the reception of modernist texts by a working-class audience — *Cahiers* speak of the need for:

> ... research on the popular forms, old and new, of narration, songs, graphic expression etc., as they appear often in the context of struggles ...[89]

If the purpose of the progressive film-maker is to reach a working-class audience (and the argument must hold good for those working within an alternative apparatus as well as for those working within a dominant one) already conditioned by dominant modes of representation, then, *Cahiers* argue, one place to start is with those modes which are 'popular' (i.e., in this instance employed by progressive elements within the working-class) and which have been utilised in the course of specific struggles; examples of this might be songs, slogans, political jokes, poster designs, banners. The justification for the adoption of such modes would presumably be that they have, already, some effectivity (however marginal) within the working-class. These various modes then have to be evaluated, in a sense judged, and *Cahiers* make it clear that they are not defending the unproblematic reproduction of that which is liked and utilised by workers, for they introduce a notion of what they call 'the most advanced experiments'. Though they are not clear about what they mean by this: are these the 'experiments' of the politically most advanced sections of the working-class, or are they the 'experiments' which show the greatest awareness of the formal possibilities of the mode of communication, and which stimulate critical consideration of the issues involved, not uncritical acceptance? What they argue for is the need:

> to carry out systematic surveys in order to bring to light the embryonic beginnings of popular initiatives in cultural expression; to evaluate the results and popularise the most advanced experiments.[90]

Brecht is perhaps clearer about the purposive nature of his conception of the popular:

> 'Popular' means intelligible to the broad masses, taking over their own forms of expression and enriching them/adopting and consolidating their standpoint/representing the most progressive section of the people in such a way that it can take over the leadership: thus intelligible to other sections too/linking with tradition and carrying it further . . .[91]

4. *'The realm of the merely enjoyable'*
In the autumn of 1969 *Cinéthique* argued that since 'it is in the interests of the bourgeoisie to conceal the work involved in producing anything, including cinematic products' that therefore it was the task of a materialist cinema to reveal the work involved in the production of meaning in the cinema, to 'perform a Marxist-Leninist analysis on the product/film itself', and to produce films which 'say everything about themselves: their economy and their means of production'. At the same time *Cinéthique* acknowledged that the films which fulfilled these demands, and which therefore constituted a radical break in the history of the cinema, ushering in the era of materialism: 'exist . . . outside the real situation of the audience' and had difficulty in reaching a working-class audience because 'workers have better things to do than to find out how capitalist exploitation manifests itself in a film'. Not surprisingly this left them in the position of sadly acknowledging the fact that in terms of the class struggle the cinema could only be 'secondary to the action of the proletariat on the political scene', and that while the films of this materialist cinema 'will not have been useless if they have swung an important fraction of the petit-bourgeoisie on to the side of the proletariat', that it would be:

> . . . utopian to expect the entire working-class to recognise (sanction) the films which objectively are serving its best interests in the present situation.[92]

While it is not difficult to see how a 'popular', mass cinema might not objectively serve the interests of the workers, it is much more difficult to see how or for how long the value of a cinema which objectively serves their interests but is *not recognised by them* can be defended. At the very least it proposes the crucial importance of the 'fraction of the petit-bourgeoisie' that is to be won over to the proletariat; and one might be forgiven for questioning the value of a materialist cinema whose whole validity depends upon that importance.

The early versions of *Cinéthique*'s materialist cinema, unwatched by workers and constructed according to the demands of the potentially infinite regressions of self-reflexivity (despite the closure implied in the statement about films which 'say everything about themselves') could hardly be more unlike Brecht's theatre for pleasure and for instruction. In the same article *Cinéthique* acknowledge that their 'notion of work is incompatible with that of entertainment', and although they try to save for themselves the notion of pleasure:

> ... the pleasure experienced in making (and seeing) a film derives from the kind of elements one uses, and the cinematographic taboos transgressed in using them ...[93]

in the end they are forced to accept that such pleasures are accessible to petit-bourgeois intellectuals but not to workers.

Brecht by contrast argues not for the kind of pleasure obtained from the formal transgression of artistic conventions, but rather for the kind of pleasure that derives from knowledge, from learning. Moreover Brecht argues that there is a connection between the degree of pleasure involved in the learning and the class position of the learner:

> Learning has a very different function for different social strata. There are strata who cannot imagine any improvement in conditions: they find the conditions good enough for them ... But there are also strata 'waiting their turn' who are discontented with conditions, have a vast interest in the practical side of learning, want at all costs to find out where they stand, and know that they are lost without learning; these are the best and keenest learners ... there is such a thing as pleasurable learning, cheerful and militant learning.[94]

Brecht's theatre for pleasure and instruction sets out to serve the working-class which, as he sees it, is the only class able to engage in 'cheerful and militant learning'. He argues that his 'representations of human social life' in the theatre are designed for these:

> ... upturners of society, whom we invite into our theatres and beg not to forget their cheerful occupations while we hand the world over to their minds and hearts, for them to change as they think fit.[95]

What Fredric Jameson calls the 'aesthetic of political modernism' (which we will here apply to *Cinéthique*'s notions of a materialist cinema) , one of the attributes of which is the defence of texts as revolutionary on the grounds that they call into question or 'transgress' existing formal values, needs to be sharply distinguished from the aesthetic developed by Brecht. For, as Jameson puts it:

> The reunion of 'science' and practical, change-oriented activity

... transforms the process of 'knowing' the world into a source of delight or pleasure in its own right; and this is the fundamental step in the construction of a properly Brechtian aesthetics.[96]

Pleasure in the modernist-materialist cinema of *Cinéthique* is a function of transgressing cinematographic taboos (that is, breaking with existing forms or conventions). In the theatre of Brecht pleasure is a function of learning about the world in order to change it. Instruction and entertainment are seen by Brecht to be interdependent, and it is this which explains his defence of the 'merely enjoyable'. Thus he states in his preface to 'A Short Organum for the Theatre':

> Let us therefore cause general dismay by revoking our decision to emigrate from the realm of the merely enjoyable, and even more general dismay by announcing our decision to take up lodging there. Let us treat the theatre as a place of entertainment, as is proper in an aesthetic discussion, and try to discover which type of entertainment suits us best.[97]

The importance of this kind of notion of entertainment in the cinema has been argued more recently by *Cahiers* in an article which rejects the 'split' between:

> pleasure-commercial cinema/duty-militant cinema ... the serious, the grave subject, the importance of the subjects treated do not need to make use of the alibis of austerity, of puritanism or of an over-weighty discourse.[98]

The article ends with a quotation from Brecht:

> With lightness of touch all the degrees of the serious are accessible.

If the modernist cinema is sometimes puritanical in its emphasis on the work to be performed by the spectator, a cinema 'for pleasure and for instruction' still remains to be constructed.

Modernist aesthetics induces a reflection upon, a consideration of, the means of representation, and for lovers of art it generates aesthetic pleasure out of a series of 'frame-shifts' (the procedures whereby the art work playfully refers to itself and its own processes of production). But too often it fails to lead its audience 'through' this first consideration and towards a second, namely, a consideration of the action represented. It is this second area of consideration which opens up the possibility of introduction to knowledge of the social world and its processes, what Brecht would have called 'instruction'. And if there is a sense in which modernism offers the only way forward, there is also a sense in which it constitutes a dead end, a graveyard. Only those who pass through it can learn from it; the rest remain buried within it.

NOTES

1. *Cahiers du Cinéma*, no. 216, Oct 1969, translated by Susan Bennett in *Screen*, v12 n1, Spring 1971, p35, and *Screen Reader 1*, op. cit.
2. Marcelin Pleynet, 'The "Left" Front of the Arts: Eisenstein and the "Young Hegelians" ', *Cinéthique*, no. 5, Sept-Oct 1969, translated by Susan Bennett in *Screen*, v13 n1, Spring 1972, p104, and *Screen Reader 1*, op. cit.
3. Ibid., pp.108-9.
4. Ibid., p.118.
5. *Cahiers du Cinéma*, nos. 220-1, May-June 1970, p.31.
6. In Luda and Jean Schnitzer (eds.), *Cinema in Revolution*, translated by David Robinson, Secker and Warburg, London 1973, p.187.
7. The text of the declaration of the First All-Russia Conference (1918) of *Proletkult* is published in Carmen Claudin-Urondo, *Lenin and the Cultural Revolution*, Harvester Press, Hassocks 1977, pp.60-1.
8. Ibid., p.61.
9. Resolution for the First National Congress of *Proletkult*, Oct 1920, in Claudin-Urondo, op. cit., p.45; and *Cahiers du Cinéma*, nos. 220-1, May-June 1970, p.31.
10. Carmen Claudin-Urondo, in her book *Lenin and the Cultural Revolution*, op. cit., advances the argument that Lenin's insistence on the need to absorb and develop bourgeois culture is the mirror image of his insistence on the need to absorb and develop bourgeois science. This double insistence may emerge more clearly in the light of two quotations from Lenin: 'For a start we should be satisfied with real bourgeois culture' (Claudin-Urondo, p.24; Lenin, *Collected Works,* Lawrence and Wishart, London 1967, Vol. 33, p.487); 'The task of the Communists . . . is . . . to be very tactful in their dealings with the scientists and technicians . . . The task is to learn from them. The Communist who has failed to prove his ability to bring together and guide the work of specialists in a spirit of modesty, going to the heart, the matter of studying it in detail, is a potential menace. We have many such Communists among us and I would gladly swap dozens of them for one conscientious, qualified bourgeois specialist.' (Claudin-Urondo, p.56; Lenin. *Collected Works,* op. cit., Vol. 32, p.144.)
11. Claudin-Urondo, op. cit., p.60; also quoted in Bernard Eisenschitz, 'Le Proletkult, Eisenstein' *Cahiers du Cinéma*, nos. 220-1, May-June 1970, p.40.
12. *Cahiers du Cinéma*, nos. 220-1, May-June 1970, p.31; Lenin, *Collected Works*, Vol. 42, p.217.
13. S.M. Eisenstein, 'Sur la question d'une approche materialiste de la forme', *Cahiers du Cinéma*, nos. 220-1, May-June 1970, p.34.
14. Quoted in A. Yermakov, *Lunacharsky*, Novosti Press Agency Publishing House, Moscow 1975, p.80.
15. Marcelin Pleynet, 'The "Left" Front of the Arts . . .', op. cit., p.108.
16. Quoted in Sheila Fitzpatrick, *The Commissariat of Enlightenment: Soviet Organisation of Education and the Arts under Lunacharsky*, 1917-21, Cambridge University Press, Cambridge 1970, p.147.
17. A. Yermakov, op. cit., p.106.
18. Walter Benjamin, 'Conversation with Brecht', *Understanding Brecht*, New Left Books, London 1973, p.121.
19. Leon Trotsky, *Literature and Revolution*, International Publishers, New York 1925, p.193.
20. Ibid., p.193.
21. Ibid., p.225.
22. Ibid., p.225.
23. Ibid., p.130.
24. *Cinéthique*, nos. 9-10, p.16.
25. Marcelin Pleynet, 'The "Left" Front of the Arts . . .', *Screen*, op. cit., p.105.
26. Leon Trotsky, op. cit., p.137.

27. Quoted in A. Yermakov, op. cit., p.95. Yermakov indicates that this statement was made in June 1925.
28. A. Yermakov, op. cit., pp.92-3.
29. Sheila Fitzpatrick, op. cit., p.123.
30. Quoted in Terry Eagleton, *Marxism and Literary Criticism*, Methuen, London 1976, p.50.
31. Claudin-Urondo, op. cit., p.60; and Eisenschitz, op. cit., p.40.
32. *Cinéthique*, nos. 9-10, p.94.
33. While it is reasonable to ascribe this position to Lenin and Vertov on the basis of the quotation offered here, it is in fact an inadequate characterisation of Vertov's position. His other writings indicate considerable sensitivity to the problems of film form, and an awareness of the need to develop new methods of communication in the cinema which would break with the traditional narrative structures of Hollywood films.
34. Dziga Vertov, 'Kino-Eye: The Embattled Documentarists', in Schnitzer, op. cit. (*Cahiers* began publishing Vertov's writings in 1970, and it is no accident that the avant-garde film group with which Jean-Luc Godard was associated after the May events called itself the Dziga Vertov Group.)
35. Gerard Leblanc, 'Direction', *Cinéthique*, no. 5, Sept-Oct 1969, translated by Susan Bennett in *Screen*, v12 n2, Summer 1971, p.124 and *Screen Reader 1*, op. cit.
36. Jean-Paul Fargier, 'Parenthesis or Indirect Route', *Cinéthique*, no. 5, Sept-Oct 1969, translated by Susan Bennett in *Screen*, v12 n1, Summer 1971, p.143.
37. Yury Davydov, *The October Revolution and the Arts*: Artistic Quest of the Twentieth Century — Tolstoy, Blok, Mayakovsky and Eisenstein, translated by B. Bean and B. Mears, Progress, Moscow 1967, p.288.
38. O.M. Brik, 'The So-Called Formal Method', *Lef*, Vol. 1, translated by Richard Sherwood in *Screen*, v12 n4, Winter 1971-2, p.43, and *Screen Reader 1*. This article was also published in *Cinéthique*, nos. 9-10.
39. Ibid., *Screen*, p.44.
40. Jean Narboni, 'Introduction à *Poetica Kino*', *Cahiers du Cinéma*, nos. 220-1, May-June 1970, p.53.
41. Gerard Leblanc, 'Direction', *Screen*, op. cit., p.127.
42. Jean-Paul Fargier, 'Parenthesis or Indirect Route', *Screen*, op. cit., p.143.
43. Jean-Louis Comolli and Jean Narboni, 'Cinema/Ideology/Criticism', *Screen*, op. cit., p.32.
44. Gerard Leblanc, 'Direction', *Screen*, op. cit., p.125.
45. Christian Zimmer, *Cinéma et politique*, Seghers, Paris 1974.
46. Eisenstein, 'A Personal Statement', quoted Eisenschitz, op. cit., p.43; translated in Jay Leyda (ed.), *Film Essays*, Denis Dobson, London 1968.
47. Ibid.
48. Eisenstein, 'On the Question of a Materialist Approach to Form', *Cahiers*, nos. 220-1, p.34. Leyda in *Film Essays*, op. cit., p.189, refers to this article by Eisenstein from 1925 as first published in Russian in *Kino-zhurnal* ARK, 1925, nos. 4-5, pp.5-8.
49. Eisenstein, 'Perspectives', in Leyda, op. cit.
50. Eisenstein, quoted by Eisenschitz, op. cit., p.44.
51. Sergei Yutkevitch, 'Teenage Artists of the Revolution', in Schnitzer, op. cit., p.18.
52. Eisenstein, 'The Cinematographic Principle and the Ideogram', *Film Form*, Denis Dobson, London 1951, pp.29-30.
53. Eisenstein, 'A Dialectic Approach to Film Form', *Film Form*, op. cit., p.46.
54. Jean Narboni, 'Questions théorique: montage', *Cahiers du Cinéma*, no. 210, March 1969, p.22.
55. 'Film and Revolution: Interview with the Dziga Vertov Group', by Kent E. Carroll, *Evergreen Review 14*, no. 83 (October 1970), reprinted in *Focus on Godard*, R.S. Brown (ed.), Prentice-Hall, Englewood Cliffs, N.J. 1972.
56. Jean-Louis Comolli and Jean Narboni, 'Cinema/Ideology/Criticism', *Screen*, op. cit., p.32.

57. But see Christian Metz, 'Methodological Propositions for the Analysis of Film', translated by Diana Matias in *Screen*, v14 ns 1-2, Spring-Summer 1973, pp.89-101; and, in the same volume, Stephen Heath, 'Metz's Semiology: A Short Glossary', discussion of 'Codes of Expression/Codes of Content', pp.219-221.
58. Jean-Louis Comolli and Jean Narboni, 'Cinema/Ideology/Criticism', *Screen*, op. cit., p.33.
59. Jean-Louis Comolli, 'Film/Politique (2) – *L'aveu*: 15 propositions', *Cahiers du Cinéma*, no. 224, October 1970.
60. See also *Cahiers*' discussion: 'Deux films: *Coup pour coup, Tout va bien*', *Cahiers*, nos. 238-9, May-June 1972, pp.5-32.
61. Gerard Leblanc, '*Coup pour coup*: Polemique entre Gerard Leblanc et Guy Hennebelle', *Ecran*, op. cit., p.44.
62. Ibid., p.43.
63. Trotsky, *Literature and Revolution*, op. cit., p.137.
64. See Gerard Leblanc, 'Quelle avant-garde?', *Cinéthique*, nos. 7-8, p.81.
65. Peter Wollen, ' "Ontology" and "Materialism" in Film', *Screen*, v17 n1, Spring 1976, p.17.
66. Gerard Leblanc, '*Coup pour coup . . .*', op. cit., p.44.
67. The notion of a 'point of ideological tension' has elsewhere been developed in terms of a theory of 'structuring absences'. The latter notion has been developed by Pierre Macherey in *Pour une théorie de la production litteraire*, and by *Cahiers* in their article, 'John Ford's *Young Mr Lincoln*', *Cahiers du Cinéma*, no. 223, August 1970, translated by Helen Lackner and Diana Matias in *Screen*, v13 n3, Autumn 1972, pp.5-44, and *Screen Reader 1* op. cit. The term 'structuring absence' found its way into cultural studies from the work of the psychoanalyst Jacques Lacan, whose critical re-evaluation of Freud has received considerable attention in France and is now receiving comparable attention in Britain. Macherey's ideas have been discussed in Terry Eagleton's *Marxism and Literary Criticism*, Methuen, London 1976, and in more detail in his book, *Criticism and Ideology*, New Left Books, London 1976.
68. 'We are searching', Editorial, *Novy Lef*, nos. 11-12, 1927, translated by Diana Matias in *Screen*, v12 n4, Winter 1971-2, p.67, and *Screen Reader 1*, op. cit.
69. Bertolt Brecht, 'Against Georg Lukacs', *New Left Review*, no. 84, Mar-Apr 1974, p.40.
70. Terry Eagleton, ' "Aesthetics and Politics" ', *New Left Review*, no. 107, Jan-Feb 1978, p.28.
71. *Brecht on Theatre*, translated by John Willett, Methuen, London 1964, p.109.
72. Ibid., p.110.
73. Ibid., p.143.
74. The remark is attributed to Lenin by Gorky, and quoted in Viktor Shklovsky, *Mayakovsky and his Circle*, Pluto Press, London 1975.
75. Walter Benjamin, 'The Author as Producer', *Understanding Brecht*, op. cit., p.100; and *New Left Review*, op. cit.
76. Ibid.
77. *Cahiers*, 'John Ford's *Young Mr Lincoln*', *Screen*, op. cit., p.7.
78. For a discussion of the semi-autonomous nature of literary production see Terry Eagleton, 'Literature and History' in *Marxism and Literary Criticism*, op. cit.
79. Masha Enzensberger, 'Osip Brik: Selected Writings', *Screen*, v15 n3, Autumn 1974, p.47.
80. Benjamin, 'The Author as Producer', op. cit., p.102.
81. *Brecht on Theatre*, op. cit., pp.34-5.
82. Gerard Leblanc, 'Quelle avant-garde? (Note sur une pratique actuelle du cinéma militant)', *Cinéthique*, nos. 9-10, Mar 1971, p.46.
85. Ibid., p.44.
86. Brecht, 'The Popular and the Realistic', in *Brecht on Theatre*, op. cit., p.110.
87. Ibid., p.112.
88. 'The Popular and the Realistic', *Brecht on Theatre*, op. cit., p.108.

89. 'Pour un front culturel révolutionnaire (Avignon 73)', *Cahiers*, no. 248, Sept 1973, p.8, translated by Paul Willemen.
90. Ibid., p.9.
91. 'The Popular and the Realistic', op. cit., p.108.
92. Gerard Leblanc, 'Direction', *Screen*, op. cit., p.130. All annotations here are taken from this article.
93. Ibid.
94. 'Theatre for Pleasure or Theatre for Instruction', *Brecht on Theatre*, pp.72-3.
95. 'A Short Organum for the Theatre', *Brecht on Theatre*, p.185.
96. Fredric Jameson, 'Reflections in Conclusion', *Aesthetics and Politics*, New Left Books, London 1978, pp.204-5.
97. *Brecht on Theatre*, op. cit., p.180.
98. Jean-René Huleu, 'Images à défendre', *Cahiers*, no. 256, Feb-Mar 1975, p.18.

3 Ideology and the 'impression of reality'

The 'base and superstructure' debate
The central problem for those theorists of art or culture operating either within — or in a way that is sympathetic to — the traditions of Marxist thought, has been the question: what is the relationship between cultural production and a society's mode of material production (often referred to as the 'economic', the 'base' of any social formation)? And, further, what is the relationship between cultural production and that system of class relations which derives from a particular mode of material production? Who produces for whom, and which class interests are served by this production?

In the period after May '68 radical film theorists in France embarked upon an exploration of these problems in relationship to the cinema; but these explorations only make sense in the context of a general understanding of certain developments in the Marxist theory of ideology, in particular those developments associated with the name of the French Marxist philosopher Louis Althusser. What characterises these developments is a calling into question of what came to be seen as the increasingly problematic metaphor of 'base' and 'superstructure' which for so long had been used by Marxists to explain the relationship between cultural production ('art') and the mode of material production ('economics').

The model of base and superstructure (of a base which determines, and a superstructure which is determined by the base) implied a simple relationship of reflection or correspondence between the base, or what Marx had called the 'material foundations' of a society, its mode of producing and distributing wealth, and the superstructure which Marx had referred to as 'the social, political and intellectual life process in general', 'forms of social consciousness', 'the legal, political, religious, aesthetic or philosophic — in short ideological forms', 'modes of thought and views of life'.

The rethinking of the categories of base and superstructure over the last fifty years or so (roughly spanning the period that begins in the twenties, or earlier, with the work of the Italian Marxist Antonio Gramsci, and ends in the seventies with the work of Louis Althusser) has resulted in the development of a theory of ideology within Marxism which, its exponents would argue, is rather more comprehensive and complex than the concept of ideology as outlined in the writings of Marx himself. However, since Marx's ideas provide the necessary point of departure for any examination of subsequent developments in this area, a brief account of his formulations around the question of base and superstructure will be offered here. References will be made here to three sources: *The German Ideology* (Marx and Engels, 1846), *The Eighteenth Brumaire of Louis Bonaparte* (Marx, 1852) and Preface to *A Contribution to the Critique of Political Economy* (Marx, 1859).

In *The German Ideology*, and beginning with the statement that:

The first premise of all human history is, of course, the existence of living human individuals.[1]

Marx sets out to relate the modes of social organisation, forms of consciousness etc., to 'the way in which men produce their means of subsistence', and to the manner in which they reproduce the conditions for their own existence. In other words he is looking for a method – to be proposed as the materialist method – for linking the analysis of any mode of social organisation to the mode of production and reproduction of the material conditions of existence adopted by these 'human individuals'.

The crucial point here is that, from a very early stage in human history, men and women enter into social relationships, modes of social organisation, in order to reproduce the conditions for their own existence. The mode of production adopted entails more, Marx argues, than simply 'the production of the physical existence of the individuals', it results also in a particular mode of social organisation, a particular way of life:

> This mode of production ... is a definite form of activity of these individuals, a definite form of expressing their life, a definite *mode of life* on their part. As individuals express their life, so they are. What they are, therefore, coincides with their production, both with *what* they produce and with *how* they produce. The nature of individuals thus depends on the material conditions determining their production.[2]

In searching for an adequate means of describing what he calls 'the life-process' of individuals, Marx searches also for a way of making a crucial distinction between individuals 'as they may appear in their own or other people's imagination', and individuals 'as they *really* are'. He defines individuals 'as they really are' in this way:

> ... as they operate, produce materially, and hence as they work under definite material limits, presuppositions and conditions independent of their will.[3]

In pursuit of this distinction between what men and women think of themselves as being, and what they 'really are', he proposes a method of analysis according to which:

> ... we do not set out from what men say, imagine, conceive, nor from men as narrated, thought of, imagined, conceived, in order to arrive at men in the flesh. We set out from real, active men, and on the basis of their real life-process we demonstrate the development of the ideological reflexes and echoes of this life-process.[4]

It is with the vocabulary of 'reflexes' and 'echoes' that the problems begin, and subsequent Marxist commentators (writers like Althusser in France, Stuart Hall and Raymond Williams in Britain) have found these terms to be something of an embarrassment, in the belief that they imply far too simple and direct a correspondence between base and superstructure. Frequently

Marx's later writings have been cited as a corrective to the too-simple notion of superstructure reflecting, 'echoing' or expressing the base. Antonio Gramsci, for example, in the *Prison Notebooks* written in the early thirties, refers readers to *The Eighteenth Brumaire* in the context of an attack which he launches upon:

> The claim presented as an essential postulate of historical materialism, that every fluctuation of politics and ideology can be presented and expounded as an immediate expression of the structure . . .[5]

Gramsci here uses the term 'structure' in place of the term 'base', but he is clearly thinking in terms of the classic base/superstructure opposition, and he goes on to argue that this 'claim':

> . . . must be contested in theory as primitive infantilism, and combatted in practice with the authentic testimony of Marx, the author of concrete political and historical works.[6]

A little later, in the same passage, he attacks 'mechanical historical materialism' on the grounds that it 'assumes that every political act is determined, immediately, by the structure'. If Gramsci's argument that political acts cannot be accounted for in terms of some immediately determining function of the economic base is accepted, how much more carefully does the concept of cultural production have to be thought through in its complex relationship to a society's mode of material production.

There are other formulations in *The German Ideology* which have come under attack for similar sorts of reasons (that is, that they suggest too simple a correspondence between base and superstructure): Marx's utilisation of the 'camera obscura' model is perhaps the best known of these, though it should be said that this formulation has remained acceptable to some Marxists. In pursuit of the argument that there is a relationship between, on the one hand, 'the production of ideas, of conceptions, of consciousness' and, on the other, 'material activity' (a proposition to which no Marxist could object), he continues:

> Consciousness can never be anything else than conscious existence, and the existence of men is their actual life-process. If in all ideology men and their circumstances appear upside-down as in a *camera obscura*, this phenomenon arises just as much from their historical life-process as the inversion of objects on the retina does from their physical life-process.[7]

According to this model what men and women 'see' in ideology is related to their material conditions, to their 'actual life-process', but they simply 'see' their real conditions reflected upside-down, inverted. It is then, clearly, not such a difficult task for someone (the materialist philosopher) to come along and turn these reflections the right way up again. The model also suggests that once the 'historical life-process' has been adequately understood, presumably through the methods proposed by historical materialism, then there will be no more ideology, no more upside-down seeing, people will see social relations, simply, as they are.

Althusser and others have taken issue with some of the implications of this model on two counts. Firstly that it proposes too simple and direct a relationship (a relationship of reflection) between 'ideology' and 'mode of production'; they would argue, rather, that ideology has its own specific mode of operation and stands in a highly complex relationship to the mode of production, and that since both ideology and mode of production are to be thought of as *processes*, constantly subject to change, never static 'moments', that consequently their relationship cannot be conceptualised in terms of 'reflection'. Secondly, the objection to the *camera obscura* model has been on the grounds that it suggests the possibility of an end to ideology.

The arguments here have been, perhaps, rather more controversial, and Althusser, in speaking of ideology as a 'matter of the *lived* relation between men and their world',[8] and therefore as something indispensable to any mode of social organisation, has claimed that ideology as such cannot be thought of as disappearing with the disappearance of class society (the position will be outlined in more detail later in this chapter).

Crucially the objections have been to the notion of ideology as straightforward *distortion*; and in relationship to the statement in *The German Ideology* that:

> The phantoms formed in the human brain are also, necessarily, sublimates of their material life-process, which is empirically verifiable and bound to material premises.[9]

It is the terminology of 'phantoms' and 'sublimates' that has been fastened on as inadequate. For if ideology is thought of as 'something that doesn't really exist' (a phantom) — as, therefore, a species of lie — then the way is left open to the thought that the simple solution to the problem of ideology lies in the advent of the materialist philosopher who, bearing the true image, will be able to uncover the falsity of the upside-down image, to correct the sight of those who previously saw the world askew. Ideology is thus abolished.

But for Althusser and others this abolition is not possible, ideology is seen as performing its own particular kind of work within the complex whole of the social formation, within the complex interaction between those aspects of the social formation traditionally referred to as base and superstructure; ideology cannot be seen as the direct expression or 'echo' of any other aspect of the social formation (for example the base). In Althusser's model ideology does not 'go away', shrieking like a vampire at the coming of the dawn, when the spotlight of a materialist understanding of the operations of the economic is turned upon it, rather it continues to perform its own 'work', only in a different way in a classless society from the manner in which it operates in a class society.

If the vocabulary of 'phantoms' and 'upside-down' reflections has proved controversial, *The German Ideology*, in introducing, in addition, the notion of 'ruling ideas', also stands at the beginning of a long line of discussions and arguments around the question of what is most commonly referred to now as the 'dominant ideology'. Having outlined a method which links the production of ideas, modes of consciousness etc., to a society's mode of material production and reproduction, Marx and Engels then go on to explain what they refer to as the phenomenon of 'ruling ideas', how it is that in any society certain ideas dominate and succeed in proposing themselves as 'the only rationally, universally valid' ideas.[10] The notion of 'ruling ideas' is developed in relation to the concept of relative access to the 'means of mental production':

> The ideas of the ruling class are in every epoch the ruling ideas, i.e., the class which is the ruling *material* force of society, is at the same time its ruling *intellectual* force. The class which has the means of material production at its disposal has control at the same time over the means of mental production . . . The individuals composing the ruling class . . . regulate the production and distribution of the ideas of their age: thus their ideas are the ruling ideas of the epoch.[11]

None of this seems very far removed from the common-sense saying that 'He who pays the piper calls the tune'. But the statement does raise some important questions as to the absolute, or relative nature of the control over the means of mental production. What Marx and Engels probably have in mind here is the work of philosophers in constructing certain systems of ideas; but there is clearly a sense in which both philosophers and cultural producers (writers, painters etc.), who may be 'controlled' by the ruling class (in the sense of patronage and censorship of the market) but are certainly not identical with it, have under certain circumstances produced works which do not immediately fulfil the ideological 'needs' of the ruling class. Such works call attention to certain contemporary contradictions, and may call into question the legitimacy of the authority of the ruling class. So there is, and has perhaps always been the 'space' for certain forms of oppositional cultural practice, which is perhaps not allowed for in the notion of (total?) control over the means of mental production.

The use of the word 'control' may in itself imply too simple and direct a 'fit' or correspondence between activities at the level of cultural production (the music of the piper) and the political programmes of a ruling class (the calling of the tune). The word 'hegemony' may serve us better, with its sense of the complex orchestration of consent, rather than the more direct, brutal and straightforwardly functionalist notion of control which seems to imply a necessarily conscious activity on the part of the ruling class. Moreover the notion of a tight class control over the production of ideas as proposed by *The German Ideology* needs to be rethought in the context of a society which, unlike the society Marx knew, is characterised by mass literacy, universal secondary education, and such peculiar concessions to the notion of feedback from those at the receiving end of the organs of mass communication as the radio phone-in programme, the television 'access' programme, and the letters pages of local and national newspapers. This is not to put forward the argument that our society is in fact characterised by a liberal pluralism founded on the free exchange of ideas among social equals, simply to call into question some of the more obviously functionalist implications associated with the use of the word 'control'.

Where the operation of hegemony comes in most sharply and most incontrovertibly, is through the mechanisms of regulating production *and distribution* to which Marx and Engels call attention in the passage from *The German Ideology* quoted above. Particularly with the development of cultural production as commodity production under capitalism, that is, the *exchange* of cultural objects whether books, films, paintings etc., through the market, the most powerful instance of ruling class control lies in the control of the market, the control over exchange or distribution. (Though a whole complex theory of mediations obviously needs to be developed to account for the operation of hegemony in a state-owned broadcasting corporation like the BBC which in so far as it produces 'for itself' has only an indirect relationship to the market.)

The most obvious question which the statement about 'ruling ideas' in *The German Ideology* seems to leave unanswered is the question: where do ideas which are not the ruling ideas come from, how do they emerge? A little later in the same passage an answer is in fact offered: such ideas do not fall from the sky, are not generated out of the superior wisdom of the philosophers, rather they are developed out of the material conditions of existence of that class (the proletariat) which has the potential for successfully challenging and historically superceding the existing ruling class (the bourgeoisie):

> The existence of revolutionary ideas in a particular period presupposes the existence of a revolutionary class . . .[12]

The emphasis on class, not on individuals, as the point of origination for the development of systems of beliefs, ideologies, or what Marx calls 'illusions, modes of thought and views of life' is continued in a brief but often quoted remark in *The Eighteenth Brumaire of Louis Bonaparte*:

> Upon the different forms of property, upon the social conditions of existence, rises an entire superstructure of distinct and peculiarly formed sentiments, illusions, modes of thought and views of life. The entire class creates and forms them out of its material foundations and out of the corresponding social relations. The single individual who derives them through tradition and upbringing, may imagine that they form the real motives and the starting point of his activity.[13]

This emphasis on the class basis for the production of ideologies, and on the relationship between ruling and subordinate classes and between dominant and subordinate systems of ideas, raises all kinds of further problems and questions, particularly for those who, having accepted the theory which proposes the revolutionary potential of the proletariat, have lived to see not the demise and supercession of the capitalist class in Western Europe and the

United States, but rather its continued, apparently successful existence, and the skill with which its corresponding modes of social organisation regulate and contain instances of class conflict.

To put the problem very crudely: why has the revolutionary class not produced revolutionary ideas? Attempts at theorising the operation of what has been called the 'dominant ideology' by Marxists over the last fifty years, including Gramsci's development of the notion of hegemony (the means by which one class organises the consent of another class to its rule) can all be related to this central problem.

The increasing interest in the development of theories of ideology in France in the period after May '68 (and before, in the case of much of Althusser's work) can be related to this obvious fact or problem — the continued existence or dominance of the capitalist class in Western Europe, fifty years after the overthrow of that class in the Soviet Union. This interest can also be related to the concern expressed by those both inside and outside the French Communist Party to 'explain' the deviations and deficiencies of the Stalinist era, the period of the 'cult of the personality' (a concept which is criticised by Althusser as a reversion to non-materialist modes of thinking) in Russia.

This explanation was in some cases undertaken on the basis of a theoretical acknowledgement of the possibility of a radical *discrepancy* between base and superstructure, between mode of production and a mode of social existence; and it was not only the *gauchistes*, the radical left, who expressed the dissatisfaction that the quality of social life in the Soviet Union was by no means fully commensurate with that state's revolutionising of its mode of material production. It is in pursuit of a solution to this particular problem that we find Althusser arguing (in a formulation rejected as inadequate by many of the non-communist left) that it is the theory of the 'relative autonomy' of superstructure from base which 'explains very simply . . . how the socialist *infrastructure* has been able to develop without essential damage during this period of errors affecting the superstructure'.[14]

To the problem of the longevity of Western capital, and the difficulties entailed in the analysis of Russian society under Stalin, can be added an interest in the principles behind the Chinese Cultural Revolution. For it is clear that the revival of interest in problems of ideology in France was in certain respects fostered by an encounter with the ideas of the Chinese communists who were emphasising, at the time of the Cultural Revolution, the importance of a struggle consciously conducted by the proletariat within the sphere of culture and cultural production even *after* the taking of power by a proletarian party and the revolutionising of the relations of production. *Cinéthique* in particular reflects the importance of this encounter, and attempts a development of some of the ideas of the Chinese Cultural Revolution, only in the context of a capitalist society — contemporary France.

A brief examination of some of the problems connected with the notion of a 'dominant ideology' may provide a useful context for some of the ideas about the operation of the cinema as an aspect of ideology explored by *Cahiers* and *Cinéthique* (some of these ideas will be looked at later in this chapter).

The notion of a 'dominant ideology' ushers in numerous problems for the radical theorists of cultural production. The most serious problems arise in relation to the examination of its 'effects' within a subordinate working class culture, what Marx called 'a definite form of expressing their life, a definite mode of life on their part'. We shall return to this problem later. But even the endeavour to think through the relationship between 'ruling ideas' and the 'ruling class' is a difficult one. In the formulation of *The German Ideology* the position of the ruling class in relation to the dominant ideology would seem to be a relatively straightforward one: this is the class which has access to the means of mental production, and which therefore controls the dissemination of ideas. But, as has already been indicated, the situation may be more complex than this. For we would run into severe difficulties and be taking the chance of a disastrous oversimplification if we proposed the organs of mass communication in Britain, for example, as simply and directly under the control of the ruling class, and as expressing in a unified and monolithic fashion only those systems of values and beliefs which are supportive of the *status quo*. The notion of a single ruling class ideology organising and uniting the organs of mass communication ignores both the presence of divisions within the ruling class, and the extent to which the ideology of free speech does open up a space for progressive journalists and media practitioners. One example of divisions within the ruling class, divisions which through a complex series of mediations might eventually find themselves transformed and reproduced within a media discourse, would be the sometimes conflicting interests of finance capital and industrial capital, a conflict between the 'free-trade' programmes of international monopoly capital and the tendency towards a policy of national protectionism – the imposition of import controls etc. – of local, national, industrial capital.

A related problem (already touched upon in Chapter 2) concerns the relationship between proletariat and cultural production in a post-revolutionary situation. After the revolutionising of the ownership of the means of production will the 'ruling ideas' necessarily be the ideas of the proletariat in the period of its political ascendancy; will the proletariat necessarily generate its own revolutionary culture? *Cinéthique*, in discussing the specificity of artistic practices in relationship to post-revolutionary Russia, pointed out that political and economic changes would not necessarily result in comparable changes at the level of artistic production:

> If the political and ideological control of the avant-garde of the proletariat is the necessary condition for a qualitative leap within artistic practices, this necessary condition is not sufficient to produce it.[15]

Despite the evident complexities in that area which has to do with the analysis of the relationship between ruling ideas and ruling class, the problems entailed in the theorising of the relationship between ruling ideas and the working class in capitalist society are in many ways very much more pressing, for such theorisation is a precondition for the development of any programme of radical cultural practice. A first question here would be this: to what extent is a particular national working class (or fraction of that class) held within the sway of ruling ideas? To what extent does a dominant ideology penetrate or suffuse, like the air that is breathed, the mode of living of the working class? This notion of an 'omnipresent ideology' is very strong in Althusser's formulation of its role: 'Human societies secrete ideology as the very element and atmosphere indispensable to their historical respiration and life.'[16] There are two extreme positions which can be taken up in relation to this question of the extent to which a dominant ideology penetrates or suffuses the culture of a subordinate class.

The first position proposes the notion that the working class, considered as an undifferentiated whole, is simply dominated by the dominant ideology, which is conceived of as an undifferentiated unity. The implication of this position is that only after a revolution with respect to the ownership of the means of production would the stranglehold of the dominant ideology be broken. Moreover, it would then necessarily be broken at the level of the superstructures as the superstructures reflect and reproduce the 'break' constituted at the level of the base. This position allows no 'relative autonomy' to the superstructures. Without a revolutionising of the mode of production and therefore of the relations of production (the relations between classes) the power of the dominant ideology cannot be called into question. This position would regard the notion of cultural struggle within capitalism as theoretically inconceivable, as at best a deviation from the main line of attack, the assault on the economic base. It might be difficult to find exponents of this position, laid out in an extreme, almost caricatural version as it is here. And yet there are *elements* of this position to be distinguished within a number of the post-'68 French debates, and we might cite in this respect *Cinéthique*'s early denunciations of the whole of the output of Hollywood considered as the monolithic representative of a monolithic entity: 'bourgeois ideology' or dominant ideology.

In opposition to the cinema of Hollywood *Cinéthique* propose the following:

> If a film in/through its forms makes apparent its links with the economic/ideological then it is a revolutionary film because in unmasking a process of production based on the exploitation of labour it contributes to the subversion of this general process.[17]

This seems rather to underestimate the difficulties entailed in 'unmasking a process of production' within a given cultural object, and to leave unanswered the question of which audiences would be addressed by these films, and the question of how a film, operating at the level of the *ideological*, could in itself 'subvert' an *economic* process. There are traces of a rather crude economic determinism (criticised in its own later work) to be found in

Cinéthique's treatment of film production under capitalism (see also *Cinéthique*, no. 4), and in its insistence on its own 'freedom' as a magazine from the constraints of being owned and published by a bourgeois publishing house (in its early days it compared itself favourably with *Cahiers* in this respect).

Cinéthique's notion of freedom from capitalist finance is predicated upon a belief in the thoroughly determining nature of such finance; the position does not allow for much in the way of 'internal contradictions' within the system, or the possibility of an oppositional practice even within dominant institutions, which might follow from the analysis of such contradictions. *Cinéthique*'s emphasis was very much on the 'break' which resulted in the setting up of alternative institutions (their own magazine) and alternative film distribution circuits, a break which was seen as the only way of avoiding the straightforward determinations of bourgeois finance.

The second position taken up on the question of the relationship between ruling ideas and subordinate classes suggests (in complete contrast to the first position) that the working class, through or because of the specificity of its own life experience under capitalism, as it were naturally and spontaneously produces, along with its own culture, *its own* ideology which is frequently inferred to be oppositional. To put the position most crudely: the eating of fish and chips in a working class community is not only different from but also aggressively in opposition to the forms of culinary pleasure of the middle and upper classes. This position both assumes that there is a one-to-one correspondence between the cultural form and the class which produces or consumes it, and that the act of production or consumption is an act of resistance to dominant cultural forms.

A related position speaks of the need for workers' self-expression (*Cahiers* engage, momentarily, with this debate in an article in which they criticise the slogan 'The Camera to the Workers'[18]), which is predicated upon the belief that the workers are 'free of', are not 'troubled by', any dominant ideology. The assumption that the working class will be able to express itself, its own needs, ignores the problem that the working class does not live in its own world, but in a world organised by capital and the needs of capital. When it expresses its needs, therefore, there is a sense in which these needs are not 'its own' but its needs understood only as they can be expressed through the structures (whether the forms of mass communication or the structures of wage-bargaining) produced by the existing relations of production and by the corresponding forms of social organisation. Any consideration of the concept of workers' self expression must encounter, and find ways of dealing satisfactorily with, the twin dangers of unprincipled populism ('if a worker says it, it must be right') and vanguardist elitism ('the workers don't know what's good for them, and must on all occasions be spoken for by the vanguard/ Party which does know').

The problem of developing cultural forms which will permit a subordinate class to 'express itself' is an enormous one, since it has to confront not only the difficulty of distinguishing the expression of 'real needs' from the expression of 'false needs', but also the existing limitations on access to a language, to a means of representation: the difficulty of 'mastery of a language' referred to in an extraordinarily acute comment made by a group of Italian peasant school children:

> True culture, which no man has yet possessed, would be made up of two elements, belonging to the masses and mastery of the language.[19]

To summarise then, briefly, these two positions on the relationship between a dominant ideology and a subordinate class: the first assumes that the dominant ideology is completely in control of the subordinate class, and that the mechanism of control is guaranteed by the mode of production, by the economic base. The second suggests that the subordinate class 'escapes' the control of the dominant ideology by virtue of its own specific life experience, and that furthermore it necessarily generates oppositional ideologies out of this differentiated life experience. Of these two extremes the first tends to a sort of quietism with respect to cultural production, for the cultural is placed firmly beneath the economic, and activity is directed primarily at the revolutionising of the economic, the base. The very possibility of cultural struggle, under capitalism and within capitalist institutions, is lobotomised out of the mind of the political activist. The second extreme offers us a very much more productive error; for it is incorrect only in assuming that the cultural forms of the working class are necessarily in a relationship of resistance to those of the ruling class. What is to be salvaged from this position is the proposition that these cultural forms are *potentially* in a relationship of resistance to those of the ruling class; but that this potentiality can be developed only in a particular historical conjuncture, and only in relationship to an understanding of other elements or aspects (to include the apparatuses of cultural exchange) of contemporary class struggle.

The summary offered above of two extreme positions on the question of the relationship between a dominant ideology and a subordinate class may help to clarify certain tendencies. But it has the great disadvantage of presenting ideology as an entity, a quantity, a thing, rather than as a process, an operation, a kind of work. For the positions outlined above rely upon the idea of the presence or absence of the dominant ideology; like a vast oil slick it either contaminates the whole sea, or leaves certain sheltered bays untouched. It should therefore be noted here that the dominant ideology may more usefully be thought of as a process, constantly changing as all aspects of social reality change, and that its operations may be thought of as being *negotiated* in different ways by those occupying different class positions. The dominant ideology may thus be thought of as working to contain the potentially oppositional cultural forms of subordinate classes. It cannot, as it were, obliterate these forms, make them vanish, any more than it could make the class which generates them vanish. Rather it works to bring these cultural forms within that vast arena of consent which enables a ruling class to assert its authority without the show of naked force. That is to say, the dominant ideology 'gathers' these subordinate cultural forms and class forces, containing them within the hegemony (to use Gramsci's term) of the ruling class.

If there has been a tendency in more recent discussion of cultural production to call attention to the inadequacy of a theory of superstructure directly determined by base and in turn simply reflecting the operations of the base, Marx and Engels also expressed certain reservations about what they saw as misleadingly mechanical interpretations of the base/superstructure model. In his 1859 Preface to *A Contribution to the Critique of Political Economy*, Marx discusses the changes effected at the level of both base and superstructure during a period of social revolution, and while pointing out the relative ease with which changes in the base, the 'economic foundation', can be discerned, clearly sees the analysis of transformations at the level of the superstructures as a rather more complex and difficult business:

> With the change of the economic foundation the entire immense superstructure is more or less rapidly transformed. In considering such transformations a distinction should always be made between the material transformation of the economic conditions of production, which can be determined with the precision of natural science, and the legal, political, religious, aesthetic or philosophic — in short, ideological forms in which men become conscious of this conflict and fight it out.[20]

The forms of struggle at the level of ideology thus have their own specificity, and are more difficult to analyse than transformations of the base. This specificity of the ideological is often discussed in terms of the notion of the 'uneven development' of the different levels of a social formation. The expression is to be found in Marx's 1857 Introduction to the *Critique of Political Economy* (also referred to as the *Grundrisse*), where in a very schematic form he notes the problem of the uneven development of forms of art and modes of social organisation:

> the uneven development of material production relative to, e.g., artistic development. In general the concept of progress not to be conceived in the usual abstractness . . .[21]

> In the case of the arts, it is well known that certain periods of their flowering are out of all proportion to the general development of society, hence also to the material foundation, the skeletal structure as it were, of its organisation.[22]

Engels, introducing in 1890 the notion, though not the vocabulary, of the specific effectivity of the superstructures, criticises the notion of the economic base as the only determining factor in social change, and emphasises the way in which the operations at the level of the superstructures in turn react upon, have an effect upon the base. Here he proposes a rather more interactive model than that suggested by the image of the *camera obscura*:

> According to the materialist concept of history, the *ultimately* determining element in history is the production and reproduction of real life. More than this neither Marx nor I have ever asserted.

Hence if somebody twists this into saying that the economic element is the *only* determining one, he transforms that proposition into a meaningless, abstract, senseless phrase. The economic situation is the basis, but the various elements of the superstructure . . . also exercise their influence upon the course of the historical struggles and in many cases preponderate in determining their *form*. There is an interaction of all these elements . . .[23]

Engels' insistence that the economic is not to be seen as the *only* determining factor, and his allocation of 'influence' to the elements of the superstructure, introduces the notion of a highly complex, differentiated social formation, with each of the elements of that formation accorded a certain effectivity. Moreover, it is Althusser's contention[24] that, by implication, this notion breaks with the idea of a tightly-knit, entirely unified social formation in which each of the upper levels of the grand edifice (the superstructures) exactly corresponds to, reflects, expresses or echoes the foundation of that edifice (the base). In other words what is implied is a notion of the social formation, comprised of the economic, political and ideological levels, which, operating in a complex and contradictory fashion, cannot be thought of as a single 'expressive totality'.[25] It is Althusser's view, however, that Engels — caught within an earlier and inadequate theoretical paradigm — lacked both the concepts and the vocabulary to think through these implications to a new and adequate formulation. It is to this task (among others), of providing a more adequate theorisation of the base/superstructure relationship, that Althusser addresses himself.

The tendency of Althusser's discussion of ideology is to insist that far from being a phantom-like illusion, a straightforward lie or distortion, a thin and easily-to-be-pierced veil that covers the truth, ideology has, rather, a reality, a materiality even, of its own. So he argues, in a 1965 article, against the notion that:

> . . . the whole social function of ideology could be summed up cynically as a myth (such as Plato's 'beautiful lies' or the techniques of modern advertising) fabricated and manipulated from the outside by the ruling class to fool those it is exploiting . . .[26]

It cannot be explained away as a device employed by one class to 'fool' another; rather, as has already been indicated, it is more like the air that is breathed ('Human societies secrete ideology as the very element and atmosphere indispensable to their historical respiration and life')[27]; and as such it is not consciously 'noticed'.

Warning against the notion 'that ideology belongs to the region of "consciousness" ', he argues that it is, rather, 'profoundly unconscious', and calls it paradoxically that 'form of specific unconsciousness called "consciousness" '.[28] It is concerned with the way in which men and women experience or negotiate their world, 'a matter of the *lived* relation between men and their world', and as such it is seen as 'a structure essential to the historical life of societies'. Because it works to adapt men and women to the conditions of their existence, Althusser argues that it is a necessary part of all societies, including communist society. It is that which, as it were, connects men and women to the real conditions of their existence, and which expresses this connection in one way or another depending upon the nature of the society. Thus:

> In a class society ideology is the relay whereby, and the element in which, the relation between men and their conditions of existence is settled to the profit of the ruling class. In a classless society ideology is the relay whereby, and the element in which, the relation between men and their conditions of existence is lived to the profit of all men.[29]

The notion that ideology connects men and women to their world, expresses their relationship to that world, with the implication that it *might* therefore say something about the real conditions of their existence, receives a further gloss as Althusser proposes the dual nature of this connection. Because ideology is the 'expression of the relation between men and their "world" ' it brings together and unites both a 'real relation' and what Althusser calls an 'imaginary' or 'lived' relation. Or, to use the better known formulation of his 1970 essay 'Ideology and Ideological State Apparatuses':

> What is represented in ideology is therefore not the system of the real relations which govern the existence of individuals, but the imaginary relation of those individuals to the real relations in which they live.[30]

Furthermore, ideologies are not mere 'lies', not the upside-down reflections of 'real relations', but systems of representations with their own complex and internally consistent (their own 'logic and rigour') mode of operating; the precise nature of their relationship to 'real relations' has to be carefully, and with difficulty, traced out.

For this 'tracing out' to occur ideology has to be understood as a system in its own right, not as merely homologous with or reflexive of the base. To summarise the point in Althusser's words:

> An ideology is a system (with its own logic and rigour) of representations (images, myths, ideas or concepts, depending on the case) endowed with a historical existence and role within a given society.[31]

In a comparable formulation, one that is cited by *Cahiers* in their 'Cinema/Ideology/Criticism' article of October 1969, Althusser writes:

> Ideology is indeed a system of representations but in the majority of cases these representations have nothing to do with 'consciousness': they are usually images and occasionally concepts, but it is above all as *structures* that they impose on the vast majority of men, not via their 'consciousness'. They are perceived-accepted-suffered cultural objects and they act functionally on men via a process that escapes them.[32]

The fact of its omnipresence, and its operation at an unconscious level, however, does not seem to mean for Althusser that it cannot be known, analysed; though he suggests that it is only when the necessity of the existence of ideology is recognised that it can then be used (presumably in a newly 'conscious' way?) for certain defined ends. Certainly the notion of a possible (conscious) ideological struggle is introduced in the statement that:

> ... ideology is not an aberration or a contingent excrescence of History: it is a structure essential to the historical life of societies. Further only the existence and the recognition of its necessity enable us to act on ideology and transform ideology into an instrument of deliberate action on history.[33]

It was this notion of the possibility of deploying, or redeploying ideology as an instrument for 'action on history', for changing society, which was, and still is, of particular interest to radical film theorists. For those theorists who were interested in film practice/production the arguments were then around the question of which ideologies? which struggles? who was to be addressed and therefore what mode of address should be employed?

Despite the importance of the arguments about the specific effectivity of the superstructures, and the valuable way in which these serve to counteract any overly mechanical or crudely determinist notion of the action of the base, these arguments can lead to certain difficulties on the very question of determination. While not wishing to accord a simple primacy to the economic, Althusser is content with the formulation of a determination 'in the last instance' by the economic.[34] Elsewhere in an endeavour to explain the concept of complex contradiction in relationship to the social formation, he speaks of it as being: 'complexly-structurally-unevenly-determined', and proposes to substitute for this inelegant expression the term 'over-determined'.[35] The difficulties of this whole endeavour have been very usefully summarised by Stuart Hall:

> ... how does Marxism enable us to 'think' the complexities of a modern capitalist social formation? How can we conceptualise the relationships between the different levels which compose it? Further, can we 'think' this problem in such a way as to retain a key premise of historical materialism: the premise of 'determination in the last instance' by what is sometimes misleadingly referred to as 'the economic'? Can this be done without losing one's way in the idea of the *absolute* autonomy of each of its levels . . .?[36]

This danger of 'losing one's way in the idea of the *absolute* autonomy of each of its levels' needs to be taken up in relation to the notion of cultural production. The notion that there is no simple correspondence between levels was taken up by *Cinéthique*, and is evident in their remark that in relation to the work of art/film etc., there should be no question of 'reducing the system of the work to reflecting the system of historical reality'.[37] But there is a problem here. For once we begin to think of the superstructures as more than the reflection, as more than the echoes of a vigorous base, once they are allowed a certain independence to, as it were, speak for themselves, then what is to prevent us from thinking of these superstructures as completely autonomous from the base? Some recent Marxist commentators moving down the primrose pathway of non-correspondence between the different levels or instances of the social formation, in pursuit of the unique specificity of each instance, have gone as far as to suggest a necessary 'non-correspondence' between the levels.[38] Where there is a notion of necessary non-correspondence, there can hardly be a concept of determination of any kind. And while much energy has been devoted to conducting an absolutely necessary attack on crude economic determinism, it is difficult to see how any proposition which finally refuses the notion of a determination in the last instance by the mode of production (considered in its most general sense), can properly be regarded as Marxist. Althusser himself, while persisting in the criticism of what he sees as the basically Hegelian notion of the social formation as 'expressive totality', in which all the elements are homologous with each other, correspond directly with each other, 'fit' exactly as a unified totality, nevertheless pulls back from the brink of asserting a complete autonomy for these elements:

> ... I talked about a *whole*, to make it clear that in the Marxist conception of a social formation everything holds together, that the independence of an element is only ever the form of its dependence, and that the interplay of the differences is regulated by the unity of a determination in the last instance; but that is why I did not talk about a *totality*, because the Marxist whole is complex and uneven, and stamped with this unevenness by the determination in the last instance.[39]

This argument about the autonomy/relative autonomy of the elements of the social formation has certain fairly practical consequences for radical film practice (or any attempts at progressive cultural production). An emphasis on the autonomy of the elements would tend to result in a cultural practice which in concentrating upon the specificity of art, sees radical practice in terms of certain advances at the level of the formal operations of the text, advances which have to do with the specific history of the art form; the radical is defined in terms of that which is radical in relation to the particular history of the system (element of the social formation) 'art'. Thus it is that the French critic and semiotician Roland Barthes emphasises in his earlier work the importance of studying 'the system's own particular time, the history of forms'.[40]

The real difficulty, however, may be posed by the need to understand the *relationship* between different 'histories', different elements of the social formation (each with their own specific history and mode of operation) at a particular historical moment. It could be argued that the position which speaks of the *relative autonomy* of the elements would be more likely — at the level of cultural production — to be concerned with these relationships between elements at a particular historical moment; that, to be more specific, the exponents of the semi-autonomous status of art/film would be more interested in developing an understanding of the relationship between cultural production and class struggle at other levels of the social formation. Such exponents might, therefore, be less likely to pose aesthetic strategies divorced from an accompanying analysis of the configurations of contemporary political life and an assessment of the most pressing problems currently confronting a particular national working class.

For the exponents of complete autonomy, by contrast, who see neither the feasibility nor apparently the desirability of assessing the relationship between the elements of the social formation (in this context the relationship between art/politics/economics), the specificity of the cultural is permitted to float elegantly free from the exigencies of the political. No attempt is made to theorise the relationship between cultural production and class struggle. *Cinéthique*, in a lengthy collective article written in 1971, criticise the notion of the complete autonomy of aesthetic practices[41] and propose instead the importance of putting 'politics in command' of aesthetic choices;[42] though this primacy of the political never slides over into a rejection of the importance of formal questions in estimating the reactionary or progressive potential of a particular film.

In France after May '68, for both *Cahiers* and *Cinéthique*, an analysis of the scope and the goals of a struggle specific to the ideological level is the primary focus of attention; radical film practice, the distribution of militant and/or 'materialist' films, as well as the production of a radical film criticism are seen to be aspects of this ideological struggle. *Cinéthique* placed considerable emphasis on its work in setting up an alternative distribution circuit which would make available films not released by the traditional commercial circuits: 'films which we think effect the "break" and contain the potential for bringing about a total reassessment of the cinema',[43] and speak also of the possibility of extending such work in distribution to include film production.[44] On the basis of a distribution network they hope to: 'elaborate its financial structure vertically to include production'.[45] In Britain groups like *Cinema Action* have placed a comparable emphasis on the need for self-financing production/distribution circuits. The question remained as to who these circuits were intended to reach, and it is interesting in this respect to consider the shifts in *Cinéthique*'s estimation of a film like *Méditerranée*.

To begin with *Méditerranée* was defended as one of the films which constituted a 'break' between an idealist and a new materialist cinema; by 1972 it was criticised on the grounds that its radical aesthetic practice was in no sense linked to a radical political practice. Its status as a radical modernist text (and *Cinéthique* criticise the journal *Tel Quel* in this context for continuing to defend the 'new formal avant-garde') is undermined. What *Cinéthique* counterposes to *Méditerranée* at this point, however, is not some popular (i.e. dominant) fiction or documentary format, but rather the work of the *Dziga Vertov* group on the grounds that their cinematic practice subordinates an aesthetic radicalism to the 'command' of the avant-garde of the proletariat.[46] This still seems to leave unanswered, however, the question of which existing aesthetic practices are accessible to the French proletariat.

By 1973 *Cahiers*' development of its notion of ideological struggle had led it to insist upon the need for very much closer links with the French working class, and to reject the notion of cultural producers/film-makers, outside and above the working class, raining radical texts down into the outstretched hands of cadre audiences:

> To pose the question of the content of revolutionary culture correctly, it is necessary to start from the position occupied by the producers and disseminators *vis à vis* the masses: to take part in their struggles is a necessary precondition for all progressive cultural work ... in all cases one must present the problems starting from a living and concrete reality.[47]

The desire to reach working class audiences of a more general kind (not cadres) is signalled by the suggestion that much more research needs to be done into existing popular forms of expression. Though there seems, at certain points, to be an underestimation of the problems that derive from any notion of the work performed by a dominant ideology. *Cahiers* state, for example:

> ... in order to elaborate a revolutionary language, one has to construct it in such a way that, hopefully, the bourgeoisie won't be able to recognise itself in it. The real problem, however, is to try and elaborate a language in which the people can recognise themselves.[48]

Such a phenomenon could only be imagined in a climate of extreme political crisis, in which one political order gives way to another, one set of ideologies is superseded by another. The proletariat could hardly 'recognise' itself (its needs as a class) in a situation in which the bourgeoisie had succeeded in organising the consent of other classes and class fractions to its own rule. To propose this as a problem should not, however, be taken as a denial of the principle affirmed by Gramsci of the 'possibility and necessity of creating a new culture'.[49]

Indeed there is a sense in which this 'new culture', with its alternative sets of beliefs and values, is constantly in the process of being produced; the arguments must be about its extent, efficacy and relationship to the balance of class forces. A voice-over near the beginning of Godard and Gorin's *Tout va bien* remarks that 'beneath the surface things are stirring', and Gramsci outlines the relations between the interests of dominant and subordinate groups in society as being in a state of constant tension:

> ... the dominant group is co-ordinated concretely with the general interests of the subordinate groups, and the life of the state is conceived of as a continuous process of formation and superseding of unstable equilibria ... between the interests of the fundamental group and those of the subordinate groups ...[50]

If this notion of there being a fundamental instability about the balance of forces within the social formation is accepted, with the dominant group, as it were, working overtime to assert its hegemony and produce the social equilibrium which stems from that successful assertion, it can be argued that a theoretical justification is available for believing in the possibility of productive work, or struggle, within the ideological field. What we find in Gramsci's formulations is a theory that underwrites and encourages a programme of political and cultural action in a pre-revolutionary period. Thus, for example, he argues:

> ... even before attaining power a class can (and must) 'lead' ... there can and must be a 'political hegemony' even before the attainment of governmental power ...[51]

And the importance of a programme at the level of ideological and cultural struggle is made rather more explicit in the remark:

> Every revolution has been preceded by hard critical thinking, the diffusion of culture, and the spread of ideas among men who are at first unwilling to listen.[52]

To return briefly to the concept of the 'uneven development' of the social formation, we may note that just as there is a possibility that a particular form of cultural production may be a 'survival', an anachronistic hangover from the class needs of an earlier epoch, so also it is theoretically possible for cultural production to *anticipate* future class needs, and to play a part in the transference of political hegemony from one class to another in advance of a radical change in the relations of production. This possibility produces that optimism which looks for the emergence of oppositional cultures and of dominated but 'protesting' ideologies. It is only this hope which justifies the continued discussion of and search for radical aesthetic practices within a social order that operates according to the exigencies of monopoly capital. The importance of this work of struggle at the level of cultural production to represent new needs and values, in advance of a radical change in the relations of production, has been usefully outlined by the English historian E.P. Thompson, in the context of a defence of the writings of the poet and political essayist William Morris:

> Morris sought in every way to implant, encourage and enlarge new 'wants' in the present, and imbue the socialist movement with an alternative notation of value, *before* the 'rupture'; and he judged that socialist success or failure in this enterprise would affect not only when the revolution came but what form it would take. In any event, Morris saw (although unclearly) that 'ruptures' in values are taking place *all the time*, and not only during moments of strike and rebellion.[53]

The 'impression of reality'
Both *Cahiers* and *Cinéthique* addressed the question of ideology in many

different contexts and in many different ways. But one key area of ideological 'struggle' for both journals was a confrontation with what was regarded as the existing, dominant, idealist tradition in film aesthetics, which stemmed in France from the writings of André Bazin, and which revolved around the question of realism, or, as *Cahiers* and *Cinéthique* referred to it, around the 'impression of reality' produced in the cinema. Since both journals were committed to analysis of the operations of cinema in capitalist society in terms of class and class interests, it may be useful to recollect one of the more polemical statements from the *Dziga Vertov* group's film *Vent d'est*:

> You know that there is no cinema above classes, no cinema which is above the class struggle . . . that means that the dominant material power in society, through the dominant class, also creates the dominant images through and in its films.[54]

If the statement suggests too simple and direct a connection between class interests and cultural forms, it does help to explain the general climate of hostility within which the radical film journals approached the analysis of 'dominant images' of mainstream, commercial cinema — for which the word 'Hollywood' often came to stand as a general, unifying, descriptive term. Though a distinction should be made, perhaps, between the straightforward, total hostility of the early writings in *Cinéthique*, and a rather more speculative approach within *Cahiers* which looked for the possibility of productive tensions and contradictions within the Hollywood monolith. *Cahiers*, for example, were interested in making a distinction between those 'films, books and magazines' which 'allow the ideology a free, unhampered passage' and those which 'attempt to make it turn back and reflect itself, intercept it and make it visible by revealing its mechanisms.[55] They clearly hoped that their own analytical work would fall within the latter category.

In contrast to their own attempts at a scientific and analytical practice, *Cahiers* argue that the 'classic theory of cinema' can only allow to the dominant ideology a 'free passage', since its notion of the camera as 'an impartial instrument which grasps, or rather is impregnated by, the world'[56] is unable even to recognise the presence of ideology. *Cinéthique* rehearsed a similar argument with the notion that the 'impression of reality' produced by the 'dominant images' allows to the dominant ideology a free rein, a free passage. Above and beyond this notion that the cinema in general acts as a vehicle for this ideology, a further argument is proposed to the effect that the 'impression of reality' in fact constitutes the cinema's own ideology. The cinema, *Cinéthique* argue, apart from reproducing existing ideologies, further:

> ... PRODUCES its own ideology: THE IMPRESSION OF REALITY. There is nothing on the screen, only reflections and shadows, and yet the first idea the audience gets is that reality is there, as it really is.[57]

This statement is at one level an underestimation of the critical faculties of most audiences. But it begins to make more sense in the context of an examination of the aesthetic of realism developed by Bazin; it becomes more comprehensible as a response to what were regarded as the potentially reactionary implications of that realist aesthetic, a brief account of which follows here.

In a 1945 article, 'The Ontology of the Photographic Image', Bazin writes of photography, and by extension of the cinema, in these terms: 'for the first time an image of the world is formed automatically without the creative intervention of man'. And he continues:

> The objective nature of photography confers on it a quality of credibility absent from all other picture-making.[58]

The key notions for *Cahiers* and *Cinéthique* are 'objectivity' and 'credibility' since both are used in Bazin's work to support the notion that the cinema shows us things as they are, that it presents reality 'automatically' with the minimum of distortion or interference from the unknown hand, eyes and brain that are situated behind the camera. Bazin's aesthetics are rooted within the mimetic theory of art; for him the proper goal of the film image, like that of Renaissance and post-Renaissance painting up to the time of the Cubists, is the production of the most perfect illusion of reality which is taken to be unproblematically 'given'. The photographic image, like a mirror, is seen to reflect the world without distortion. Moreover, in a development which takes on a rather more metaphysical edge to it than most mimetic theory, the cinema/photography is proposed as having the capacity to restore to the spectator a fresh and uncorrupted vision of the world:

> Only the impassive lens, stripping the object of all those ways of seeing it, those piled-up preconceptions, that spiritual dust and grime with which my eyes have covered it, is able to present it in all its virginal purity, to my attention.[59]

Since the work of editing, and Eisensteinian montage in particular, threatens to contaminate this 'purity', to distort it, Bazin's aesthetic proposes and defends as the finest exemplifcation of its principles the cinema of the 'long take'. Refusing the notion of film, the devices of narrative and so forth as an *account*, or version, or construction of reality, Bazin writes as though the finest films for him were authored by reality itself, not by men or women or the processes of production. Thus his praise for the films of von Stroheim seems to be on the grounds that von Stroheim's authorial presence offers the least possible impediment to the real author which is reality:

> In his films reality lays itself bare . . . He has one simple rule for direction. Take a close look at the world, keep on doing so, and in the end it will lay bare for you all its cruelty and ugliness.[60]

The hint of a radical pessimism is of interest in view of Bazin's Christian beliefs (perhaps a residual Manichaeism?). But the real importance of this remark for an understanding of the post-'68 assault on realism is the metaphysical quality of the assertion that reality itself speaks through the impassive lens, the director has only to look (presumably without preconceptions, fictional characters or narrative structure) and reality will reveal itself. It is not difficult to see why the radical film theorists (who believed firstly that reality itself was socially constructed, secondly that the work of film-making introduced a further level of constructedness, and thirdly that ideology as an inflection of 'real relations' was an operative concept) found these ideas impossible to accept, and devoted some energy to combating them.

The real nature of *Cahiers*' and *Cinéthique*'s objections to the 'impression of reality' or the 'depicting of reality'[61] in the cinema is that this impression is offered from the point of view of the ruling class — in other words, that it is an instance of dominant ideology. It is objected to on the grounds that it 'presents the existing abnormal relations of production as natural and right',[62] that it 'is never anything other than a method of permitting the audience to live an imaginary life within a nonexistent reality';[63] that it registers 'the vague, unformulated, untheorised, unthought-out world of the dominant ideology'.[64] What the cinema offers is not the marvellous, refreshing reality of Bazinian aesthetics, but an impression or account of social reality which is supportive of existing social relations, and which assists in the reproduction of those relations.

Both journals would agree that any attempt at subversion of this cinema-as-ideology would entail a consideration of the means of representation employed, a re-organisation of those means with a view to undermining the power of that cinematic illusion generated by the 'impression of reality'. But beyond this, they map out rather different areas of work for themselves, and are more (in the case of *Cahiers*) or less (in the case of *Cinéthique*) interested in exploring significant differences between films within the arena of mainstream, commercial cinema.

Cinéthique's programme of action involves the notion of a 'break' (derived from the Althusserian terminology of a 'break' between ideology and science) within cinema history between 'idealist' and 'materialist' films, and an attempt at encouraging the distribution and production of this 'materialist' cinema (a cinema which 'does not give illusory reflections of reality', which 'starts from its own material nature' and 'produces specific knowledge about itself').[65] While they speak of the need to produce a cinema which will 'really be of use to the proletariat in its struggle for power' the examples of materialist films which they cite are all experimental works within the modernist tradition (*Octobre à Madrid*, Marcel Hanoun; *Méditerranée*, Jean-Daniel Pollet; *Le joueur de quilles*, Jean-Pierre Lajournade), and indicate a strategy aimed at a highly specialist, cadre audience. This strategy is accompanied by an insistence on the need for a cinema of 'theoretical practice' (another Althusserian term linked to the ideology/science distinction, theoretical practice being the proper activity of 'science');[66] this notion is criticised by *Cahiers*,[67] and subsequently recognised by *Cinéthique* itself to be a theoretical impossibility[68] since the cinema's inclusion within the realm of ideological practices makes conceiving of it as a candidate for theoretical practice impossible. This assumes, of course, that the knowledge which a film produces about itself is of a lower epistemological order than the knowledge generated by theoretical practice.

Both journals have had to confront the problem of offering a theoretically adequate account of working class responses to different types of cinematic practice (mainstream, militant or experimental). *Cinéthique* attempt this account in terms of a notion of 'recognition' or 'mis-recognition', arguing that bourgeois and petit-bourgeois audiences 'recognise themselves in the representations on the screen',[69] and identify with a mode of life with which they are familiar; but that working class audiences, by contrast, because the mode of life represented is generally not their own (an argument that would require careful scrutiny) are mystified by what is represented:

> They identify with what happens on the screen (mechanically) but they *cannot*, or ought not to be able to, recognise themselves in it.[70]

The 'ought not' betrays the weakness of the argument, which seems both to underestimate the manner in which fictional structures modify in complex ways the procedures of recognition, and to underestimate the presence and 'work' performed by the dominant ideology. Why is it that the working class 'ought' not to recognise itself? Could it be because it 'ought' not to be dominated by the dominant ideology? Such statements would indicate that the whole question of class-differentiated 'readings' of films remains to be explored, and a little empirical research might be preferred to the 'ought not' of this passage.

Cahiers encounter some related difficulties in the context of a comparison of the film *Coup pour coup* by Marin Karmitz, a film made in a fairly straightforward naturalist style, and relying heavily upon workers instead of professional actors, with the more experimental film *Tout va bien*. They point out that a voice-over (which says: 'You have understood that your enemy is the boss') used at the end of *Tout va bien* would be inconceivable within the style of filming characteristically employed by Karmitz. They suggest that it would be difficult to imagine such a statement being made within a shot in *Coup pour coup*, and ask why this is. They continue: 'Should we reply that the workers would not have wished it?'[71] This seems to imply that, despite the objective 'correctness' of the statement, it would be impossible to find any workers who would actually agree with the remark, and agree to say it in front of the camera.

Perhaps more than anything else this comment betrays the difficulty that radical film critics (and film-makers?) have in engaging with advanced sections of the working class, with all of the problems (of being isolated within an intellectual ghetto, with little realistic sense of the direction or variety of directions of the contemporary working class movement) which stem from this difficulty. The real question is perhaps whether or not radical film critics are interested in understanding or constructing a relationship between their own proper theoretical and critical activity and the needs of the working class movement at the level of ideology. Is their work understood to be purposive in this sense? Is it love of the cinema, alone, which moves them, or a love of the cinema linked, by whatever means are appropriate (and this is not an easy question to settle) to a concern with the needs of contemporary class struggle? A recent interview (1977) with one of the editors of *Cahiers* would seem to indicate that it is love of the cinema above all else which has won the day, a 'cinephilia' which speaks of itself as 'not just a relationship to the cinema' but also 'a relationship to the world through cinema'.[72] A statement which might leave us wondering whether film lovers do not also know the world through work, newspapers, trade union activity and so forth. This 'cinephilia' of 1977 rejects 'sectarian films made hastily by people who didn't care about cinema'. In addition, the question of political power (which clearly must be linked to the progress of class struggle at the level of ideology) is, apparently, to be placed on one side in favour of a new interest in 'morality':

... morality becomes a living question again because everyone has experienced the fact that there exists no morality for someone who thinks in terms of power (to be seized, held onto or dreamed of), and therefore no morality on the left or in Marxism. Morality is something individual; it's natural that returning to a certain *politique des auteurs* should reintroduce morality.[73]

Cahiers' once radical aesthetic has travelled a long way, and appears here to have returned to those principles from which it broke away in the late sixties, namely to the categories of individual creativity and individual morality, long proposed as the central values of bourgeois aesthetics.

Film criticism and 'radical readings'

If *Cinéthique* placed emphasis on the need to produce a 'materialist' cinema and to deal with the problem of ideology at the point of its production, it would be fair to say that *Cahiers* placed its emphasis rather on the problems of criticism and 'reading', on the difficulties entailed in the analysis of ideological operations at the point of consumption (that is at the point 'where' the text is consumed, seen, read). But the work of criticism which they have in mind is, in the first instance, to be sharply distinguished from those impressionistic movie reviews (referred to as 'specious raving'[74]) designed to sell or not sell movie tickets; rather *Cahiers* are interested in 'rigidly factual analysis of what governs the production of a film'. But they also, perhaps more surprisingly, distinguish their project from the production of 'commentary' and 'interpretation'; the traditional exegetical work of criticism — producing interpretations and accounts of the text — is thus apparently ruled out. The *Cahiers* collective analysis of John Ford's *Young Mr. Lincoln* (August 1970) explains some of the reasons for this position, and outlines some of the goals of their own critical project. This article can be seen as an attempt at in-depth analysis of one of those category (e) films, the existence of which is hypothesised in 'Cinema/Ideology/Criticism' (see above, p. 35). A brief review of the arguments proposed in the *Young Mr. Lincoln* article may be useful here.

Firstly, they criticise that work of commentary which aims to 'distil an ideally constituted sense, presented as the object's ultimate meaning', on the grounds that any such attempt at fixing the meaning is impossible — the meaning 'remains elusive indefinitely'. Moreover, this attempt at fixing a reading which amounts to a kind of re-duplication of the text can only end up by ignoring the very specificity of the text: in offering an account of what the text means, it forgets to look at the ways in which the text is able to produce meanings, it forgets to examine the specific signifying practices of the text, or, as they put it, the attempt at fixing a meaning 'misses the reality of the inscription'.[75]

The only problem with this notion of opening up the broad vistas of a text's capacity to generate an infinite number of meanings is that it tends to militate against the task of discovering precisely what (or what range of) meanings are attributed to a given text by particular readers at a particular historical moment. For if critics cannot begin to map out a range of possible meanings they can scarcely begin to account for the text as a socially operative phenomenon.

A related point (one not drawn out in this *Cahiers* article, but one which is developed by a number of the *Tel Quel* writers from whom *Cahiers* draw many of their theoretical premises) is the notion that the work of exegetical criticism, of fixed meanings, is a fundamentally repressive work, that it cuts short the pleasures of the 'sport' of meaning between reader and text. The infinite productivity of the text, the pleasure which the text offers to a reader who knows that its meanings are inexhaustible[76] is, this argument would propose, cut short by an authoritarian criticism which attempts to fix and limit meaning.

But a question that has to be asked by any critic who is interested in reading as a social and historical phenomenon is: for whom is this pleasure available, for whom is this range of meanings available? Who benefits most from the supposed infinite productivity of the text? It is this sort of problem which accounts for the rather sour tone adopted by an English critic,Terry Eagleton, who criticises some of the political implications of this argument about textual productivity; his tone in reproducing the argument is heavily ironic, and he then moves in to the attack:

> Criticism as the repressive father who cuts short the erotic sport of sense between text and reader, binding with the briars of its metasystem the joyfully pluralist intercourse of meanings between them. A *libertarianism* of text and reader, in short, typical of the *Tel Quel* group, which like all libertarianism fatally inverts itself into a mirror image of bourgeois social relations.[77]

The criticism here may be rather too harsh, with its notion that the defence of a plurality of readings (the 'libertarianism of text and reader') quickly becomes the mere mirroring of bourgeois freedoms and the confirmation of existing bourgeois social relations. But it none the less raises important questions with respect to some of the implications of the first point in *Cahiers*' programme, and the problem of historically and socially specific readings.

Cahiers' second point has to do with the notion of criticism as meta-system or meta-language. In attacking the principles of 'interpretation', *Cahiers* object that the language of criticism can never adequately transpose or translate the meanings of the text; it can never fully reproduce the meaning of the text in a parallel language, can never comprehensively interpret the text, transforming it from one system of discourse (its own) into another (the language of the critic). Like the first point, this one is concerned with the irreducibility of the text which, constructed by its specific signifying practices, can never be fully accounted for, or shadowed by, the language of criticism. A criticism which knows its own limitations, and which respects the inviolate 'body' of the text, will not, therefore, attempt such an operation.

Thirdly, *Cahiers* criticise what they call a 'mechanistic structural reading': the attempt to break down an object which is 'conceived of as a closed structure'[78] into its supposedly discrete elements. Rather *Cahiers* propose the notion of a 'dynamic of the inscription'; their notion of signifying practice, of the processes for the production of meaning employed by the text, implies a constantly working process of meaning production within the text, not a fixity or final achievement of meaning. A critical method must therefore engage with the processes or operations of the text and not seek to allocate fixed meanings to individual elements.

Finally, criticism is made of what is regarded as the reductionist method employed by *Cinéthique* which seeks to demystify the film, to re-locate it 'within its historical determinations', to force it to yield its secrets of meaning, to 'reveal' its assumptions, declare its problematic and aesthetic prejudices and criticise its statements'.[79] This method seeks, as it were, to squeeze the reactionary meanings out of a film 'in order to see it collapse and feel no more needs to be said'.

It is not that *Cahiers* are against the notion of 'historical determinations', but they are concerned to point out that the work of analysing a cultural object in terms of its socio-historical context is no easy task (and the reason for this is that whole long history of arguments about 'uneven development' and about superstructure not simply reflecting or expressing the base). Any attempt at producing a properly historical reading of a film must therefore both recognise the specific textual operations of that film (its specific signifying practices), and be aware of that complex network of mediations which comes into play 'between' the text and its historical context. For the text does not directly reflect the mode of economic production and attendant political and ideological systems which are contemporaneous with it. *Cahiers* argue the case in this way:

> ... that an artistic product cannot be linked to its socio-historical context according to a linear, expressive, direct causality (unless one falls into a reductionist historical determinism), but that it has a complex, mediated and *decentred* relationship with this context, which has to be rigorously specified (which is why it is simplistic to discard 'classic' Hollywood cinema on the pretext that since it is part of the capitalist system it can only reflect it).[80]

This notion of a decentred relationship is then further explored in terms of the concept of *structuring absences*, the notion that a film is organised around the principle of displacement (a concept drawn from psychoanalysis, in particular from Freud's method for the analysis of dreams), that it is organised around its significant absences, around that which it cannot say. At worst this proposal to search out 'structuring absences' grants the critic the most extraordinary licence to claim the presence of precisely that which is not 'there in the text' (an unacceptably paradoxical procedure for traditional literary criticism which takes the organic and meaningful unity of the work as its premise). At best, and for those who accept Freud's theory of a principle of (finally meaningful) displacement at work in dreams, it opens up the possibility of a symptomatic reading of the text which seeks to draw out from certain points of tension within it the presence of that which the text strives to 'say' but cannot 'say'. This method looks not for the organic unity of the work, but for its significant 'gaps', 'breaks' or 'fissures'. The concepts and the critical method are outlined in this way:

> What will be attempted here through a re-scansion of these films in a process of active reading, is to make them say what they have to say *within* what they leave unsaid, to reveal their constituent lacks; these are neither faults in the work . . . nor a deception on the part of the author . . . they are *structuring absences*, always displaced . . . the unsaid included in the said and necessary to its constitution. In short, to use Althusser's expression – 'the internal shadows of exclusion'.[81]

What this search for the 'internal shadows of exclusion', or the 'structuring absences' opens up is the possibility of certain radical readings of film texts (though this is not an expression that is used by *Cahiers*). No matter how far removed the text may seem to be from contemporary social and political reality, no matter how fantastic its fiction, this method proposes a way of searching out the significant points of ideological tension, and therefore of thinking about the text in relation to its historical context. It is this method of symptomatic reading which Roland Barthes has in mind when he asks:

> . . . if it is possible to teach people to read or not to read, or to re-read beyond the confines of educational and cultural conditioning.[82]

Of course, despite the existence of a proposed method for radical reading, the answer to Barthes' question is not an easy one. And it would be a great mistake to assume that the recognition of a method of analysis within a highly elite intellectual circle meant its inevitable and rapid transmission to large numbers of people. A whole massive primary and secondary educational apparatus with its own dominant notions of what reading is all about (consuming for pleasure, raiding for 'facts', recognising that richness of text attributed to it by its official interpreters) intervenes to *form readers*, and to impose expectations about the proper goals of the act of reading, long before the radical critic or the modernist film-maker arrive on the scene.

The re-examination of the notion of reading, linked with theories of the reading subject (the reader), and of signifying practice derived from psychoanalysis, forms one of the most fertile and most controversial areas within film studies at the present time. It will be possible here only to touch upon a few of the issues raised in this debate.

The single most important achievement of this rethinking of reading is perhaps that it, as it were, opens out the text (no longer conceived of as a discrete, autonomous entity, resplendent with its finely polished, finished and finally achieved meanings) onto or into a number of different processes. The text is no longer frozen into the timeless vacuum which it had been permitted to inhabit by virtue of its eternal value as art, rather it is seen as the complex sum of *both* those processes of meaning production contemporaneous with the moment of its production *and* those processes of meaning production contemporaneous with the moment of its consumption or reading.

What seemed at first like a method which simply abolished history by insisting that the text was in no simple relationship of reflection with its historical moment, turns out rather to be reinstating the text within a number of histories, a number of processes. To put it another way, the method now recognises that, as one writer has suggested:

We and the texts are in process together.[83]

The intentions of the author, the formal operations of the text, the apparent intransigence of the reader (him/herself subject to historical process and change), begin to be reworked into a theory of the relationship between the moment of the author, the moment of the text and the moment of the reader. But each of these moments is itself part of a process or history of its own. Each can be thought of in terms of various socially and historically specific processes for the production of meaning, or as the 'products' of various already existing systems of signifying practice (the text is called into already existing systems of literary production, the individual human subject is called into, or 'produced' by, already existing systems of social and psychic organisation).

It is not just that, as *Cahiers* put it, films are to be studied in relationship to:

. . . the codes (social, cultural . . .) for which they are a site of intersection . . .[84]

but that, in addition, both authors and readers can be studied in relation to those often different codes (processes for the production of meaning) for which *they* are the site of intersection. The encounter between reader and text is thus the complex sum of a number of different histories, the histories of the different codes for which author, text and reader are the site of intersection. The moments of writing and of reading are not timeless, but the products of those several histories which have made them possible.

A rather more practical aspect of this theory of reading (one not without its dangers) is proposed by the Italian semiotician Umberto Eco. Eco suggests that the 'gap' between the moment of the text's production (the moment of 'encoding') and the moment of the text's reception or reading (the moment of 'decoding'), could — perhaps should — be opened up and exploited; not closed down or smoothed over after the manner of critics who seek to bring the reader up to the level of the text, to minimise the 'gap', to ensure that the reader 'buys' all the meanings which the text has to 'sell'. The theory of reading based on a notion of signifying practice rejects, in any case, the notion that the text 'has' — holds, contains — a fixed number of elements of meaning which it is the job of the critic or 'skilled reader' simply to make over to the ordinary, less skilled reader (a kind of consumer protection service that enables the reader to answer the question 'Am I getting the full value of the text?'). Eco proposes the possibility of opening up this 'gap' between transmitted and received message; methods of radical reading, like conceptual tool kits, would be made over to the reader to enable him/her to decode meanings other than those intended by the encoder.

The method seems like a desirable one for combating the effects (the constant process of socialising into homogeneity, the ideological binding operation), of television in particular. But it may result in an evasion of the task of opening up certain contradictions at the encoding end (for the broadcasting institutions are not entirely monolithic and impenetrable). It may also lead in the dangerous direction of seeing all cultural texts (whether movies, plays, newspaper articles or television transmissions) as simple 'Rorschach blots' (unformed blots of ink or paint offered to patients for interpretation in the course of certain psychology tests), which have no structure of their own, and which can be read in whatever way the reader chooses.

Despite these reservations, it is still possible to argue that Eco's proposal offers a starting point for thinking out productive strategies of reading. He writes:

> In my *La struttura assente*, I proposed, also, the possibility of a 'semiotic guerrilla warfare'; the gap between the transmitted and the received message is not only an aberration, which needs to be reduced — it also can be developed so as to broaden the receiver's freedom. In political activity it is not indispensable to change a given message: it would be enough (or, perhaps better) to change the attitude of the audience, so as to induce a different decoding of the message — or in order to isolate the intentions of the transmitter and thus to criticise them.[85]

The question which remains is: how is this 'semiotic guerrilla warfare' to be disseminated? It is here that any strategy for radical readings cannot afford to ignore the problems generated by the particular placement of working class children within the primary and secondary educational system. For it is presumably not only university graduates and the mandarins of higher education who are to benefit from the liberating effects of the methods of radical reading. And a whole area of study, that of existing class-differentiated readings, is only beginning to be opened up.

Eco proposes the idea of opening up the 'gap' between encoder and decoder with a view to turning the transmitted message back upon itself, reading it in ways which were never intended by the producer. But the theory of radical criticism based on the notion of signifying practices is less and less happy with the notion of a message, of a given structure which is transmitted from one place to another place, from the place of the producer to the place of the consumer, with more or less damage to its integrity as a given set of elements. It is perhaps this breaking down of the notion of message as a fixed quantity of elements, shunted from one place to another in the process of transmission, that accounts for an occasional confusion within radical criticism as to whether the attribute of 'radicalness', of the 'progressive', is seen to pertain to the text or to the act of reading.

This radical criticism sometimes finds itself caught between two sets of vocabularies and therefore between two conceptual fields (the field constructed by traditional information theory on the one hand, and the field constructed by a theory of signifying practices on the other). It therefore sometimes fails to be clear about whether it is proposing the text which it studies as a radical object (whether the 'open' text of modernism which apparently and categorically does not force or require a particular reading, which leaves the spectator free to construct his or her own passage 'through' the text, or the statement that, for example, the film *Jaws* is 'really' a critique of the auto-destructive tendencies of late capitalism; both these positions propose the 'radical' as a necessary, inherent attribute of the text), or whether it is proposing a radical method of reading that text. Which is 'radical', the reading method or the text?

Any theory of cultural production which is based on the notion of signifying practice (the complex interaction of reader and text within a particular historical conjuncture) *cannot* in fact propose a text as being 'radical' in and of itself, simply by virtue of the fact of its textual operations; it can only operate in a radical way or not within the process of reading. It is the reading process itself, in relationship to the particular operations of the text, which introduces the possibility of the radical; the 'radical' or the 'progressive' can then clearly be seen to be the attribute of a process (reading) not of an entity (the text). Once this point has been clarified, it can then be allowed that certain sorts of textual operations invite or encourage certain sorts of readings; the cultural producer who has an interest in encouraging radical readings will therefore think carefully about the selection of one set of textual operations rather than another.

****

The discussions generated in France by the May events were themselves only one contribution, though an important one, to a longstanding debate within Marxism conducted around the question of radical aesthetics. In terms of both film production and film criticism these discussions may be helpful to the furtherance of this debate in Britain. But it must be emphasised that the content of these discussions cannot be simply imported, for at the point at which theory transforms itself into practice it must be aware of its specific economic, political and ideological context. A theory of cultural production must be aware of the specific historical struggles to which it seeks to make its contribution, and aware also of the specific aesthetic and institutional forms which it seeks to analyse and then to reconstruct.

A series of developments in British film culture, following in the wake of the 'May of film theory' has brought us to the point where some — whether film-makers or film viewers — are rejecting as unhelpful the dry cracklings of cultural theory, others are insisting upon the importance of a theory of radical aesthetics but are unsure of its areas of application, and a few, through their engagement in particular political struggles, and in their attempts at developing a cultural practice that will carry these struggles forward, have entered that small clearing in the forest where the theoretical illuminates and serves the work of transforming the old world.

NOTES

1. Marx and Engels, *The German Ideology*, Lawrence and Wishart, London 1974, p.42.
2. Ibid.
3. Ibid., pp.46-7.
4. Ibid., p.47.
5. Antonio Gramsci, *Selections from the Prison Notebooks*, edited and translated by Quinton Hoare and Geoffrey Nowell-Smith, Lawrence and Wishart, London 1971, p.407.
6. Ibid.
7. *The German Ideology*, op. cit., p.47.
8. Louis Althusser, *For Marx*, translated by Ben Brewster, New Left Books, London 1969, p.233.
9. *The German Ideology*, op. cit., p.47.
10. Ibid., p.66.
11. Ibid., p.64.
12. Ibid., p.65.
13. Marx, *The Eighteenth Brumaire of Louis Bonaparte*, in Karl Marx and Frederick Engels, *Selected Works* in one volume, Lawrence and Wishart, London 1970, p.117.
14. Louis Althusser, *For Marx*, op. cit., p.240.
15. 'Texte collectif', *Cinéthique*, nos. 9-10, 1971, p.16.
16. Louis Althusser, *For Marx*, op. cit., p.232.
17. *Cinéthique*, no. 4, p.26.
18. 'Pour un front culturel revolutionnaire', *Cahiers*, op. cit., p.9.
19. *Letter to a Teacher*, by the School of Barbiana, Penguin, London, 1970.
20. Marx, Preface to *A Contribution to the Critique of Political Economy*, in Marx and Engels, *Selected Works*, op. cit., p.182.
21. Marx, *Grundrisse*, translated by Martin Nicolaus, Penguin, London 1973, p.109.
22. Ibid., p.110.
23. Engels, 'Letter to Bloch' (1890), in Marx and Engels, *Selected Works*, op. cit., p.682.
24. See Louis Althusser, 'Contradiction and Overdetermination', in *For Marx*, op. cit.
25. For Althusser's discussion of the Hegelian notion of totality, see 'On the Materialist Dialectic', in *For Marx*, op. cit., especially pp.202-204.

26. Louis Althusser, 'Marxism and Humanism', *For Marx*, op. cit., p.235.
27. Ibid., p.232, and *For Marx*, op. cit., p.240.
28. Ibid., pp.232-3.
29. Ibid., p.236.
30. Louis Althusser, 'Ideology and Ideological State Apparatuses', in *Lenin and Philosophy and Other Essays*, New Left Books, London 1971, p.155.
31. 'Marxism and Humanism', *For Marx*, op. cit., p.231.
32. Ibid., p.233.
33. Ibid., p.232.
34. Louis Althusser, 'Contradiction and Overdetermination', op. cit., p.113.
35. Louis Althusser, 'On the Materialist Dialectic', op. cit., p.209.
36. Stuart Hall, 'Re-thinking the "Base-and-Superstructure" Metaphor'. in *Class, Hegemony and Party*, (ed.) Jon Bloomfield, Lawrence and Wishart, London 1977, p.44.
37. Gerard Leblanc, 'Quelle avant-garde?', *Cinéthique*, nos. 7-8, p.81.
38. See, in Britain, the debate between Ros Coward and the Birmingham Centre for Contemporary Cultural Studies. Ros Coward, 'Class, "Culture" and the Social Formation', *Screen*, v16 n1, Spring 1977, pp.75-105, and the response from the Centre, 'Marxism and Culture', *Screen*, v18 n4, Winter 1977-78, pp.109-119.
39. Louis Althusser, 'Is it Simple to be a Marxist in Philosophy?', first published in France in 1975; published in English in *Essays in Self Criticism*, translated by Grahame Lock, New Left Books, London 1976, p.183.
40. Roland Barthes, *Elements of Semiology*, Jonathan Cape, London 1967, p.98.
41. 'Texte collectif', *Cinéthique*, nos. 9-10, p.49.
42. Ibid., p.44.
43. Gerard Leblanc, 'Direction', *Cinéthique*, no. 5, p.129.
44. See, for example, *Cinéthique*'s own film, *Quand on aime la vie on va au cinéma* (1974).
45. Gerard Leblanc, 'Direction', op. cit., p.129.
46. 'Programme pour une lecture publique de *Méditerranée*', *Cinéthique*, no. 13, 1972, pp.78-9.
47. 'Pour un front culturel révolutionnaire', *Cahiers*, no. 248, op. cit., p.6, translated by Paul Willemen.
48. Ibid., p.8.
49. Antonio Gramsci, ' "Wave of Materialism" and "Crisis of Authority" '. 1930, *Prison Notebooks*, op. cit., p.182.
51. Ibid., p.57, footnote.
52. Gramsci, 'Socialism and Culture', *Avanti*, June 1916, quoted and translated in *Antonio Gramsci and the Origins of Italian Communism*, by John M. Cammett, Stanford, California 1967, p.42.
53. Edward Thompson, 'Romanticism, Utopianism and Moralism: The Case of William Morris', *New Left Review*, no. 99, Sept-Oct 1976, p.111.
54. Quoted by Gerard Leblanc in 'Quelle avant-garde?', *Cinéthique*, op. cit., p.74.
55. **Jean-Louis Comolli and Jean Narboni, 'Cinema/Ideology/Criticism', Part One, op. cit., p.29**
56. Ibid., p.30.
57. Jean-Paul Fargier, 'Parenthesis or Indirect Route', op. cit., p.136.
58. André Bazin, *What is Cinema?*, Vol. I, essays selected and translated by Hugh Gray, University of California Press, California, 1970, p.13.
59. Ibid., p.15.
60. Ibid., p.27, from 'The Evolution of the Language of Cinema'.
61. This is the term that *Cahiers* use in 'Cinema/Ideology/Criticism', op. cit.
62. Jean-Paul Fargier, 'Parenthesis or Indirect Route', op. cit., p.138.
63. Gerard Leblanc, 'Direction', op. cit., p.124.
64. 'Cinema/Ideology/Criticism', Part One, op. cit., p.30.
65. See Jean-Paul Fargier, 'Parenthesis or Indirect Route', op. cit.

66. Althusser's notion of theoretical practice which has implications far beyond the realms of film theory was developed in Britain in the journal *Theoretical Practice*, which published seven issues between 1971 and 1973. One of the editors of *Theoretical Practice* subsequently (1974) became the editor of the British journal of film theory *Screen*. For a critique of Althusserian positions on theoretical practice and on the science/ideology distinction see: J. Rancière, 'On the Theory of Ideology' (1970), in *Radical Philosophy*, no. 7, Spring 1974, pp.2-14; Robin Rusher, 'What is it he's done? The Ideology of Althusser', in *Working Papers in Cultural Studies*, no.6, pp.70-96; Alex Callincos, *Althusser's Marxism*, Pluto Press, London 1976; and Althusser's own *Essays in Self Criticism* (1974), New Left Books, London 1976.
67. 'Cinema/Ideology/Criticism', Part Two, *Cahiers*, no. 217, November 1969; translated by Susan Bennett in *Screen*, Summer 1971, p.148. Reprinted in *Screen Reader* no. 1.
68. See *Cinéthique*, nos. 9-10, 'Ideologie/Art/Science', p.46.
69. Jean-Paul Fargier, 'Parenthesis or Indirect Route', op. cit., p.137.
70. Ibid.
71. 'Le Groupe *Dziga Vertov*', *Cahiers*, nos. 238-239, May-June 1972, p.39.
72. 'Les *Cahiers du Cinéma* 1968-77', Interview with Serge Daney, in *The Thousand Eyes*, no. 2 (New York), p.24.
73. Ibid., p.30.
74. 'Cinema/Ideology/Criticism', Part One, op. cit., p.34.
75. 'John Ford's *Young Mr. Lincoln*', *Cahiers*, no. 223, August 1970; translated by Helen Lackner and Diana Matias in *Screen*, Autumn 1972, Vol. 13, no. 3, p.6.
76. See Roland Barthes, *Pleasure of the Text*, Jonathan Cape, London 1976, and *S/Z*, Jonathan Cape, London 1975.
77. Terry Eagleton, *Criticism and Ideology*, op. cit., p.42.
78. 'John Ford's *Young Mr. Lincoln*', *Cahiers*, op. cit., p.6.
79. Ibid.
80. Ibid., p.7.
81. Ibid., p.8.
82. 'A Conversation with Roland Barthes', in *Signs of the Times. Introductory Readings in Textual Semiotics*, edited by Stephen Heath, Colin MacCabe and Christopher Prendergast, Granta, Cambridge 1971, p.47.
83. Geoffrey Nowell-Smith, 'Six Authors in Pursuit of *The Searchers*', *Screen*, v17 n1, Spring 1976, p.33.
84. 'John Ford's *Young Mr. Lincoln*', op. cit., p.6.
85. Umberto Eco, 'Towards a Semiotic Enquiry into the Television Message', *Working Papers in Cultural Studies*, no. 3, Autumn 1972, p.121.

Appendices

The history*

Monday, May 13. After a week of student revolt and the barricades of rue Gay-Lussac, nearly a million demonstrators march from the Place de la République to Denfert-Rochereau.

Wednesday, May 15. Four young technicians create the Cinema Commission within the framework of the Sorbonne Action Committees. From May 14, the inter-faculty Commission undertakes to provide screenings. Some fifty films go into regular circulation in the four important centres: Sorbonne, Censier, Jussieu, Nanterre. Screenings are organised in various Parisian and provincial *lycées*, as well as in a number of factories. They include both the classics and films made for the struggle which do not always carry the censor's certificate.

Thursday, May 16. Pupils of the Ecole de Vaugirard agree to their school becoming the general headquarters for a permanent film information service, both short and long term. A viewing theatre is set up in the annexe amphitheatre of the Sorbonne. The beginnings of a distribution movement are seen in the universities, lycées and factories.

Friday, May 17, 12 noon. The central office of the film technicians' union *(Syndicat des Techniciens de la Production Cinématographique)*, brings together film-makers, technicians, members of the actors' union *(Syndicat Francais des Acteurs)*, students from IDHEC *(Institut des Hautes Etudes Cinématographiques)* and ENPC *(Ecole Nationale de Photographie et de Cinématographie)*. The latter ask for the participation of both union and non-union professionals in an information and action meeting to be held in the premises of their occupied school in rue de Vaugirard. The idea grows to the dimensions of a general assembly of cineastes, to be convened at the ENPC, to show solidarity with the students' and workers' struggle, protest against police repression and propose an action by the profession as a whole.

In the afternoon, another meeting takes place at the headquarters of the technicians' union, with the editors of *Cahiers du Cinéma*. A decision is taken not to limit the Assembly to simple consultation between cineastes, but to turn it into the starting point for a true movement of challenge, even of the present structures of French cinema. The name 'Estates General of French Cinema' is proposed and adopted. The same evening more than a thousand people meet at the ENPC. The following leaflets bring them there:

   1.   May 17, 1968.
Given that in present conditions, a free Cinema and Television do not exist, given that an infinite minority of film-makers and technicians have access to the means of production and expression,

---

* Reprinted from *Cahiers du Cinéma*, no 203, August 1968, with permission.

Given that for all professional categories decisive changes are called for at all levels,

Given that the cinema has a major mission to fulfil today and that it is gagged at all levels in the present system,

Film-makers, technicians, actors, producers, distributors and critics in film and television, resolved to bring an end to the present state of affairs, have decided to convene the Estates General of French Cinema.

We invite you all to take part in the Estates General, the date of which will be announced later. Revolutionary Committee of Cinema-Television.

2. The film technicians union central office calls all film-makers and all collaborators in the film profession to take part in the opening of the standing sessions of cinema this evening at 9 p.m. in the premises of the ENPC, 85 rue de Vaugirard, Paris 6, occupied by the students since 6 p.m. Wednesday. Paris, May 17, 1968, 2 p.m.

The same day at the ORTF *Service de la Recherche,* a group of film-makers and critics demand of Pierre Schaeffer and his collaborators, that they put technicians and film material at the disposal of students and workers. Soon a film is shot by the Renault workers with the collaboration of the *Service de la Recherche* team in the Boulogne-Billancourt factories.

At the Estates General: Motion passed on the principle of a strike by production workers, technicians, laboratory employees; motion passed concerning the Cannes Festival, to be telephoned through immediately to the film-makers, critics and journalists present at Cannes:

The information and action assembly of French cinema which, on May 17, 1968, brings together more than a thousand professionals at the ENPC in rue de Vaugirard, occupied by its students since May 15, asks all film-makers, producers, distributors, actors, journalists, jury members, present at Cannes, to oppose, in collaboration with their foreign counterparts and and by the means appropriate to them, the continuation of the Festival in order to show solidarity with the workers and students on strike, to protest against police repression and express thereby their will to oppose the gaullist government and the present structures of the film industry.

Saturday, May 18. Total strike at the Saint-Maurice studio *(Le Cerveau,* Gérard Oury). The Estates General organise themselves: creation of working parties: 1. internal functioning of the Estates General; 2. External action; 3. Education; 4. Film-television; 5. Information; 6. Opposition.

The working parties are open to all. A permanent core of officers ensures continuity without a designated president. The point is to avoid professional pigeon-holing and bureaucracy. The cinema has been suffocated by the compartmentalisation that came from fragmentary struggles. This is what has to be shed first.

The extraordinary general assembly of the film technicians' union, meeting May 19 at the Labour Exchange, issues an order for a total strike and publishes the following declaration:

> The film profession in its entirety has long been in a tense situation. Present events are developing with lightning speed. It is our duty to take emergency measures.
>
> The students of ENPC-Vaugirard, the students of IDHEC, and the staff of *Radio-Télévision Scolaire,* have gone on strike and occupied their premises; the studios are on strike; the Cannes Festival has been interrupted, as have the majority of films in the process of being made; the film-makers are on strike.
>
> Everyone must clearly grasp the serious nature of the present situation and understand that the order for a total strike does not confine itself to traditional claims, but implies a real questioning of the petrified structures in which we work.
>
> Everyone must clearly grasp that an order for a total strike is an order for general mobilisation, not imposed by recruiting sergeants, but dictated and put into operation by the freedom of all.
>
> All must clearly grasp that this is not a matter of manifesting some straightforward dissatisfaction in a superficial way.
>
> All must clearly grasp that at the present time, the true and only future of our profession is each one of us.

Strike.

Occupy your places of work with order and discipline.

An immense task awaits us.

The Estates General of the Cinema has been proclaimed.

We call on you to take part.

The Estates General for its part published the following motion:

> We (cineastes/film-makers, technicians, workers, students and critics) are on total strike to denounce and destroy the reactionary structures of a cinema which has become a commodity. We shall not cease our struggle except as agents and controllers of our profession.

Sunday, May 19. More advanced than many other union directives confined to 'traditional demands', these directives have the courage to recognise that film work is inseparable from the conditions in which it is exercised. Challenging the "now petrified structures" means taking a political position.

The decision is taken to make direct contact with the projectionists (who belong to seven different unions) to urge them to go on strike.

Arrival of the festival-goers from Cannes.

Monday, May 20. Establishment of the Repeal Board *(La Commission de Dérogation)* allows for filming to go on, despite the strike, on the workers and students' movement and on the negotiations on Vietnam.

Decision taken not to approve the films shot on the events.

Paris cinemas sectioned up between three hundred people with the task of encouraging projectionists to strike. Groups are formed to go into the forty-five cinemas of Paris. They come up against the isolation of the projectionists who are divided into multiple unions.

Bringing together technicians according to professional categories was a union decision. The film-makers' meeting in a cinema on the rue de Solférino brings out the pressing need for arriving at a definition of the new structures of our profession without delay.

Tuesday, May 21. Meeting of the CGT union projectionists. Motion of support at ORTF where the objectivity of the television news programme *Le Journal Télévisé* is interfered with. Creation of a liaison committee for Cinema-ORTF. The Estates General affirms that the *Centre National du Cinéma* (CNC) no longer exists. For some this is easier said than done. They voice the need for a vote and ask that everyone personally sign the motion. Reaching agreement on the wording of the motion is not easy. There is protracted argument over the need to use the word 'present' in the text of the motion: whether to deny the existence of the CNC, or to deny the existence of the CNC in its 'present structures'.

The following motion is passed and signed by a certain number of those participating in the Estates General:

> The Estates General considers the reactionary structures of the CNC abolished. Consequently, they affirm that its existence, its representativity and its regulations are no longer recognised by the profession. New structures for our profession must be born of the Estates General. At the close of the Assembly on May 21, we sign and invite the whole of our profession to join in witnessing this fact.

The Estates General working party on education holds its sittings in the premises of IDHEC and brings together students and teachers from IDHEC and the Vaugirard school, as well as cinema and television professionals. The meeting decides on the creation of a single school of audio-visual education. Dissemination of a leaflet from the inter-university Cinema Committee:

> Cineastes, what are you doing for the revolution?
> The insurrectional situation has allowed you to begin your professional revolution. What are you doing today for the revolution?
> It is vital to achieve an awareness of the absolute need to put all the means you have in the service of the revolution. We must support the strikers. We must screen films in the factories and on a very large scale. We must distribute documentary material filmed during the demonstrations, in company premises, public places and cinemas. Other actions are equally urgent. With this in view, we invite you to make contact with the worker-student action committees of Censier (meetings every evening at 8 p.m.).

The Estates General of the Cinema demanded the creation of a body common to Cinema and Television, composed equally of representatives from the technical, artistic and worker staff of these two branches of audio-visual expression. This body to be charged with promoting the re-organisation of the whole of audio-visual production.

With this aim, the Estates General proposes:

1. An increase in television viewing time and a fixed minimum percentage for the national production of 'new' programmes.

2. The free circulation of technicians based on the harmonisation of salaries and professional criteria;

3. The free circulation of films and programmes through the various systems of distribution.

The historical development of the Estates General of the Cinema has since been marked by three general assemblies, meeting at the *Centre culturel de l'Ouest Parisien* at Suresnes. At the first two (May 26 and 28), 19 projects for new structures were presented. After a vote, four of these projects were upheld, submitted to a more detailed examination by the Assembly and defended by their authors. The third (June 5) was devoted to a reading and criticism of a synthesis project resulting from the four previous ones. This was so clearly a 'patchwork' project that it was set aside after discussion. In the end agreement was reached on a more general motion defining the directing principles of action by the Estates General.

translated by Diana Matias.

Film journals and politics*

Introduction

Like the film-industry, film criticism is going through a crisis. It all began in May '68, with the revolutionary dream and the need to 'change life'. But because the world could not be changed immediately, one tried to change the cinema or, rather, the way we view the cinema.

Another important phenomenon which helps an understanding of the problems raised by film-criticism is this: in the wake of the reformist wave which swept over our educational structures, for the first time in France film criticism forcibly entered the Universities. Not only were academics passionately interested in the cinema able at last to teach their chosen subject, but people who had little to do with teaching—a certain number of film critics and historians of the cinema—were also given the opportunity to lecture in Parisian and provincial colleges.

Marxism-Leninism, in a way, became a kind of yard-stick, an indispensable reference upon which was erected, if not a scientific mode of criticism, at least a more methodical criticism which could go beyond the simple impressionism prevalent in newspaper columns. Both *Cahiers du Cinéma* and *Cinéthique* were in the vanguard of this movement. However, there is a reverse to this coin, a danger of too systematic an approach which would sever the cinema from its day-to-day life, from its real practice in the spheres of production and consumption. Other reviews—like *Positif*—seem more aware of this danger, and so would not engage in pure speculation.

Here the teams of the three reviews—*Cahiers*, *Cinéthique* and *Positif*—explain their positions.

Positif: 'to be readable'

Our ambition is to produce a review which is not esoteric. Although it cannot always be avoided, we refrain from commenting on films that few would have an opportunity to see. But we are not interested in vulgarisation. We do not wish to be caught up in the snobbish attitudes of the elites, although we do not want to talk about everything. What we set out to do is to be exacting and readable. We reject pedantry and demagogy and we would use humour if need be. But this, of course, does not please everyone.

Like any living organism, a review must evolve. *Positif* has no 'hard' line, but keeping in mind that it has been going for twenty years and that its editorial staff has gradually renewed itself, one can perhaps see three main lines of development emerging from no 1 to no 133.

1. An interest in popular cinema: slapstick, horror, musical comedies, westerns. Thus, from early on, a sharp interest in American cinema.

2. Support for film-makers who are young or little known. Very early, *Positif* talked of Antonioni, Wajda, Franju, Bunuel, Resnais, Kubrick and Jerry Lewis. More recently, we have looked at Cinema Nuovo, Bellochio, Bertolucci, Skolimovski.

* Translated from *Le Monde*, 13 January 1972, with permission.

3. A particular way of talking about the cinema. *Positif* is not tied to any Party or to any given political tendency. It is a meeting point of various left-wing critiques: Communist, Maoist, Trotskyist, Surrealist.

We always try to tackle a film by placing it in its context. Frank Capra, to whom we have for instance devoted our last issue, is a prime example of a certain kind of American cinema in the thirties and is linked to a specific sort of populist ideology.

With regard to political films, *Positif* would defend *Hands over the City, Salvatore Giuliano, Os Fuzis, The Hour of the Furnaces,* but not *Z* or *The Confession* which we think are cinematically poor and politically vague; nor would we defend certain works which would pretend to be preparing the revolution by doing no more than destroying the language.

Cahiers du Cinéma: 'historical document'

1. The review's work, which consists in ideological struggle and the elaboration of a theory in the field of cinema, is based on historical and dialectical materialism, on Marxism-Leninism.

2. This implies the recognition of '*the primacy of politics*' (Lenin) in all forms of class struggle, as well as the recognition of the economy as the ultimately determinant factor of a mode of production. Economistic revisionism 'forgets' the primacy of politics.

Against revisionism...

3. The struggle against the bourgeoisie cannot be divorced from the struggle against revisionism, viz—on the ideological level—against petit bourgeois ideology as it is assumed by revisionism and made to serve, in the last analysis, the interests of the bourgeoisie.

its continuation in modernism...

4. This two-sided struggle—against the declining bourgeoisie and against revisionism which perpetuates it—spreads out, according to specific modalities, to all ideological practices and therefore to the ideological apparatus of the cinematic State. On this specific level of class-struggle in France, as on all other levels, there are decisive lessons to be learned from the Great Chinese Proletarian Cultural Revolution.

5. Mostly on the basis of the positions outlined above, but also using relevant concepts of psychoanalysis and semiology, we therefore set out to: a) struggle in support of avant-garde films whose *work* is based on Marxism-Leninism; b) analyse, with a view to transforming them, those practices which do not claim to be Marxist-Leninist but are important in the struggle for a materialist conception of the cinema because of their anti-naturalist and anti-formalist expressions; c) lay bare the ideological mechanisms and the significant constitutive processes of the high points of cinematic idealism which today still animate practically all films that are *seen;* d) denounce not only overtly bour-

geois and reactionary films, but also modernist films which really take over from them: political exploitation films, dabbling in formal games of all kinds. . .

. . . *and dogmatism.*

6. Since Marxism-Leninism is not a dogma but a guide for action, its principles could not be dialectically applied in any given field without grappling with the specific contradictions of this field. To declare that avant-garde films must present an active and revolutionary image of the contradictions of a social formation without analysing the concrete application of the words 'active' and 'revolutionary' is to go inevitably from a voluntarist/leftist position to a liquidationist/rightist position on the specific practice one is engaged in. Nor has Marxism-Leninism anything to gain from dogmatism.

Cinéthique: 'to divide the spectators'
Unlike the bulk of other cinema reviews, *Cinéthique's* autonomy *vis-à-vis* the ideological and economic apparatus of the bourgeoisie (publishers, art-patrons—another name for capitalism—or film society federations) guarantees the specificity of its work; and this, not out of some predilection for marginality or for the sake of some 'underground' myth. *Cinéthique's* autonomy also constitutes a *commitment to a position:* first, a refusal to facilitate the reproduction of the conditions which make the cinema of the dominant class possible, be it monopolistic, experimental or parallel (one always parallels a right line),[1] and second, a rejection of the discourses which accompany, replicate and reinforce this cinema.

Cinéthique's words may not therefore be taken as 'a new-wave critique' or as some 'original' variation on the old theme of the cinema-review, with discussion of films, interviews with film-makers etc. . . As against these incessant repetitions, the babblings of the dominant ideology, there is a need for a political and theoretical analysis of products (films) which exist only in and through a class apparatus. Thus the study of discourses concerned with *censorship* requires that one considers their functioning within class ideologies whose institutional expressions are called National Cinema Centre, Federation of Film Societies, Technicians' Unions, Film Schools, etc.

A historical and dialectical materialism
When elaborating these analyses, the written texts relate dialectically to a practice of 'dissemination' which, through the kind of film considered and the political work aimed at, can have no area of agreement with any traditional writing of criticism, for this traditional writing does no more than provide additional fuel to the development of experimental and parallel cinema. Thus *Cinéthique* does have an aim: to divide the spectators.

This struggle against dominant practices and discourses implies a commitment to a radically different position, one which directs the whole of our work. The point of departure of this position is the science of social formations and of their history (historical materialism) as well as the philosophy of this science (dialectical materialism). There is no question of improving or duplicating the apparatuses of the bourgeoisie, but, on the contrary, of hastening their downfall by setting up in their place proletarian apparatuses. This work requires a sharp break from obfuscating discourses parading as formal avant-garde or as Freudian Marxism.

Thus our interventions in a specific practice (the cinema) and gradually in other artistic practices call for more and more political analyses and investigations in the field of historical and dialectical materialism. Whilst avoiding eclecticism, work of this kind is[2] and will continue to be published in *Cinéthique*.

Notes

1. Tr. note: This is a pun which cannot be reproduced in English. In French, the word *droite* means both 'straight line' and 'right'.
2. Cf., our latest issue (nos 11-12): 'Politiques de la censure' (Politics of Censorship), 'Pratiques de diffusion' (Dissemination Practices), 'Les pratiques artistique dans le marxisme-leninisme' (Artistic Practices in Marxism-Leninism), 'Du reflêt au procès' (From Reflection to Process).

translated by Elias Noujaim

Polemic on *Coup pour coup**

Gérard Leblanc—Cinéthique

An advance on box office takings, acceptance by *Art et Essai*† exhibitors who, as the number of cinemas under their management grows, are increasingly turning into producer-distributors,[1] a censor's certificate obtained without problems. All this seems to confirm Jacques Duhamel's speech to the National Assembly, reproduced by various organs of the press, in which he said: ' There is no political censorship in France '.[2]

Coup pour coup is part of the ideological class struggle towards the overthrow of the bourgeoisie by the proletariat and its allies. The film aims to produce a particular *reflection* of a *reality* evolving in the factories at the present moment: the spontaneous struggle of men and women workers against the bosses, and their discovery of the necessity, if they are to assert their economic demands (struggle against the reduction of real earnings, struggle against the demand for increased rates of production, struggles against worsening working conditions, etc.), to fight against the revisionist unions (which subordinate working-class economic demands to a cringing application of the 'social compact' policy the bourgeois state is striving to impose on the two so-called social partners, bosses—working-class).

What could or should be demanded from the revolutionary viewpoint[3] of a film which takes as the object of reflection certain aspects of the most advanced struggles, led by the working-class and what is more, by one of its most exploited segments (women workers, who undergo a second level of exploitation within the family unit, a unit which bourgeois ideology seeks to reproduce within the working-class since it contributes to the reinforcement of capitalist relations of production; if a working-class couple obey the call of bourgeois ideology, the woman has the function of contributing through servile work—upkeep of home, husband and children, the latter moreover educated by the dominant bourgeois ideological apparatus, the school—to the reproduction of the worker's labour power, without costing the bourgeoisie a penny)?

Not a simple documentary report on these struggles (though this would be an advance on the films distributed in the *Art et Essai* circuit at the moment), and not simply the reduplication of those struggles, but an active *reflection,* a reflection which makes room for a rise in working-class consciousness and progress towards victory against the class enemy (the establishment of the dictatorship of the proletariat in France).

This concept of the role of the revolutionary film-maker in France would mean combatting the kind of declaration Karmitz makes in *Ecran 72* (which

* Translated from *Ecran 72,* no 4, April 1972, pp 41-4, with permission.

† A government-subsidised art-house circuit.

conveys something of Karmitz's erroneous conceptions of class struggles and the place of cinema within those struggles); 'We have confidence in those who struggle; this is not a film which offers them a strategy or form of organisation.' While we agree with Karmitz in thinking that the question of *revolutionary content* (what we at *Cinéthique* call the ideological struggle within the non-specific cinematic codes) is a determining factor in the making of a revolutionary film, resolving the question is certainly not a matter of investigating the power of the film-in-itself, in an abstract way (leaving out the analysis of class contradictions at the present moment and the reflection of these contradictions within the specific contradictions of a film made at the same moment). Resolving this question means:

    1.   determining the political line which must regulate the making of a film seen as an active and specific reflection of the concrete situation analysed by Marxist Leninist theory within its creative development;
    2.   determining the specific transformations implied by putting this political line to work in film practice. Resolving the question of revolutionary content means first resolving the problems which every *militant* (whether film-maker or not) faces in practice.

Does this mean that Karmitz's error is a result of the 'modesty' of his pretentions with regard to cinema? Not at all. The specific error is dictated by a false political line, being developed at the moment by *La Cause du Peuple*. It is principally characterised by its spontaneism and opportunism. To demonstrate briefly: the line elaborated by *La Cause du Peuple* at the present moment hooks the work of communist propaganda onto the spontaneous mass movement. Now, that spontaneous mass movement is not revolutionary in itself, although it is the effect of the development of class antagonisms. If it is not directed (and consequently *transformed*) by Marxist-Leninist theory, it will never 'spontaneously' culminate in the overthrow of the bourgeois dictatorship by the dictatorship of the proletariat. The role of revolutionary intellectuals in the present period, whatever their specific practice, does not consist *solely* in allying themselves to the spontaneous mass movement. It *also* consists in raising their theoretical activity to the level of that movement. *The development of the spontaneous mass movement calls for, demands and is dialectically linked to the development of revolutionary theory*. And out of the efforts made by the workers and intellectuals of the avant-garde in this direction will come the revolutionary *organisation* (party), rendered objectively necessary by the development of the internal contradictions of French society.

The *economic* class struggle against factory bosses (even though it takes on forms as violent as holding prisoners) is not yet the *political* class struggle (even though it is inseparable from it) against the bourgeois state apparatus. It is useless to make an attack on the CGT, only to fall back into an economism of a new type. In the course of the film, the women workers learn that they can fight the bosses, earn the respect of the managerial staff (administrative, supervisory), assert through violence the satisfaction of their economic demands (the state apparatus features in the form of a Deputy who advises the imprisoned boss to negotiate, since the strike by women workers is provoking movements of solidarity in other factories). Some shots of demonstrations are thus inserted into the sequence of images. But nothing is said on the *conditions* that need to operate in order to transform this strike (which focuses the lessons drawn from numerous strikes by women workers in the recent period) and this spontaneous movement into a revolutionary movement (i.e., a movement which subordinates tactics—struggles to be led within a definite, limited time period at all levels of the social structure—to a *strategy* of take-over of power by the proletariat and its allies). The reflection presented by the film is resolutely passive and tag-along. The spontaneist political line rises 'obviously' (i.e., dialectically) in the film practice which sets it in motion. In this fiction film without actors, what dominates is the ideology of the 'experienced', the well-observed, the detail stamped accurate. In other words the ideology of the mirror, which allows women workers to contemplate themselves in a factory as *real* as the one in which they have struggled at some time. The dialectical materialist process of knowledge (the philosophy of the proletariat in struggle) is in radical opposition to this ideology. It does not remain at the stage of perceptions and representations. It links the concrete struggles against capital to knowledge of its internal mechanisms and this knowledge acts in return on the concrete struggles, charging them with a revolutionary content. It is not confined to lining up a few stereotype representations of the repressive state apparatus, it breaks down the processes which determine its intervention and the processes which allow it to be combatted and overcome. It proposes political resolutions to the economic contradictions within which the working-class is held.

Only films of this kind (which put into operation within their specific contradictions a dialectical materialist progression in knowledge) can claim to contribute to revolutionary practice in a historical period characterised by the absence of a Marxist-Lenninist party (and consequently by the impossibility of making mass films).[4] The formal filmic transformations made necessary by *our* concrete situation are considerable. But the formal transformations are not 'formalist'. They are in step with new, revolutionary, content to be set in motion. And it is clearly in order not to set such a content in motion that Karmitz adopts bourgeois film practice uncritically.

Guy Hennebelle—Ecran 72
I consider Marin Karmitz to be one of the most important French film-makers of the day. He is one of the few to have drawn coherent conclusions from the failed rising of May 1968. While the majority of the reedy tenors of our cinema hurriedly closed their memories to bad recollections, or at best, acquitted themselves of responsibility by scattering delicate 'allusions' through their films, as they did during the Algerian war, Marin Karmitz undertook to place the seventh art at the service of popular struggles in a real way.

In so doing he marked a break with a whole current of utopianism and 'culturalism', which saw in May 1968 simply a will to change life without really overthrowing the structure of French capitalist society. The observation of their failure moreover often leads the followers of this line, mystical prophets of the hippy tribes, to the escapist excesses of the beats, denouncing the famous consumer society on the basis of an erroneous concept, and extolling, as does Diourka Medvecsky in *Paul* and Jean Rouch in *Petit à petit*, a return to origins and the golden age, through a withdrawal to bucolic life or a voyage to some faraway elsewhere.

By allying himself with the real life of French people, Marin Karmitz also accomplishes a leap forward as far as French cinema is concerned, in the sense that he goes beyond the stage of humanist denunciations and the vaguely progressive. Such it seems to me is the basic requirement of a revolutionary cinema today, in this country in particular and in Western Europe in general. It is no longer enough to appeal to the emotions of a well-intentioned audience against the misdeeds of an unjust society. We have to go further, to show the way towards the overthrow of capitalism by describing in concrete terms the popular struggles going on from day to day on all fronts, and by placing them within the framework of a strategy and method.

For Marin Karmitz that method is obviously Marxist-Leninist. In this respect it is useful to recall something of his personal evolution. To me it seems significant and even in many cases exemplary. Marin Karmitz comes from a bourgeois milieu and began by shooting shorts which today he rejects. *Nuit noire, Calcutta,* made in collaboration with Marguerite Duras, makes an interesting comparison with the last of these films, *Jaune le soleil;* the path Marin Karmitz traced in order to escape the anguished but self-congratulatory problematic of an intelligentsia continually resifting its own fantasies is clearly observable. In his first long film, *Sept jours ailleurs,* after dwelling at length on the existential anguish of a bourgeois artist, the film-maker can only offer an infantile revolt, expressed in gunshots, against the supposed cause of that alienation—the object (telephone, television, various machines). The same erroneous perspective is shared by René Allio in *Peter and Paul.*

Then came *Camarades.* This film which set out to describe the proletarianisation and awakening of consciousness of the young offspring of a petit-bourgeois tradesman, marked a notable stage in the evolution of both Karmitz and the French cinema in the search for new paths. Of course on both the political and the formal level the film was still marked by the ideology of the traditional left film, especially its first part (as I said in *Cinéma 71,* no 3). But it constituted an important advance, particularly in the second part.

In the interview published in no 3 of this journal, the film collective of *Coup pour coup* stressed the aesthetic faults and political deficiencies of *Camarades.* The point needs making that *Coup pour coup* owes much to the criticism and self-criticism provoked by the preceding film. Unlike many film-makers, Marin Karmitz did not retreat into the offended dignity of the *auteur,* but accepted the challenging of his *work.*

Filmed in conditions unprecedented for French cinema, this third long film has primarily the advantage of setting its action in the heart of the working-class. Not a very common phenomenon. Second, it makes the heroines women, a sex which the Paris cinema has often relegated to the level of titillating and useless toy. Third, the film tells the story of a strike, a hard strike without any fancy trimmings. Fourth, it constitutes a call to revolt against exploitation by the bosses. Fifth, it takes violent issues with the failure and betrayal of the union leadership.

The canvas is rich! It is possible in a sense to 'understand' the reaction of the employers' federation for the Paris region (see *Le Monde*, February 24), which denounced in alarm 'this film of incitement to misdemeanours, to taking the law into your own hands, occupying factories, and locking up the owners, a crime punishable by Article 341 of the penal code' and qualifies *Coup pour coup* as a 'particularly aggravating piece of provocation'.

To digress slightly: The 'revolutionary films' so praised by two *aesthetically* ultra-left journals, with titles like *Othon, Lutte en Italie, Vent d'est, Mediterranée, Le joueur de quilles,* and other products of the laboratory, have never aroused so much ire among those gentlemen and that is not surprising. The 'cinema revolution', which to this day has only produced worthless and boring films and which does not even have the merit of proposing new forms, does not distress the French employers' federation.[1] It is a different thing where the true revolutionary cinema is concerned. It is time to put an end to the *telquellian* illusion according to which intellectuals have the special task of promoting a 'proletarian line' on the 'language front' against the 'bourgeois line', while the workers have as their objective the take-over of power in the factories. Behind the screen of this logomachy without risk lurks the badly repaired corpse of a new art for art's sake. This does not mean that a revolution in the forms of expression is not necessary, but it can only arise in a progressive way through patient work effected in collaboration with the people for whom one claims to be fighting. This is the case for *Coup pour coup*. This is the only way of resolving the eternal and difficult problem of the relation between the artistic and the political avant gardes.

The form of *Coup pour coup* is much more consistent and much more elaborated than that of *Camarades*. I think that, this time, the double snag of populism and workerism has been avoided overall, as has the pitfall of socialist realism in the Soviet version of the late thirties. The film-makers, taking their inspiration in a believable way from the Yenan Proposition, declared that they wanted to combine realism on the level of description with a certain romanticism in perspectives. The result, although it may not initiate a new art as yet, seems to me remarkable in its power and accuracy. The dissolution of the individual hero into the collectivity will be noted.

The film will no doubt be reproached for resorting to *spectacularisation*. I should say first that the term here has nothing to do with what is practised in the films of the 'Z series' (as defined in no 3 of this journal). Second, whatever may be said of it, the cinema will always be a spectacle. 'Deconstruction' (as distinct from Brechtian 'distanciation') rarely opens up anything more than boredom. Moreover, I would defy anyone to mobilise a significant mass of people or even arouse their interest on the basis of a film as admirable and intelligent (in spite of a certain confusion) as *Oser lutter, oser vaincre* (a documentary account of a strike at Flins by the Maoist 'Ligne rouge'). It is much too austere.

What remains to be considered is the delicate point in *Coup pour coup*— its virulent anti-trade unionism. While I am absolutely convinced that the image of the officials (whether CGT or CFTD, it is not made clear) given by the film is true to reality, I nevertheless believe that there is a confusion there between the *trade union leadership* and *trade unions as a whole* and that the film tips into spontaneism. Why 'squash' the character of the shop steward (not to be confused with the general secretary, in a tailored suit), who is on strike and seems discreetly to direct it? Of course, faced with the omnipresence of revisionism which preaches collaboration of the classes, it is not easy to construct a true revolutionary strategy, but the evidence condemns spontaneism out of hand.

But to be justified in regretting this error, it is necessary first to denounce the opportunist policy which gave it birth. Lenin in fact said that leftism was simply punishment for the sins of opportunism. He wrote: 'In a few advanced countries modern imperialism has created a situation of exceptional privilege which has fostered the growth of leaders of the treacherous opportunist, social-chauvinist type, the labour aristocracy, defending the interests of their own social stratum. The victory of the revolutionary proletariat is impossible unless we fight this evil, denounce it and make it wither away, unless we throw out the opportunist, social-traitor leaders.'

This is why it seems to me the mistake of *Coup pour coup* remains minor in the light of its qualities. Looking at this very remarkable 'incitement to revolt' and to the 'uplifting of life' as Maurice Clavel would say, brings to mind Dominique Grange's poignant song, *Les nouveaux partisans,* which extols 'the sharp-shooters of the class war' and abuses 'the galley-slaves of the working-class and the official flunkeys who stick to pontoon.'

A man died at the age of 23 because he wanted to unmask them. He was called Pierre Overney.

Notes
Gerard Leblanc
1. The brothers Rochman will be familiar names. New owners of the '3 Elysées', they are, with a German television network, co-producers of *Coup pour coup.*
2. The same period saw the creation of a 'committee for measures against political censorship', which aims to set Duhamel's statement into contradiction with his practice. The committee intended to present the film censorship board with some forty 'militant' films (shot before and after May 68) *en bloc,* the majority of which had not been given a certificate on completion.
   Such a step does not seem to me to be of a kind to bother the minister for culture or the censorship board. It would undoubtedly have been useful, before taking such a step, to carry out a concrete analysis of the phenomenon of film censorship in France (what I say here is based on work in progress begun in *Cinéthique*

nos 11-12 and continued in *Cinéthique* no 13). At the level of empirical observation, we note that *Coup pour coup* obtained its censor's certificate without difficulty. And this is a film no less politically 'advanced' than the majority of films the committee plans to present to the board. Moreover, its careful presentation makes it perfectly acceptable in the *Art et Essai* circuit.

All well and good. But getting a certificate would allow some forty films to be exhibited in the non-commercial circuit without risk of being seized. The question then posed is that of the political work possible using these films as a starting point. To my knowledge this *basic* question has not been raised.

3. A revolutionary viewpoint is a viewpoint which strives to resolve contradictions from the viewpoint of the secondary, and at the moment dominated, aspect of the principal contradiction, in which the bourgeoisie at the moment constitutes the principal aspect. The secondary aspect in question is the proletariat.

4. In *Ecran 72* no 3, Guy Hennebelle identifies with the Chinese and Albanian audiences and accuses us of 'ultra-leftism' for defending films—i.e., the films of the Dziga Vertov Group—which those audiences would 'reject'. We advise Hennebelle to begin with a political analysis of the contradictions of French society before throwing out such statements. At the same time we might submit a new problem for his wise consideration: *Cinéthique* also distribute Chinese films (including *The Red Detachment of Women*). We hope he'll be there. For those who are interested in *Cinéthique's* positions on the Dziga Vertov films we refer to the magazine *VH 101* no 6.

5. Although the general line of this text seems correct to us, the complexity of the problems broached, which are fundamental in nature, would require much longer treatment. The space accorded to us in this journal makes it impossible. Obviously we are ready to produce the discussion if such a debate were to interest the readers and editors of *Ecran 72*.

Guy Hennebelle

1. Not the Communist Party of France, as Jean Delmas emphasised in *Jeune Cinéma* 52.

translated by Diana Matias.

Interview with Paul Séban *(La CGT en mai '68)**

The interview with Paul Séban (author of the film *La CGT en mai-juin '68*) brings us back to the question we have tried to pose since the first issues of *Cinéthique:* the definition of a class cinema. This topic will be extended in no. 6, notably out of the workshop in cinema/politics, which the journal organised in the early days of September...

Cinéthique: A film is not like other products; it's an ideological product. In your film, *La CGT en mai '68, La vache et le prisonnier* [Fernandel] is shown to the workers on strike. This conjuncture throws remarkable light on the principle contradiction of the complex process of relations between cinema and politics.

Séban: I kept this passage because it's part of the reality. The guys at Ugines sent it to me on cassette. I was very struck. I would have preferred them to see *Strike* or *Salt of the Earth*. But I kept it because it expresses the power of the dominant class well. Workers on strike against the propertied bourgeoisie only show the films of the bourgeoisie, and never think for a moment of sharpening their weapon, which is the strike, with an ideological struggle through film. To omit this passage is to falsify reality: it's to make believe that the working-class possesses the same ideological formation, the same resistance, at all levels.

Cin: How did you obtain this document?

Séban: You know how we went about things. We asked all the strike committees for what they had shot, what they had recorded. So I received this cassette among others. It seemed to me to be symptomatic. A strike is a moment of struggle; it's also people to occupy behind the walls, the closed gates. It's difficult to hold out all the time; things must be found to occupy them. This points to our responsibility because we don't have the films which are necessary for such periods.

Cin: It's one of the deficiencies of all the political and trade union organisations of the working-class never to have given attention to the cinema as a political arm.

Séban: Hold on, I want to make a comment. It makes a difference whether I am speaking as a militant or as an individual. There are considerations which

---

* Translated from *Cinéthique* no 5, Sept-Oct 1969, pp 9-13, with permission.

hardly concern Paul Séban, but which are of consequence for the political militant.

Cin: These differences should be analysed...

Séban: Of course... If you say, up to now the CGT and the PC[F] have barely been aware of the importance of the audio-visual as a means of propaganda, I agree...

Cin: (Yes, your film is the first they've made since '36.)

Séban: Yes, but they're changing: buying video-recorders, attempting to produce films on such and such an aspect of the struggle at a particular moment. Films of 10 or 20 minutes, immediately available for distribution in multiple copies, as with this film. Regional branches buy a copy and distribute it themselves in their area. For each film there'll be 90 copies, exhibited throughout France. This week, for example, *La CGT en mai '68* was shown 6 times in Hauts-de-Seine.

Cin: Does the CGT reckon only to show militant films on this circuit? They don't envisage also distributing films which deconstruct films carrying the dominant ideology?

Séban: This is their first concrete experiment. They envisage a series of other experiments; if these work they'll be able to go further. But the CGT can't take the place of us film-makers. They can produce certain films, but can't become like other production organisations. That would demand too big an organisation.

Cin: However, it is they who have taken the question furthest. You only have to listen to the film-makers' group at Git le Coeur.

Séban: Yes, them insofar as they're communist film-makers, but not the CGT as such. Yes, the CGT can encourage films which would show up the dominant ideology, but can't be the financial promoter of them. Well, I can't see them in that situation, but perhaps it's in their plans.

Cin: The CGT is one of the few organisations powerful enough actually to set up such an infrastructure.

Séban: What was done for the distribution of *La CGT en mai '68* will be of great use. Through it they've been able to get an idea of the importance of the thing. They'll produce 20-30 minutes a year.

Cin: Doesn't the CGT envisage equipping itself with video-recorders which would allow the gathering of even more interesting information than you received on mini-cassettes?

Séban: Personally I hope so, because the mini-cassette is valuable but a bit poor. The union committee of each large work-place ought to be able to buy a video-recorder. What a wonderful reserve of images! But it's not the CGT as an organisation that can do it, rather the local committee...
These questions make me uneasy. I can't speak for the CGT. I can speak for the Syndicat Français de Realisateurs de Télé, because I'm a member of its Executive. But as soon as you ask me, a rank-and-file member of the CGT, questions about their reactions as a whole to the 'audio-visual', I can only give you personal impressions of what concerns Paul Séban.

Cin: What definition would you give of a class cinema for today?

Séban: Its content or its distribution?

Cin: The two are linked.

Séban: Of course. I don't see, given that the cinema demands considerable means, that one can do anything other than engage in smuggling films which remain clandestine, which don't have 'presence' and whose glory is in not being distributed. On the other hand, if one can project these films, then I am in agreement with putting all my communist ideology, all my competence, into it.

Cin: The CGT has an official existence. They could distribute films which no other group could.

Séban: That's also why they can make films about daily struggle. *Not only to reproduce* these struggles, but also to illuminate them. Today three-quarters of the interesting films have a strength of impact solely because they *reproduce* reality well. One admires the cineaste's having had courage to film the reality. He's saying: this is a 'statement'. Personally I understand the notion of a 'statement' very well, in so far as one is not master of the film distribution. Presenting what is.

Cin: (That's what you did with the television series *Les femmes aussi*?)

Séban: It's the highest level of what I can do within the system. But it's not the cinema I'd like to do. What I'd like to do is take such and such element of reality, film it as it is and illuminate it in the light of class struggle while dismantling the ideological mechanism. Television always stops at the moment where it begins to get interesting. I'm for a didactic cinema, close to the ground, clear, explanatory, which indicates the responsibilities, the causes... It's terrible to think that finally misery, struggle, are always presented on television as a spectacle. They show rats, and the children who will eat them, the sordid picturesque, but say nothing about the imperialism which is the cause of it. Everything becomes accidental.

Cin: The film of the CGT also confines itself to the 'official statement'. The analysis could have been pushed much further. If we come back, for example, to the case of *La vache et le prisonnier* (since we're touching on the principle contradiction mentioned earlier), you could have, starting from that material, carried out a critique of an ideological behaviour, perhaps through a discussion.

Séban: I agree, but the film was two and a half hours. You can't go beyond that. It was made to be projected at factory gates. You get the guys together, you say to them: come on, there's a film telling this story—*La CGT en mai '68*... It was reduced to 1 hr. 35 mins. That already poses problems for the comrades organising the screenings. The guys have to go home... For example, everything concerning Flins was much more complete, it was 25 minutes of film.

Cin: (Flins is a little short in fact.)

Séban: Yes, I regret that, but it was necessary to choose. There have been books on May; they don't exhaust the events, however. So you can't ask me to be comprehensive in one film. For me to make this film, that meant fixing a date, establishing what developed at that time and, secondly, taking some big themes and dealing with them.

Cin: There's something else: all bourgeois films play on the impression of reality one experiences in front of a screen. Don't you think that watching your film it is equally possible to have this 'impression of reality', be caught by the bourgeois idealism of the spectacle, not because of your political analysis, but because of a negligence with regard to the natural ideological tendency of the cinema.

Séban: I only half understand what you mean. But it seems to me you're right. The workers' reaction was: 'It's our strike, we can see ourselves.' There's a deep identification. For my part, I find that important. But this identification rules out analysis, it's dangerous. We'll analyse presently why the film is made in this way and not another.

Cin: Let's make it clear that the Etats Généraux films—which you call *'gauchistes'*—have this in common with yours: they play on the impression of reality, they invoke identification.

Séban: I'm beginning to understand your question. What was the sense of the film when I was thinking about making it? When the CGT spoke to me about it, it happened to overlap with my preoccupations as a militant (not as a director because, as you remarked, it's a film which, from the production point of view, has come from everywhere). I said to myself: the most important thing for me, as a militant, is to see at which point during the events of May '68 a particular form of labour structure and organisation played its part: in setting off the strike, the factory occupations, and what followed; how people who had never been militant caught up with the most advanced segment of the working-class. Beginning there, I didn't pose myself other questions. When the images came, when I received all these films, I noticed that they all presented the same composite structure; you know, those composite images one spoke of in philosophy class: to know the features of a family, you superimpose a photo of the grandfather, the great-grandfather, the father, etc... and little by little the main features, the lines of force stand out. The same phenomenon could come into play for these films. First one saw some backs in front of a gate; they unroll a banner: total strike; they withdraw towards the camera a friend is holding and make a small sign. Then, second sequence: the guys organising the strike inside; they get their own food, they prepare beds. Third shot: big procession in the town to assert their strength to the population which is not yet engaged in the struggle. Fourth shot: the group responsible for order. One sees the guys who control their friends—who goes home, who goes out. Fifth shot: a meeting, a comrade speaking. Sixth shot: the return to work. This was the schema which kept cropping up systematically.

Cin: That should have been analysed.

Séban: I wanted to retrace the idea, starting from the album of photos the comrades are turning over because it became a page of their struggles.

Cin: Hence your film is the development of the structure of a photo album.

Séban: Yes because that's how I experienced the films which the guys had sent me from everywhere. From that I felt that this manner of seeing comrades during the shooting of their films had influenced me. What they were expecting wasn't inconsequential speeches but their strike, the way they'd actually experienced it and in which, practically, they had been masters of a given moment. Masters of the factory, masters of the town. Consequently the film took this form.

Cin: That's linked to *La vache et le prisonnier*. Maybe the style of filming workers was invested with bourgeois ideology...

Séban: That's certain. Hence I proposed to the leadership of the CGT, and to all the committees where I present the film, to come with friends when they want, take their film and do an ideological critique of all their films: not the form, I don't care about that. As for *La CGT* the critique comes immediately after the screening. The way it was filmed is a very precise ideological content. Simple things like giving the impression of a deserted factory pose a problem when you aren't used to it. Most people naturally, spontaneously, film the place deserted; now, nothing shows up the emphasis of something so much as a person just passing through, or something as it stops moving. Well, they don't know that. So each time they want to show the desertedness of places of work they use a static shot of something which doesn't move, which has no soul. However, there are some who did in fact show two guys dropping in and so, suddenly, the empty aspect appears.

Cin: There's a film to be made, from these little films you received, which would analyse their ideological content, their relationship with the cinema of the dominant class. Do you reckon to make such a film, which would be very important for a raising of consciousness?

Séban: I've proposed speaking about it with those who made them. Making a film about that requires many things. A whole infrastructure, my own freedom, the freedom of the guys... If now is not the time, it will always be possible because all the elements on 8 which I retained have been blown up to 16 and are part of the CGT *cinémathèque*. Likewise the sound elements have been re-done and conserved.

Cin: You're saying then that you reproduced the structure of the workers' films, to 'inform' your film. Wouldn't it have been possible, at the time you made this film, to introduce a critique of the photo album, souvenir portrait dimension?

Seban: I tried to do this at one point in the shape of a question I put to a guy at Nantes: 'And the claims and the struggle, what becomes of them in this grand fete?' But I didn't push in this direction because having seen the film-documents, it didn't seem to me to fit what the film was going to become. At this stage, rather than introduce the critique in the film, I prefer it to come from the hall. Given the way cinema is received at the moment, introducing this type of critique in the film, would be a damp squib.

Cin: So perhaps one can suggest that you've made a film reproducing the bourgeois vision the worker actually has of the cinema?

Seban: I don't share this idea. In any case, if that's what I've done, it's not what I wanted to do.

Cin: To the extent that their style of filming, which is not questioned in the film, is invested with the dominant ideology, you have necessarily reproduced it.

Seban: When you say that their style of filming is invested with the dominant ideology because they've only seen bourgeois films, it's true, but it's a formal way of approaching the matter. The second way, the content, is not bourgeois. The content is the sharp aspect the class struggle took on in May '68: factory occupations, general paralysis of the economy, demonstration of the strength of the working-class mustered together... If one only looks at the film's formal aspect...

Cin: One can't separate the two.

Seban: Yes, but I had the impression that you risked separating them; that you took only the formal aspect while forgetting the content which is, after all the strikes of May–June. The content of this film is not the style of filming which a certain number of comrade workers had with their 8mm cameras. They filmed, first of all, a content which is a strike in which they were the most dynamic actors.

Cin: It seems to me that there's a dissociation. Of course, it's necessary to re-place May in an historic continuity, but it's necessary to *re-place it in cinema,* that's to say, in a specific place which has its laws, etc... and reproducing the real on a screen is, all the same, an idealist way of making films. One can't separate the two.

Séban: I agree with you. It's in this sense that I struggle in television. I'm for fiction as the basis of reality, but worked upon by the director. I can't tolerate filming what is.

Cin: In short a didactic fiction. But why then doesn't the film on the CGT make an analysis of the political implications of, for example, what amounts to the internment of the boss. Why just give a narrative account of it: they did this, they said that, etc... In order to make class awareness, progress, this bitter form of the struggle should have been analysed.

Séban: That comes from the project of the film: to deal with 30 days of strike in 1hr. 30 mins. I couldn't go off the track, but I needed to.

Cin: There were two directions to take. The first you took: the account of a certain number of events, of the continuity of the struggle; a second: an analysis of this event.

Séban: In short, I couldn't make anything other than an 'enlightened account' of what had happened. But it's certain that beginning from the elements retained by the film, there is a theoretical reflection to be made (the imprisonment of Duvochel, the occupation of factories). When I present the film, I spend two hours discussing that, theorising on these events. Otherwise, it presupposes another film. One question I have not dealt with voluntarily: was the situation revolutionary or not? I wanted to deal with it solely by interview.

Cin: You give some reactions to this topic after de Gaulle's speech.

Séban: Yes, but I wanted to do otherwise: to take Krazucki and two or three workers. They would have analysed the situation. I did it with Krazucki and two guys; but this alone required 40 mins. If not you end up with gratuitous and rapid assertions. Consequently it would have been necessary to put another film inside the film. Finally you must take into account that it's the first film I've made on May and that it's made in a narrative form, but there are other films to make in the shape of political analysis. They must be made. The CGT must produce them. If they have the means to do it, I'm sure they'll produce them. But as with a story: first it's told, then comes reflection. But it's necessary to make this reflection theoretically.

Cin: Yes, because the simple reproduction of events doesn't produce progress in class awareness as an analysis could have. It's difficult for this film to progress, to lead beyond the contradictions of May since it's a simple establishment of a moment of struggle. So that now what needs to be done (if it hasn't been already) is analysis of May with a view to going further and not along routes where one's been astray.

Séban: Is it the cinema's role? Would one manage to seriously discuss the situation of May other than by the intervention of political analysis? One comes back to fiction. Situations created by an author can push and explode the contradictions: 'Was the situation revolutionary or not?' But that's a film still to be made, a real film.

What is the impact of the film, actually? At the end of screenings, workers come and say to me: 'We're recharged, mate; we're ready to go back for another go.' I receive a letter from Sochaux: 'The film moved us. But above all, it recharged us.' That's not negligeable. Another wrote me: 'Seeing on the screen how many we were, I realised our strength.' It's important for the essential problem of the trade union movement: conducting the collective struggles without neglecting the partial ones. The film helps towards progress on this point. To come back to theoretical analysis: how to conduct it in a film? I've done enough journalistic stuff to know how to conduct it by interview. But an interview, as such it's nothing. At that point I prefer to film Krazucki or a union group in discussion than to have to deal with the analysis of these events, especially as it's complex. It brings into play so many elements which are complicated to analyse by means of cinema. Or else one reads.

Cin: There is a theoretical reflection to be made precisely on the forms which will be necessary to conduct these analyses, montage, etc. . .

Séban: It's a reflection which needs to be conducted, but isn't for very precise reasons. Because, finally, one is afraid of foundering in the driest didacticism, the driest illustration. In fact our bourgeois intellectual reflexes are thoroughly in play here. This has been reported to me. Workers see the film and say: 'That's our strike'. Engineers and office staff see it and say: 'It's well made. The images are beautiful.'

Cin: It's a hundred times worse.

Séban: One last thing on these impressions which have been reported to me and which conceal a deep desire to change things, it's to what point the Nantes sequence—the holding of the director—gives pleasure; that's to say, the moment when the struggle takes on its sharpest aspect.

Cin: The film will undoubtedly have contributed to re-boosting the workers who see it, but it won't have made them progress at all on the cinematic level; that's to say, they will still be vulnerable; they will still go to see bourgeois films. Now, a film must also (and perhaps even first of all) make them progress on its own terrain: the terrain of ideological struggle. We must think about that. . . . If not, what will happen in France, even if we have a socialist regime—is what happened in the USSR, for example, after Eisenstein.

Sèban: I know, it's an incessant struggle, but difficult to conduct because we conduct it with reduced and practically non-existent weapons. Our whole struggle is still developed with words. Let's suppose that the film *La CGT en mai '68* had had the character of ideological struggle we're talking about, that it was a political-analysis-in-cinema, perhaps it might not have had the impact it has with the working-class and we would have missed our mark. People would say: 'We don't like that, it's too wordy.' We're stymied by the fact that the whole working-class watches television.

Cin: The PC[F], for example, is equipped from the press point of view, but is totally bereft from the point of view of images and sounds, and above all from the point of view of audio-visual theoretical reflection. But perhaps the problem poses itself in another way: there is an urgency to reach people; so to produce a film which breaks down the ideology of spectacle, which the workers (and electors) accept, is to take too big a risk.

Sèban: I wouldn't go so far, but the problem is to be understood by the masses to whom one's addressing oneself. One can't go further than their actual level of comprehension. 'To be one step ahead of the working-class, but not two', said Lenin. To make a film mildly ahead, but not too much. If not, what would be the purpose of a revolutionary avant-garde cut off from the masses?

Cin: To take these questions further, perhaps it's necessary to pose them at the top of the CGT and try to transform their attitude?

Sèban: The contact we've had on this subject has been positive. Those we've talked to are now convinced that in order to conduct the class struggle on the ideological level against television and the cinema, it's necessary to be equipped. To be the 'reverse shot' of the television news. One always sees the police side and never the other; one never knows why the other side is fighting. Hence the need to make propaganda. They agree about doing this. But they haven't yet arrived at the need to break down the bourgeois ideology which invests the workers through the cinema.

Cin: How does one arrive at that stage?

Sèban: Everything must be overthrown. We have to have the revolution.

translated by Angela Martin.

Economic - Ideological - Formal*

Cinéthique: Amongst the films you have seen, which seem to you to be political?

Pleynet[1]: I don't believe you can ultimately operate with the concept 'political' when you mean to apply it to film-making. Indeed, how could one say of a film that it is not political? Be it *Les Souliers de Saint-Pierre, La Chinoise,* or *Le Gendarme se Marie,* all films are political. This is so insofar as they are, I grant you, more or less consciously determined by the dominant ideology. But, on the other hand, I take this concept of ideology to be more operative by way of indicating in the effect (here the film) under scrutiny the extent of the vacuum left by the theory — a vacuum always filled in for the dominant ideology. The kind of question, it seems to me, which can be asked today with regard to the cinema must be something like this: which films appear to be determined by theoretical work — work, that is, which endeavours to consider the cinema in the manner of what Althusser calls 'differential specificity'?[2] The only answer to this question is that today there is more than one cinematic practice which could be inscribed within a theoretical perspective. There are political films and more or less politicised films but, primarily because their practice is empiricist,[3] they are all without exception invested by bourgeois ideology. It is rather surprising that this question of the specificity of the cinema has never really been raised (except in Russia in the twenties) even after this vogue of linguistics and structuralism we have just gone through, and which film journals have not failed to echo. Here, in France, more than in any other country in the world, the cinema has given rise to a literature as enormous as it is inane (think of the esoteric critiques of Hitchcock, Minnelli, Ford, etc... not to mention studies in aesthetics).

Thibaudeau: To answer your question, I will consider some of the criticism that Godard levels against Pollet in an interview in the first issue of *Cinéthique*. Godard's point is that in *Méditerranée* the theoretical function of the film overshadows its militant value, primarily because the film fails to show the class struggle.
It is true that the film is entirely removed from its explicit referent: the Mediterranean. In other words, here is a film that produces itself, but does not reproduce. Godard bemoans the absence of class struggle from the film as others would miss the 'Look at Life' tour, the documentary, the love story, or

*Translated from *Cinéthique*, no. 3, 1969, pp7–14, with permission.

the drug-trafficking, all of which could have been included in the film — you might say that *Méditerranée* is not distributed for this reason. And, no doubt, in a film as elsewhere, one can put forward the class struggle in the same manner as one might put forward the affairs of the Carlton Club — or anything else. All this, however, does not make it any the less necessary to try to posit the ideological struggle at the level of the 'differential specificity' of a particular practice. By the systematic de-construction of representative phenomena and the rigorous construction of signifier series, *Méditerranée* provides us with a positive work of cinema critique; which means that it gives us a revolutionary work, even though it does not include the political signifieds of films like *Hands Over The City, Le Vent des Aures* or *Z*. (But then the fact of reducing a Mediterranean periplus to a voyage through something like death — although in the film the heroine is alive on an operating table — gives you, unfortunately, quite a good account of today's political reality.)
If I concentrate on what Godard says, it's because he is almost the only one to confront — through his montage practice (montage in the sense of the best silent Soviet cinema) — the question of cinema as ideological production: being ahead of others in his practice. Godard finds himself somewhat obliged to assert his ideology, an ideology which could be described as right-wing — anarchist.
This ideology of course upsets the balance of bourgeois ideologies but nevertheless is subsumed in them since basically it ignores the real class struggle — the struggle of the proletariat. This is why, in my view, the most interesting of Godard's films are those where he sets himself the task of contesting the use of ideology (*Le Mépris*). When he seriously assumes his own version of bourgeois ideology, the result sometimes can be successful (*Made in USA*), suspect *(Le Petit soldat)* or objectionable (the humanism of *Alphaville* and the train conversation of *La Chinoise*). By rejecting the function of theory in the name of a class struggle in which nevertheless he does not participate, Godard is thus limited to agitational dissent.
To conclude this point, note that in *Tu imagines Robinson* Pollett does not at all set out to exclude any political signifieds: although he had to keep the Greece of the Colonels out of the film, he has, on the other hand, allowed me to write a text which inscribes *in the film* the repression of History and the critique of bourgeois ideology that had dominated the making of the film. Finally, note that the film does not 'take place' in Greece, but here, in this very place where we are.

Pleynet: Thibaudeau is absolutely correct. This shows very well that Godard has never concerned himself with the question of the cinema's specificity. In *Méditerranée*, however, we have a film that can deal with such a question. The very fact of candidly admitting that the functions of theory and militancy are opposed to each other implies a recognition of one's own militant activity as being an empiricist practice (a practice in any case invested by bourgeois ideology).

Cinéthique: But isn't the specificity of the cinema also linked to the conditions of production of films?

Pleynet: Quite so, and I didn't mean to deny this. A practice which could not think about the condition of production of its object would be an empiricist practice (non-theoretical), unable to take stock of its own specificity. As far as the cinema is concerned, you have psychological theories, formal theories . . .

Cinéthique: Christian Metz . . .

Pleynet: Yes, quite. Metz's work, based on the model of linguisitics, is no doubt of great importance. But it must be stressed that by not saying anything about the function of ideology or the economic determinations of the object of his analysis, Metz adopts a position which, insofar as it presents itself as scientific, not only leaves the field open to the dominant ideology but also becomes a justification of it. If you counterpose to this 'formalist' approach that of Godard, as Thibaudeau outlined it . . . it becomes obvious that in both cases . . . one aspect of specificity is claimed to be specific totality . . . and this amounts to an approach which censors and excludes from its field a whole part of the real activity of the object under consideration, thereby creating a vacuum which, once more, will be inevitably filled by the dominant ideology.

Cinéthique: In the cinema, the overthrow of bourgeois ideology goes through a transformation of the economic conditions of production.

Thibaudeau: The overthrow of bourgeois ideology generally goes through the appropriation by the workers of the means of production. Any transformation of the economic conditions of film production would be powerless to 'overthrow' an ideology which has behind it centuries of crushing dominance and in front of it, no doubt, a future: even in the socialist countries, the struggle has not ended and remains open – and it will continue to remain open as long as capitalism survives in the face of socialism, and beyond. In view of these obvious facts, the eventuality of 'cinema power' is as unreal as all these fragmentary 'powers' which May '68 has rendered fashionable; it would be as visible as those 'black power', 'white power', 'Jewish power', 'student power' etc . . . badges which are sold indiscriminately in the boutiques of Greenwich Village. And as far as the cinema is concerned, when you hear Milos Forman (on the French radio station Europe I) rejecting the Eisensteinian reference, and referring himself to Carné instead, you begin to realise that we are nowhere near the time when this question of the overthrow of bourgeois ideology in the cinema will be settled.

Pleynet: Whether you're talking about cinema, painting, literature, or music, I don't believe you can have a very original answer to such a question. But you're quite right in wanting to emphasise the economic mode of production of films; it is a reality that will never be taken enough into consideration. However, we must not pose the reality of an economic system of production as a thing in itself, as a kind of cumbersome monument which one would then only need to avoid. This leads to the sort of attitude: 'I live in a capitalist economy, but the films I make do not depend on this economy.'; which is, literally, nonsense, utopia. The economic reality you emphasise is the reality of the cinema; it concerns the so-called commercial cinema as well as the marginal cinema, professional as well as amateur cinema — only an idealist would deny this. Current attempts to oppose commercial cinema to marginal cinema must concentrate on what determines this opposition; this determination is not primarily economic. Although the two types of production have different-sized budgets, they both, in fact, belong to the same economy. So if this opposition is to be thought, if we are to be able to think about it (and make a theory of it), then it must be situated in its own terrain; but the most evident aspect of this opposition — so evident that it might at first be overlooked — is the contrast between *academicism* in commercial cinema and *formal research* in marginal cinema. If we are to reject a position of naïve avant-gardism and see the birth of a cinema whose political effectiveness is real, then we must primarily examine the materials potentially available to it . . . By this I mean that before we can declare it to be 'revolutionary', we need to know in what sense the cinema can be so, we need to answer the question concretely. Now this idea that marginal cinema is politically more interesting than commercial cinema comes from the film-makers' illusion that to use less capital means to have more freedom. But we still need to understand the modalities of this freedom. Does a film-maker looking for 'more freedom' want this freedom because he intends to use it in order to serve his political ideas (couldn't he do this through the commercial system of production), or because he wants to be able to undertake a work of formal research? Both aims, you might no doubt answer, go together. So be it. But then the question of formal research becomes very pressing, and as far as I know no one as yet has dealt with it. It is not enough to conceive of a plan against all conventional rules and to set about systematically transgressing these rules, in order to produce a cinema ready to overthrow bourgeois ideology. Plus the fact that, insofar as formal research is concerned, where the marginal, low-budget film gives an illusion of 'more freedom', this illusion remains entirely moral: the low-budget film, by reducing the technical possibilities of cinematic production, also narrows down the field of research. I don't mean to say, of course, that the entire Hollywood machinery should be made available to every film-maker . . . but it is clear that below a certain budget, the resulting film can in no way fulfill the requirement of minimum formal research needed for the *de-construction* of the apparatus of ideological production, which the cinema is. It is perfectly understandable that the cinema should want to transform its conditions of economic production; but we still need to know whether it is capable of doing so . . . that is not to say that we need to know whether film-makers in the future will be able to form themselves into co-operatives, for instance . . . but that we need to know whether the formal investigations which characterise marginal cinema are, or will soon be, capable of being thought in a theoretical manner, whether they will be able to break from the empiricist practice which they now have; this, indeed, is the *sine qua non* of all transformation, whatever it may be. The contradictions I have just tried to outline between low and high-budget films, between formal research and academicism, between moral freedoms and subjection to technical means, these contradictions have never been theorised; which shows well that the cinema is far from the level of maturity necessary for the fulfilment of its ambitions of change. Before considering any possibilities of transformation we must therefore first resolve the question concerning essentially *the real force of transformation* available (viz. the theoretical force of the object). But how important can this force be for a film-maker who opts out of the commercial circuit and becomes then primarily preoccupied with the problem of finding funds . . .

Cinéthique: It is also a question of creating a new distribution circuit.

Pleynet: The decision to create new distribution circuits may derive from an idealist view-point. Do you believe that it is really more effective to re-think the whole distribution circuit — an impossible task, in any case — rather than act upon the circuit as it now exists? Should one's work be inserted dialectically in relation to the political reality in which one finds oneself ('work' being here a theoretical force capable of thinking the transformative effects of its dialectical articulation), or should one simply decree (as from an idealist view-point): I will deny this reality and create another one instead? But, I ask you, what will it be created with? In a recent article published by *L'Humanité,* Pierre Juquin, with reference to Lenin's text on 'The tasks of the Youth Leagues', correctly underpins 'the dialectical character of the development of science in a bourgeois régime.' 'Science', he says, 'progresses thanks to the efforts which researchers make inside, through, and despite the socio-economic and ideological conditions imposed upon them by the bourgeoisie.'

Cinéthique: So according to you it's impossible to combat the dominant ideology unless from inside the system?

Pleynet: Quite; it can only be combated from the inside. Here is what Lenin says in this connection: 'We cannot resolve this problem unless we understand that only a perfect knowledge of the culture created by the development of humanity and of its transformation enables us to create a proletarian culture.

Proletarian culture does not emerge from nowhere, it is not the invention of men who pretend to have specialist knowledge of the matter . . . ' We must note in this text the dialectical relation established between *knowledge* and *transformation*, as well as Lenin's warning against the *inventions* of specialists.

Thibaudeau: To combat the dominant ideology other than from the inside you need to be on the outside, which can never be the case. Any work must be carried out in some place, and it is at that place that the fighting must be done. Ideological struggle is never anything but first and foremost a civil war. And this all the more so because ideological production always appears in a network, in an extremely precise and tightly-knit context; since it is concerned with the modification of this context, it could not be limited uniquely to the text as bourgeois thought, with its notion of the *oeuvre*, would have it.

Cinéthique: This may well be right for literature, but it seems more difficult to achieve in the cinema, precisely because of the size of the funds involved in any attempt to make a film within the system. The publishers of *Tel Quel*, Seuil, are absolutely reactionary, and if they publish *Tel Quel* it is because the expenses incurred are relatively minimal compared to their overall budget, and because *Tel Quel*'s circulation is so small and so élite-oriented that it does not represent any direct and immediate threat to the ruling-class.

Pleynet: All right, let us take a look at *Tel Quel*. 5000 copies will be printed of the next issue; and you should normally multiply this figure by three to get total readership. As you can see, this represents quite a large readership and any talk of élites and 'élitism' is definitely beside the point. Because of the specificity of *Tel Quel*'s object, because it was able to articulate its position dialectically vis-à-vis the real situation (socio-economic and ideological) of this object, it became possible for it to accomplish a certain type of work. I am not trying to say that the two fields of activity (cinema and literature), as types of social inscription, completely overlap; I am only stressing the idealist character of a viewpoint which deliberately places itself outside the structures by which it is conditioned.

Thibaudeau: One of the most serious projects conceived by the Estates General for a 'revolution' in the cinema consisted in a highly revealing schema of the way it was supposed to work: in this schema, money, to begin with, would fall from heaven once and for all, and then continue to circulate indefinitely, as in a closed circuit. In short, it was a (naïve) image of a capitalist enterprise . . . And a sympathetic image too, half-way between Gaullist 'participation' and Yugoslavian-type self-management, but wholly irrelevant. The main problem for French cinema is, I believe, to impose on

the State — the State of monopolies — a certain number of 'rights', inside the system. It is probably much more important to succeed in 'leaving a mark' on commercial cinema and television than to make small, individual, militant films.
I want to say that, in the face of capitalism, we must attempt to impose demands which would force capitalism to retreat, in the same way as on the industrial front — and here it can be said without the slightest ambiguity — we must attempt whenever possible to win nationalisation demands, trade union rights, etc . . . the 'artisanal' solution being totally inadequate. Still, we may well want to make small, militant, individual films which would be distributed as stealthily as they were made: but for the purposes of what organisation, party or group, and from what class position?

Cinéthique: The dissemination of class films in trade-union branches can be an interesting initiative.

Thibaudeau: Yes, it will be fine to have film-making teams available to trade-union branches, neighbourhood committees, etc . . . This would fall entirely within the current line of struggle against the anti-democratic strengthening of the state's central powers which the next referendum aims to secure. But on this level, it would be a matter of using the cinema — and here perhaps video would do a better job — as an instrument of news-coverage, information, propaganda and political education against the conditioning disseminated by the ruling class: We are at any rate opposed here to Garrel, and some important difficulties will have to be taken into account.

Pleynet: In any case, there will no question of relying here on some private initiative. It is a problem, I would have thought, which should precisely concern trade-union organisations. However, this sort of cinema does nothing to answer the question you raised initially, namely: what is a political film? Under a bourgeois régime, what is a class cinema? Have you noticed how discourses whose object may be film and cinema (and there are many of them) all assume *a priori* the non-signifying existence of an image-producing apparatus, as if this apparatus could be indifferently put to this or that use, for the benefit of the left or of the right? Don't you think that before wondering about 'their militant function', film-makers would do well to look into the ideology produced by the apparatus (the camera) which determines the cinema? The cinematographic apparatus is a strictly ideological apparatus; it disseminates bourgeois ideology before anything else. Before a film is produced, the technical construction of the camera already produces bourgeois ideology.

Cinéthique: Less so in the case of 16mm. than 35mm. or 70mm.

Pleynet: Absolutely not. Whether in 16mm. or in 35mm. a film by Rohmer remains a reactionary film in its ideological production as well as in the materials it utilises. The problem is the same for 16mm., namely a camera which produces a code of perspective directly inherited from and built upon the model of the scientific perspective of the Quattrocento. I should like to expand this point . . . show how the camera is carefully built so as to 'rectify' any anomaly in perspective, so as to reproduce in its full authority the code of specular vision as it was defined by Renaissance humanism. It is interesting to note that precisely at the time when Hegel announced the end of the history of painting, at the time when painting became conscious that the scientific perspective which determines its relation to forms depends on a specific cultural structure . . . at this precise point in time we find Niepce[4] inventing the photographic process, a process which was to reinforce the end declared by Hegel as well as produce, in mechanical fashion, the ideology of the code of perspective, its norms and its censorships. I take the view that only when a phenomenon of this kind has been thought, only when the determinations of the apparatus (the camera) that structures reality by its inscription have been considered, only then could the cinema objectively examine its relation to ideology. We can say that the montage theories exhibited by the Russian cinema of the twenties (Kuleshov, Eisenstein) were a development of this return to the camera. To my knowledge, there hasn't been anything similar since then; as a result, cinematic practice is now entirely caught in empiricism and could not, in any case, use the 'freedom' it is asking for, primarily because the ideology produced by its apparatus of thought (the camera) has never been taken into consideration.

Cinéthique: If it was, the economic pressures of the system would prevent it from being realised.

Pleynet: I am not sure . . . In any case, before venturing any answer, I think that, as far as the social inscription of the cinema is concerned, you need to know first the tactical possibilities inherent in this or that particular type of investigation. And in a capitalist system, I am far from certain that to be politically effective a film must necessarily talk about politics. *La Chinoise,* for instance, is a film splashed with politics; nonetheless, it is entirely invested by bourgeois ideology. You put a slogan on a wall and you film it; by doing so, however, you put it through a particular apparatus, built for particular purposes, possessing, so to speak, a particular mental ideological structure (which is, in short, monocular scientific perspective). From there on, it is no longer your slogan which speaks, but your apparatus which uses the slogan, which produces doubleness, a specular image. You have a bloke sitting in the dark looking at an image, he is forced to accept what bourgeois society has always offered him, namely the possibility of acting only by proxy. This consideration is far-reaching. One of my film-maker friends has pertinently pointed out to me that the effect of distancing, which is possible in the theatre because the spectator sees all the scenes from the same viewpoint and in the same framework, is considerably more complicated to achieve in the cinema: here, point of view and framework happen to be determined by a sovereign will (the director's) . . . whilst the spectator can only master them through the fiction, even if this fiction is only the fiction of monocular perspective. So, for all these closely related reasons, before proceeding further we must first tackle one of the most pressing problems of cinematography in France; and that's a problem of deconstruction of the ideology produced by the camera. There is systematic work to be done in this area, and it should be done on the level of making a film as well.

Cinéthique: That could give rise to yet more purely formal work.

Pleynet: Not if this move goes back to providing a critique of the mode of production of the apparatus (the camera). Not if the cinema ceases to be thought as *autonomous specificity,* and instead as *differential specificity.* It is because of the particular way in which it is produced that the cinema condemns itself today to purely formal effects: deconstruction of the story, of shots, of modes of camera movement, deliberately arbitrary montage, etc. . . . all this left to the whims of avant-gardist empiricism. It must be recognised that, to this day, no film-maker has been led to think his practice theoretically (systematically).

Thibaudeau: Eisenstein.

Pleynet: Yes, in a socialist country.

Cinéthique: Couldn't the un-thought of the cinema be found precisely in its anchorage in industry?

Pleynet: You must understand that in fact I am not opposed to what you are suggesting. I would be opposed to it if the emphasis on economics served to blot out the ideological, in a practice which is primarily ideological. At any rate, the economic problems of the cinema should not only be seen from the point of view of *mise en scène.* You mustn't forget that in the cinema you have about 90% unemployment. I think this would be the first economic aspect to remember if you want to stress the economic problems of the cinema . . . Here you have a social situation unlike any other . . . And it is only on the basis of this situation that one can tackle the economic problems of the cinema in their reality.

Thibaudeau: Insofar as film work is dependent upon some capital, some practical necessities become inevitable: first, you need various means (at the stages of shooting, laboratory processing, editing) which must be used according to norms and within set time-limits. So to make a film is to involve oneself in a process of automatic accumulation – the actor is added to the set, the sound-track to the image-track, colour to black-and-white, etc . . . But these accumulations cannot be thought as soon as the process is under way. I have the feeling, however, that most marginal cinema falls into exactly the same basic error of not realising that by making a film in three days one speeds up the process, but one does not avoid it; nor, as a result, is one in a position to take each element in isolation and enquire why and how they can be made to interact on their own terms. The film-maker who wants to avoid the process must therefore find the means to work without the alibi of having a particular film to make; otherwise, all he will ever manage to do is add yet another film to the stock of already existing films. Besides, and talking about this enormous quantity of celluloid exposed in the last fifty years, the film-maker should be able to use film-archives in all sorts of ways – as writers use libraries not only to 'read' but also to 'write'; he should be able to quote, plagiarise, appropriate, deform, re-make, as he wishes . . . material and institutional problems of the cinema are always thought of in terms of shooting, never in terms of montage.

Cinéthique: On the theoretical level, it would be interesting to ask why the CGT technicians identify the director with the class-enemy (the producer). Therein might lie the explanation why the working-class adopts a line of least resistance in the face of films that disseminate bourgeois ideology.

Thibaudeau: If a film gets made at all, at least here in France, it's almost always because of the director, be it Gérard Oury, Tati, or Garrel. The director is rarely a pure and simple wage-earner (except for industrial, scientific or advertising films). As often as not, he appears as the boss, more or less the agent of the capital invested, in charge of a temporary factory. But, of course, he is not responsible for this state of affairs.

Pleynet: Now on this question of the relation between technicians and directors, assuming you're right about what you say . . . the explanation, it seems to me, is very simple: first, the majority of directors do not join the technicians' union (the CGT), and second, throughout the history of the cinema, from the early days on, the director has always tried to boost profits on the funds invested in his film. Mme Maurice Champreux, Louis Feuillade's daughter, remembers, for instance, that her father often used to say: 'I have been entrusted with capital, my duty is to make it grow . . .' Perhaps you know the story of Gaumont reminding Feuillade of the example of the Danish company Nordisk, which would produce films with the well-known Asta Nielsen at 6.50F. per metre of negative celluloid? Feuillade, offended, apparently retorted: 'I'll do it at 6F.' The history of the cinema is littered with anecdotes of this kind . . . you could also find instances of close solidarity between technicians and directors − but these, I must admit, are rather rare.

Cinéthique: Let's take the example of the CGT's minimum crew requirement. There can be no doubt that if all those involved in making a film had access to the film's meaning, if there was at this level any real contact between director and technicians (within a perspective of proletarian cinema), then the CGT might re-consider its position, *inter alia*, on the minimum crew issue.

Pleynet: This is an aspect of the contradictions in which today's cinema is caught. These contradictions must not be ignored, and any attempt to throw light, as you like to do, on the economic problems faced by the cinema must begin with these contradictions. The setting up of alternative networks of production, of new distribution systems can only be thought about (if at all) in terms of the 90% unemployment in the film industry. And, in fact, it must not be forgotten that marginal cinema (we have talked about it too much, perhaps) is produced mainly by groups of non-professionals and amateurs (scabs, in short), and not by film technicians. Isn't that a political position and a social attitude worth looking into . . . and shouldn't marginal cinema, before anything else, explain itself on this question.

Thibaudeau: As long as the State − which produces and distributes films and owns television, but which is not socialist − has not been forced into democratic reforms, it will have to be fought inch by inch in the cinema as well as in other areas. But the cinema cannot be compared to the steel industry or to public transport: as far as the cinema is concerned, it is not clear what one means by 'service' or 'national interest'. If there is a need in the cinema for trade union solidarity, there is also a need, not for the film-makers to take power, but for the film-makers to help bring active power into the hands of democratic authorities. On the other hand, I wonder if, in an actual piece of work, it would not be desirable to have some critical contribution from the crew instead of having a director who, throughout the shooting and editing, behaves as if he was the sole repository of the 'meaning' of a work which, after all, is collective.

Thibaudeau: This is a contradiction which at present is insurmountable. Capital only gives money to the cinema where it can make money profits or . .

Cinêthique: Ideological profits . . .

Thibaudeau: Yes, or for prestige reasons: either totally commercial cinema, or big-name directors.

Pleynet: If Godard's practice was not empiricist, I think he could make any film he likes tomorrow, and if he doesn't make it, it is because he is incapable, because he hasn't thought his practice.

Cinêthique: Godard occupies a privileged place inside the system and he is, precisely, turning presently to marginal cinema. This is significant.

Pleynet: Godard's practice is inconsistent.

Cinêthique: Maybe, but he shares your point of view that all the films he's made within the system are reformist.

Pleynet: I am sorry if I repeat myself, but it seems to me that we are constantly skirting around the problem without ever coming face to face with it. I can well understand that your most immediate concerns lead you to consider the economic circuit . . . But this mustn't blind you to the extent of believing that, on the basis of these concerns alone, you could tackle the problems besetting French cinema today. You cannot do it so long as you do not determine the specificity of the cinematographic field, so long as you have not tackled the question of whether the cinema produces primarily an economy or an ideology.

Cinêthique: It seems that, because of the larger place it occupies in the economic circuit, the cinema could hold the power of unmasking this circuit, that is, of establishing links with the real life of the spectator.

Pleynet: Of course. The cinema has a very considerable ideological importance and it can have an immense influence.

Cinêthique: On condition, however, that these problems are raised *in* films.

Pleynet: The kind of films which do not raise all these problems are the films which are produced at the moment; all these problems need to be raised in films.

Cinéthique: But the system does not allow them to be raised. Any script inclined to raise them would not receive any advance payments from the CNC. So you're forced to work outside the system, forced to use 'amateurs', because you can't afford technicians.

Pleynet: From an empirical view-point, we can recognise that films made outside the official circuit can affect the official circuit, insofar as they can make the latter appear cut off from the life of the cinema. But this does not imply that one situation is better than the other.

Cinéthique: The question is: is this the only possible situation?

Pleynet: From the point of view of social practice, I do not think that this is the only possible situation, far from it. But it is another matter from perhaps the point of view of the film-maker, the *metteur en scène*, viz. the 'creator' who wants to 'express' himself, to produce an 'oeuvre' — that's another matter . . . I am not so sure, however, that the old picture of the creative artist is a very contemporary problem. Keeping in mind the economic situation of the cinema we've talked about (90% unemployment), in fact it may well turn out that, as a social activity, the cinema doesn't produce any 'oeuvres' or films (at least, in the first instance). But wouldn't this social activity be otherwise more real than, for instance, all these full-length and medium-length films produced by May '68? We must not forget that today in the so-called non-commercial cinema, or marginal cinema, although we may perhaps find the best, we also find the worst . . . I personally cannot see any great difference between Garrel and Louis de Funès, not to mention the American Underground . . .

Cinéthique: To us, a defence of marginal cinema in no way implies a defence of 'artists producing their oeuvre'. It is very much a question of grasping present-day reality.

Pleynet: Then the work you propose to do with your journal, and which could be very important, will only become important to the extent that the two types of activity (economic and ideological) will be stressed whilst insisting every time on the over-determining role of the ideological.

Cinéthique: What do you think of the present state of 'film criticism'?

Pleynet: It's practically non-existent. In one way or another, it serves the ideology which is kept going by the cinema. Godard is, if you like, absolutely right when he says 'All that's written about the cinema is of no purpose, save that its use is to put value on a product.' And bear in mind that all these films which are not going to be commercial and which will claim to be experimental art cinema . . .

Cinéthique: Certainly not! The films we defend are against the reactionary ideology of the 'experimental art' cinema.

Pleynet: Other problems, other contradictions. In the final analysis, the only objective role of the marginal film, the avant-garde film or the experimental art film is to stand cultural (or even political) surety for the commercial cinema . . . to put value on a product, the cinema product . . . whereas the first thing to do would be to warn the public very seriously against this product. The question: what is cinema? has never been answered, it remains suspended. Look at what happened to *Cahiers du Cinéma* . . . objectively, they have always 'promoted the wares', but they will disappear without ever becoming a film journal . . or rather they will never become anything but a film journal . . . just another one, that is. I would say that for a group of people who want to start a journal, there are quite a lot of lessons to draw from reading *Cahiers*.

Cinéthique: Had Pollet not produced *Méditerranée* outside the system, it would never have got made.

Pleynet: That's true. *Méditerranée* is a film which in fact is much more political than *La Chinoise,* for instance, since it is a film which acts upon the spectator in an absolutely decisive manner, a film which forces the spectator to ask himself at the end questions like: What is cinema?

Cinéthique: If the system digested *La Chinoise*, it must be because the film did not pose a great threat to it.

Pleynet: The system even paraded the film throughout the United States, through all the American universities.

Cinéthique: So we come back once more to marginal cinema. This expression has unfortunate connotations. In the marginal cinema, there are all kinds of films that we reject; but, at present, we believe that is where the films which shake the system will be made.

Pleynet: From a practical point of view, it would be better to make them there, but from the point of view of social effectiveness, it would be better to make them within the system.

Cinéthique: Both aspects being connected ...

Pleynet: Yes, they are connected. I quite agree that they must not be separated from each other, otherwise you would get a Garrel or a Deval, that is, the bloke who is there to express his little personality. But if you say that they are thus connected, then you must reverse your proposition ... You are forced to say that the marginal cinema can occasion a cinema production of more consequence than the large, commercial production (we must not pretend that low-budget commercial films do not exist ... *Adieu Philippine* and *Chronicle of Anna Magdalena Bach* were both produced by commercial cinema) ... so you must say that marginal cinema can give the opportunity of producing films of greater consequence, but in the same breath you must recognise that one is dealing here with, precisely, marginal effects which must be incorporated in the reality of the cinema's social situation as it appears today (90% unemployment).

Cinéthique: What is your definition of a working-class cinema for today?

Thibaudeau: In France today, working-class cinema would be the cinema of the big working-class organisations, the Communist Party and the CGT. Having said this, I must repeat that the cinema as such is a particular locus of practical, ideological and theoretical work. In France today any 'experimental' or 'avant-garde' film is the work of a bourgeois aiming at a bourgeois audience. This is the very starting point which must be used in challenging this necessary starting basis and in finding, in present-day conditions, the 'materialist' answer to the constituent idealism of the cinema. We are not in Russia in the twenties and if an attempt is made to link revolutionary practice to revolutionary ideology and theory, then the most pressing, as well as the most hidden, problem is without doubt the problem of theory.

Pleynet: I would like to consider your question and everything we have been able to say so far in the light of two statements which, I think, have particular relevance to the problems around which we have been circling. Both statements come from a text by Lenin published in March 1923. 'Better Fewer, But Better'. The first statement is concerned in fact with your question: 'What is your definition of a working-class cinema for today?' and it is this: 'In questions of culture, haste and large-scale projects are most harmful.' With specific regard to the cinema produced today, that is the cinema which claims to be political, to be a class cinema, the second statement tells us that 'a veritable boureois culture would be enough to begin with'. Now, what are we to make of this, for the point of view of your question? Well, primarily (the two statements in my view being complementary) that a class cinema will be a cinema that could effect as complete a return as possible to bourgeois culture (we're far from achieving this), a cinema which will have located its class determinations on the practical as well as on the theoretical level (we're far from achieving this too). As you can see, I am only repeating what I have said; but it can all be summed up by saying that there can be no practice of consequence without theory. The present-day situation of a working-class cinema is closely dependent upon the possibilities of a theoretical work which film-makers of today can set themselves . . . It is through this work, and only through this work, that the cinema will be able to free itself from the ideological pressure that weighs it down more than any other mode of inscription.

Interview conducted by Gérard Leblanc and translated by Elias Noujaim.

Translator's Notes

1. Marcelin Pleynet, and his colleague Jean Thibaudeau, were editors and regular contributors to the influential literary review *Tel Quel.*

2. Through the interview, both Pleynet and Thibaudeau rely heavily on the philosophy of L. Althusser. Since the interview does not clarify what is meant by 'differential specificity', for this concept as well as others which appear in the interview (e.g. 'autonomous specificity') see Louis Althusser and Etienne Balibar, *Reading Capital,* translated by Ben Brewster, New Left Books, London 1975.

3. For the distinction between theoretical/empiricist practice, as well as other concepts relating to practice, cf. Louis Althusser, *For Marx,* translated by Ben Brewster, Allen Lane, The Penguin Press, London 1971.

4. Niepce (1765-1833) was a contemporary of Hegel (1770-1831).

Bibliography

Althusser, L., *Essays in Self Criticism*, translated by Grahame Lock, New Left Books, London 1976.
Althusser, L., *For Marx*, translated by Ben Brewster, New Left Books, London 1969.
Althusser., L., *Lenin and Philosophy and Other Essays*, New Left Books, London 1971.
Barthes, R., *Mythologies*, Paladin, London 1973.
Barthes, R., *Elements of Semiology*, Jonathan Cape, London 1967.
Barthes, R., *S/Z*, Jonathan Cape, London 1975.
Barthes, R., *Image/Music/Text*, essays selected and translated by Stephen Heath, Fontana, London 1977.
Bazin, A., *What is Cinema?*, essays selected and translated by Hugh Gray, University of California Press, Berkeley 1970.
Benjamin, W., *Understanding Brecht*, New Left Books, London 1973.
Bloomfield, J. (ed.), *Class, Hegemony and Party*, Lawrence and Wishart, London 1977.
Brecht, B., *Brecht on Theatre*, edited by John Willett, Methuen, London 1964.
Breton, A., *Manifestoes of Surrealism*, translated by Richard Seaver and Helen Lane, University of Michigan, Ann Arbor 1972.
Brown, R.S. (ed.), *Focus on Godard*, Prentice-Hall, Englewood Cliffs N.J. 1972.
Cassou, J. and others, *Art and Confrontation: France and the Arts in an Age of Change*, Studio Vista, London 1970.
Callincos, A., *Althusser's Marxism*, Pluto Press, London 1976.
Claudin-Urondo, C., *Lenin and the Cultural Revolution*, Harvester Press, Hassocks, 1977.
Cohn-Bendit, G. and D., *Obsolete Communism: The Left Wing Alternative*, Penguin, London 1969.
Debord, G., *The Society of the Spectacle*, (1967), translated for Practical Paradise Publications, London 1977.
Andrew, J. Dudley, *The Major Film Theories: An Introduction*, O.U.P., New York and London 1976.
Eagleton, T., *Criticism and Ideology*, New Left Books, London 1976.
Eagleton, T., *Marxism and Literary Criticism*, Methuen, London 1976.
Ecran '78, special issue: *Cinéma action I – dix ans apres mai '68, aspects du cinéma de contestation*.
Erlich, V., *Russian Formalism*, Mouton, The Hague 1955.
Fitzpatrick, S., *The Commissariat of Enlightenment: Soviet Organisation of Education and the Arts under Lunacharsky: October 1917-1921*, Cambridge University Press, Cambridge 1970.
Gaudibert, P., *Action culturelle: intégration et/ou subversion*, Casterman, Paris 1972.

Godard, J.-L., *Godard on Godard*, translated by Tom Milne, Secker and Warburg, London 1972.
Gramsci, A., *Selections from the Prison Notebooks*, edited by Quintin Hoare and Geoffrey Nowell-Smith, Lawrence and Wishart, London 1971.
Heath, S., MacCabe, C. and Prendergast, C., *Signs of the Times: Introductory Readings in Textual Semiotics*, Granta, Cambridge 1971.
Hobsbawm, E., *Revolutionaries*, Pantheon, New York 1973.
Jameson, F. (ed.), *Aesthetics and Politics: Debates between Ernst Bloch, Georg Lukacs, Bertolt Brecht, Walter Benjamin, Theodor Adorno*, New Left Books, London 1978.
Johnston, C. (ed.), Edinburgh '77 Magazine, No. 2, *History/Production/Memory*, Edinburgh Film Festival, Edinburgh 1977.
Lebel, J.-P., *Cinéma et idéologie*, Editions Sociales, Paris 1971.
Lenne, G., *La Mort du cinema*, Editions du Cerf, Paris 1971.
MacBean, J.R., *Film and Revolution*, Indiana University Press, Bloomington 1975.
Marx, K., *Grundrisse*, translated by Martin Nicolaus, Penguin, London 1973.
Marx, K. and Engels, F., *Selected Works* in one volume, Lawrence and Wishart, London 1970.
Marx, K. and Engels, F., *The German Ideology*, Lawrence and Wishart, London 1974.
Metz, C., *Film Language*, Oxford University Press, 1974.
Metz, C., *Language and Cinema*, Mouton, The Hague 1974.
Nichols, B., *Movies and Methods*, University of California Press, Berkeley 1976.
Posner, C. (ed.), *Reflections on the Revolution in France 1968*, Penguin, Harmondsworth 1970.
Seale, P. and McConville, P., *French Revolution 1968*, Heinemann and Penguin, London 1968.
Singer, D., *Prelude to Revolution: France in May 1968*, Hill and Wang, New York, 1971.
Stansill, P. and Mairowitz, D.Z., *Bamn: Outlaw Manifestoes and Ephemera (1965-1970)*, Penguin, Harmondsworth 1971.
Society for Education in Film and Television, *Screen Reader I: Cinema/Ideology/Politics*, introduction by John Ellis, London 1977.
Todorov, T., *The Poetics of Prose*, translated by Richard Howard, Blackwell, Oxford 1977.
Touraine, A., *The May Movement: Revolt or Reform*, translated by Leonard Mayhew, Random House, New York 1971.
Trotsky, L., *Literature and Revolution*, International Publishers, New York, 1925.
Tudor, A., *Theories of Film*, Secker and Warburg, London 1974.
Willener, A., *The Action-Image of Society: On Cultural Politicisation*, translated by A.M. Sheridan-Smith, Tavistock, London 1970.
Williams, R., *Marxism and Literature*, O.U.P., Oxford 1977.
Wollen, P., *Signs and Meaning in the Cinema*, Secker and Warburg, London 1970.

Zimmer, C., *Cinéma et politique*, Editions Seghers, Paris 1974.

Readers interested in developments in semiotics and the theory of the subject might find useful the bibliographies included in the following books:

Hawkes, T., *Structuralism and Semiotics*, Methuen, London 1977.

Coward, R. and Ellis, J., *Language and Materialism: Developments in Semiology and the Theory of the Subject*, Routledge and Kegan Paul, London 1977.

Edinburgh '76 Magazine, No. 1, *Psycho-analysis/Cinema/Avant-garde*, Edinburgh Festival, Edinburgh 1976.

Journals (in English) reflecting developments in these areas include:

Camera Obscura (California)
Diacritics (USA)
Film Reader (Northwestern University, Chicago, USA)
Ideology and Consciousness (London)
Screen (London)
Semiotica
Substance (USA)
Twentieth Century Studies (University of Kent)
Yale French Studies, no. 48, 1972 (USA)
Working Papers in Cultural Studies (Birmingham)